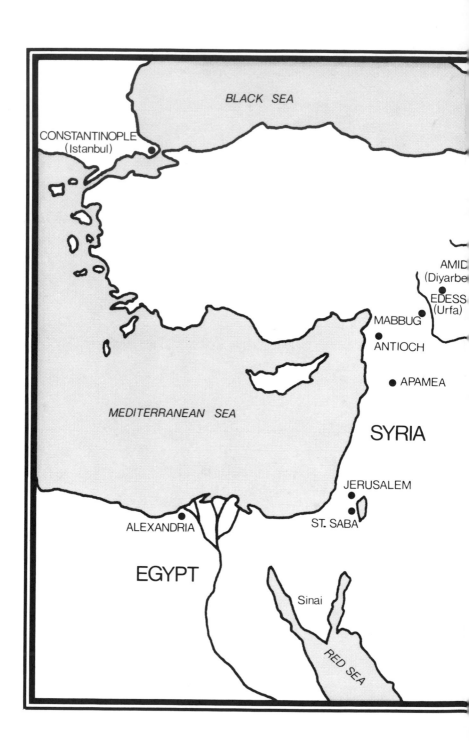

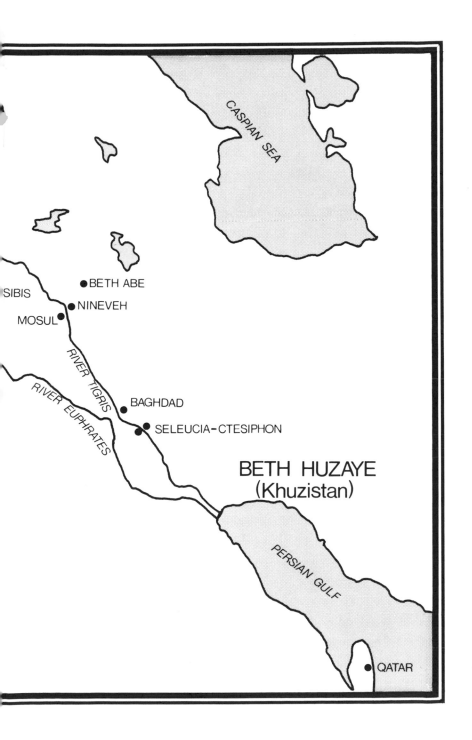

CASPIAN SEA

SIBIS
● BETH ABE
● NINEVEH
MOSUL ●

RIVER TIGRIS

RIVER EUPHRATES

● BAGHDAD
● SELEUCIA—CTESIPHON

BETH HUZAYE
(Khuzistan)

PERSIAN GULF

● QATAR

The
Syriac Fathers
on
Prayer
and the
Spiritual Life

Introduced
and
Translated
by

Sebastian Brock

CISTERCIAN PUBLICATIONS INC.

Kalamazoo, Michigan

Available in Britain and Europe from
A. R. MOWBRAY & CO. LTD
ST THOMAS HOUSE
BECKET STREET
OXFORD OX1 1SJ

Available elsewhere (including Canada) from the publisher

Cistercian Publications Inc
WMU STATION
KALAMAZOO, MICHIGAN 49008

The work of Cistercian Publications is made possible in part by support from Western Michigan University

This book has been published with aid from the Koch Foundation of Clearwater, Florida

Library of Congress Cataloguing–in–Publication Data:

The Syriac fathers on prayer and the spiritual life.

(Cistercian studies series; 101)
'Selection of excerpts translated from Syriac writers'—Pref.

Bibliography: p. xliii
Includes index.
1. Prayer. 2. Spiritual life. 3. Fathers of the church, Syriac. I. Brock, Sebastian P. II. Series: Cistercian studies series; no. 101.
BV209.S9 1987   248.3'2' 09015   87–6369
ISBN 0–87907–601–1
ISBN 0–87907–901–0 (lib. bdg.)

TO MILITZA ZERNOV
IN MEMORY OF NICOLAS

Table of Contents

v

Abbreviations

CSCO	Corpus Scriptorum Christianorum Orientalium (Louvain)
DSpir	*Dictionnaire de Spiritualité* (Paris)
OCA	*Orientalia Christiana Analecta* (Rome)
OCP	*Orientalia Christiana Periodica* (Rome)
PG	Patrologia Graeca (Paris)
Philokalia	G. E. H. Palmer, P. Sherrard, K. Ware, edd., *The Philokalia*, I (London, 1979).
PO	Patrologia Orientalis (Paris/Turnhout)
RAM	*Revue d'Ascétique et de Mystique* (Toulouse)

Preface

THE AIM of this selection of excerpts translated from Syriac writers, mainly on the topic of prayer, is to introduce this little known tradition of Eastern Christian spirituality to a wider audience. Many of the texts have never previously been translated into English (or sometimes indeed into any European language); in a few cases the translation has been made from works whose original Syriac text has not yet even been published (thus the opportunity has been taken to include some newly discovered works by Isaac the Syrian, or Isaac of Nineveh). For the reader who is unfamiliar with this tradition the General Introduction is intended to provide a brief orientation. Some supplementary information on the individual authors will be found in the introductions to each chapter.

Those wishing to explore this territory further will find some guidance in the Bibliographies (where details of the sources from which the translations were made are also located). The section numbers in the translations are those introduced by the editors of the Syriac originals (or, in rare cases, by the authors).

I take the opportunity to thank Sister Martha Reeves, not only for her help with typing many of the translations, but also for the encouragement she has given in the later stages of preparing this book.

S.P.B.

General Introduction

ACCORDING TO A PATTERN familiar from many standard handbooks, Christian tradition is to be divided historically into the Latin West and the Greek East; *tertium non datur*. Such a dichotomy is both unfortunate and inadequate, for it completely overlooks the existence of the oriental Christian Churches which constitute an important third stream of Christian tradition, quite distinct from the other two familiar streams. Among the oriental Christian Churches those within the Syriac liturgical tradition may be said to hold pride of place, since they are representatives of, and to some degree direct heirs to, the Semitic world out of which Christianity sprang. It is a matter of pride for them still today that they employ as their liturgical language Syriac, a dialect of Aramaic, the very language of Jesus. The form of the Lord's Prayer used in the Syriac Churches today is indeed not all that much different from the words that Jesus himself must have uttered in first-century Galilaean Aramaic: Syriac (the local Aramaic dialect of Edessa, the traditional birthplace of Syriac Christianity) and Galilaean Aramaic would certainly have been mutually comprehensible.

Although Syriac Christianity, like Latin Christianity, soon came under the very strong influence of Greek-speaking Christianity, its earliest literature is usually expressed in a manner much more characteristic of the Semitic—and biblical—world out of which it grew. In the writings of the greatest representative of this early form of Syriac Christianity, St Ephrem of Nisibis (*c.* 306–373), poetry not prose holds primacy of place as the vehicle for theology, and his profound theological vision, expressed in poetry by means of paradox and symbol, rather than by analysis and definition in prose, is one that retains its value, *mutatis mutandis*, even today. Furthermore, as the sole representative of a Semitic Christianity which was for the most part still unhellenized—in other words, uneuropeanized, and unwesternized—early Syriac Christianity takes on a new relevance in the modern world where the Churches of Asia, Africa, and South America are rightly seeking to shake off the European cultural baggage from the Christianity which they have usually received through the mediary of European or North American missionaries: here, in the early Syriac tradition, we encounter a form of Christianity whose theological expression is as yet uninfluenced by the Greek philosophical tradition, but which employs thought forms that are far more conducive to these Churches' own cultural backgrounds.

From this point of view it is the earliest Syriac writers—and above all the theologian-poet Ephrem—who are of most importance, for from the fifth century onwards the Syriac tradition came to be increasingly influenced by Greek thought–forms and modes of expression. This hellenophile process reached its climax in the seventh century; by that time it has often become very difficult to tell whether a particular Syriac text was composed in that language or whether it is in fact a literal translation from Greek. Ironically it was at precisely this point in history that the Arab invasions effectively cut the Syriac Churches off from the Byzantine world to which they had for the most part belonged. In the ensuing centuries the theologians of the Syriac Churches systematized the scholastic theology that they had inherited from the Greek world in the course of the sixth and early seventh centuries (Porphyry's *Eisagōgē*, or introduction to Aristotelian logic, had been translated into Syriac at about the same time that Boethius translated it into Latin). More or less contemporary with St Thomas Aquinas, the great Syrian Orthodox scholar Barhebraeus compiled his own *summa theologica*, equally based on the Aristotelian tradition.

Syriac Christianity thus comprises two quite distinct poles, which we can for convenience term the Semitic and the Hellenic. Between these two poles there is, of course, a continuum, and even a writer like Ephrem, one of our main witnesses to the Semitic pole, is certainly not free from the influence of Greek thought, but this influence affects, as it were, only the surface, and never the deep structures, of his thought patterns and mode of expression.

THE SYRIAC CHURCHES

One reason for the neglect of oriental Christian tradition in many standard works on Church history and the history of doctrine lies in the fact that many of these Churches became separated from the 'mainstream' Church of the Graeco-Latin world during the fifth and sixth centuries as a result of the christological controversies of the time. The doctrinal formulation put forward by the Council of Chalcedon (451), in particular, proved a stumbling block, for the statement that the incarnate Christ was one hypostasis 'in two natures' seemed to many, not only a logical impossibility (given their understanding of the technical terms), but also dangerously heretical, in that it appeared to them to deny the full reality of the incarnation. In the heat of the ensuing controversies, the various parties were not willing to step back and consider whether or not their verbally conflicting definitions might just be due to the use of different conceptual models and a different understanding of the key terms in the debate. The lamentable result of all this was the emergence in the sixth and seventh centuries of separate Chalcedonian and non-Chalcedonian hierarchies in the Near East.

The non-Chalcedonian Churches, today usually known as the Oriental Orthodox Churches,[1] all belong to the Alexandrian christological tradition of Cyril of Alexandria. Among their number is the Syrian Orthodox Church.[2] At the other end of the theological spectrum comes another important representative of Syriac Christianity, the Church of the East. For this Church, whose centre of gravity lay outside the Roman Empire and in the Persian (Sasanid) Empire to the east, it was the Antiochene theological tradition, represented above all by Theodore of Mopsuestia, which constituted the norm of orthodoxy.[3] In the course of the fifth and sixth centuries the Church of the East (which was already a separate patriarchate beyond the frontier of the Roman Empire) came to feel more and more alienated from the theological developments that were taking place within the Roman Empire. For them the 'ecumenical councils' were just internal affairs of the Roman *oikoumenē*: the Council of Ephesus (431) they viewed with open disapproval, whereas Chalcedon was regarded as only a partial (and hence unsatisfactory) remedy to the ills brought about in the years intervening between 431 and 451; the Fifth Council, of Constantinople (553), was seen as wholly retrogressive.

Almost all extant Syriac literature dating from the mid-fifth century onwards belongs to one or other of these two Churches. For the sake of completeness, however, two further representatives of Syriac Christianity need to be mentioned. These are the Maronite and Melkite Churches, both belonging to the Chalcedonian theological tradition.[4] Both have their roots in Syriac Christianity, and emerge as separate Churches in the seventh century as a result of the monothelete/dyothelete controversy. Whereas the Melkite Church changed its liturgical language from Syriac to Arabic and its rite from Antiochene to Constantinopolitan in the Middle Ages, the Maronite

Church has retained Syriac as a liturgical language into the twentieth century, although it is now being replaced by Arabic in the Middle East and by English in the diaspora; its liturgy, however, retains many archaic features, characteristic of early Syriac Christianity.[5]

The Syriac Christian tradition is thus the heritage of several different oriental Churches, and it is today represented wherever these Churches are to be found in the world; this means not only in the Middle East, but also in South India (Kerala), where the connections with Syriac Christianity go back to earliest times, and in the large diasporas that have grown up in the present century (sometimes indeed in the last few decades) in Europe, the Americas, and Australia.

It is from Syriac writers of the early, and most creative, centuries of this tradition that the excerpts on prayer and the spiritual life in this volume have been drawn. In date they range from the fourth (Chapters I and II) to the eighth century (Chapters XIV and XV). Geographically they belong to the area covered by modern north Syria, south-east Turkey and north Iraq. The texts in Chapters I–V all pre-date the divisions brought about by the christological controversies of the fifth century; the remaining texts are taken from both Syrian Orthodox writers and from those of the Church of the East (as we will see, many of these texts had no difficulty in travelling across ecclesiastical boundaries).

SYRIAC LITERATURE

How do these writings fit within the history of Syriac literature as a whole? Syriac has been in use as a literary language for nearly two thousand years, and in certain limited circles (mainly Syrian Orthodox) it continues to flourish even today. Over the course of these centuries, but above all from the millennium or so between the third and the fourteenth century, Syriac has been employed for the writing of poetry, history, philosophy, medicine, and

science, as well as theology. A small purely secular literature survives, but owing to the circles in which the older
Syriac literature was handed down, most of what has been
transmitted to us can broadly be described as specifically
Christian in character. The golden age of Syriac literature
may be said to extend from the fourth to the seventh
century, and it is from this period that almost all the
excerpts translated in this book derive.

Very little literature in Syriac earlier than the fourth
century survives, but this includes the Old Syriac translation of the Gospels (made from Greek), the beautiful but
mysterious *Odes of Solomon*, and the *Acts of Thomas*.[6]
From the fourth century we have two writers of prime
importance, Aphrahat and Ephrem, both of whom are represented below (Chapters I and II). The literature of this
period, prior to *c.* 400, constitutes the best witness to the
Semitic pole within Syriac Christianity; we are thus fortu-
nate in having an extensive corpus of writings, in both
prose and poetry, by Ephrem, who certainly ranks as the
finest poet in any language of the patristic period.

The fifth and sixth centuries saw great literary activity,
both by way of creative writing and by way of translations
from Greek into Syriac. Early in this period, from approximately 400, comes the first great monument of Syriac
literature devoted specifically to the spiritual life, the *Liber Graduum* or *Book of Steps* (*Ascents*), represented in
Chapter III. Like Aphrahat before him, the author was
writing somewhere in what is today the modern state of
Iraq, but was then the Persian Empire, lying beyond the
eastern frontiers of the Roman Empire. Writing perhaps a
few decades later, and an approximate contemporary of
Theodoret of Cyrrhus, was John of Apamea (Chapter V), a
Syriac author whose true stature is only now beginning to
emerge. Both John and Theodoret belong to Syria, and
both men were probably bilingual in Greek and Syriac, but
since Theodoret wrote in Greek and very much within the
Greek rhetorical tradition, while John wrote in Syriac,

they sometimes give the appearance of belonging to two quite separate worlds; in particular, the idiosyncratic Syrian ascetics described with such gusto by Theodoret in his *Historia Religiosa*[7] seem a long way removed from the ascetic communities (clearly not at all uncultured) for whom John was writing.

Much Syriac literature of the fifth century happens to be anonymous. This applies above all to the rich hagiographical and martyr literature, some of which proved so popular that it was translated into Greek; this includes, for example, the original Syriac form of the life of the 'Man of God'[8] (subsequently given the name Alexius) which in due course came to enjoy great popularity in the medieval west. To the end of the fifth century belong two major poets, Narsai in the Church of the East, and Jacob of Serugh in the Syrian Orthodox tradition (Jacob's life continued into the sixth century; he died in 521). Both were prolific in the production of verse homilies, usually on biblical or liturgical topics.[9] A long quotation from Jacob, the better poet of the two, is incorporated into the anonymous text translated in Chapter VIII. Jacob clearly found theological controversy utterly distasteful and it is only in his letters that he manifests, and then only under pressure, his position within the doctrinal controversies. In this he stands in sharp contrast to his exact contemporary, Philoxenus of Mabbug (died 523), from whom the excerpts in Chapter VI are taken. Philoxenus acted as the main spokesman in Syriac for those who refused to accept the definition of faith laid down at the Council of Chalcedon. Unlike Severus of Antioch, the other great advocate of the Syrian Orthodox theological position but who wrote in Greek (though his works *survive* for most part only in Syriac translation), Philoxenus did not simply develop and refine Cyril of Alexandria's christology; instead he proved in many ways a much more creative theologian and in his writings he offers a very original fusion of elements drawn from both Greek and Syriac tradition.

The most important Syrian Orthodox writer of the second half of the sixth century was John of Ephesus, author of an *Ecclesiastical History* and of *The Lives of the Eastern Saints*, a collection of delightful sketches of the lives of holy men and women from his native region of Amid (modern Diyarbekr, in south-eastern Turkey.[10] Among the many anonymous texts of this period will probably belong the two short pieces on prayer translated in Chapters VIII and IX. The second of these is little more than an anthology of earlier texts.

During the course of the fifth and sixth centuries a vast number of works by the Greek Fathers were translated into Syriac. These included much of the extensive literature of early Egyptian monasticism, such as the *Life of Antony*, Palladius' *Lausiac History*, the *Historia Monachorum* (attributed ironically to Jerome, rather than to Rufinus), and various collections of *Apophthegmata*.[11] A Greek writer who proved particularly influential in Syriac translation was Evagrius of Pontus,[12] and owing to the condemnation of his works at the Fifth Council in 553 many of his writings survive only in Syriac and Armenian translation. So much was Evagrius seen as a spiritual authority by later Syriac monastic authors that it has seemed excusable to include in the present collection one text surviving only in Syriac (Chapter IV); some justification for this procedure can actually be found in the fact that this particular discourse eventually came to be attributed to a Syriac writer, Abraham of Nathpar.

Abraham of Nathpar was a product of the monastic revival in the Church of the East which took place in the sixth century; this spread from the reforms of Abraham of Kashkar, whose monastery on mount Izla, to the north east of Nisibis, still stands. Abraham of Nathpar, who flourished perhaps around the turn of the sixth/seventh century, has accredited to his name a considerable number of treatises on the spiritual life, most of them still unpublished. Several of these evidently do little more than recycle older material, and this applies to the text under his name translated in Chapter X: this proves to be a slightly modified form of a short work originally by John of Apamea.

Probably, but not certainly, dating from before Abraham of Kashkar's reforms comes the Letter of Babai to Cyriacus (Chapter VII). Although this work definitely emanates from within the Persian Empire, the home of the Church of the East, it is transmitted only in Syrian Orthodox manuscripts. This was made possible by the identification of the author as the martyr Baboway, the last Catholicos-Patriarch of the Church of the East who was recognized as orthodox by the Syrian Orthodox. If the identification were to be correct (which is not very likely), then the text would date from before 484, when Baboway was martyred; more probably it belongs to somewhere in the following century. Its author is not to be confused with the great theologian of the Church of the East of that name, who died in 628.

Whereas in the Syrian Orthodox Church monastic writers of the sixth to eighth century seem to have occupied themselves mainly with works of translation and scholarship (most famous among them was Jacob of Edessa, who died in 708), those in the tradition of the Church of the East produced a truly remarkable body of literature on the spiritual life (though it was not always appreciated by the ecclesiastical authorities at the time). It is intriguing to reflect that the best known representative of these writers, St Isaac the Syrian, was a contemporary of St Cuthbert of Lindisfarne: in these men we have two remarkable witnesses to the eremitical life, living at the two opposite extremities of the Christian world.

These monastic writers of the Church of the East draw both on earlier Syriac writers (notably John of Apamea) and on the Greek monastic literature that had been translated into Syriac (as it happens, probably mainly by Syrian Orthodox monks) in the course of the fifth and sixth centuries: Evagrius, the Macarian Homilies, the *Asceticon* of Abba Isaiah, the Dionysian Corpus, Mark the Hermit, and Nilus seem to have been particularly influential for them. Several of these authors also make use of a lost work *On perfection* by Theodore of Mopsuestia.

Martyrius (the Greek translation of the Syriac name Sahdona), from whose long *Book of Perfection* the extract in Chapter XI is taken, belongs to the early seventh century. A victim of the *odium theologicum* of his times, he was deposed from episcopal office on the grounds that he failed to adhere strictly to the doctrinal formulations of the Church of the East (he was accused of adopting the Chalcedonian position). He found refuge near Edessa and it was there that he wrote his *Book of Perfection*, a work of great fervour, remarkable especially for its strongly biblical orientation. It is a matter of some interest that one of the spiritual advisers who had left a great impression on Martyrius was a woman.[13] By far the most famous of the monastic writers of the Church of the East is Isaac of Nineveh, also called Isaac the Syrian (late seventh century), author of a large number of short works on various aspects of the spiritual life. The extracts translated in Chapter XII are taken both from the 'First Part' of his writings, long known to English readers from Wensinck's translation, and from the recently recovered 'Second Part', preserved complete in a manuscript in Oxford. It was evidently thanks to communities of monks from the Church of the East resident in Palestine[14] that Isaac's works came to the notice of bilingual monks at the Greek Orthodox monastery of St Saba, in the Judean desert, for it was there, in the eighth or ninth century, that part of Isaac's writings was translated into Greek.

The other representatives of the East Syrian monastic tradition included in the present book are Dadisho, a contemporary of Isaac (Chapter XIII) and two eighth-century writers, Joseph the Visionary (a convert from Zoroastrianism; Chapter XIV), and John of Dalyatha, also known as

John the Elder (Saba), some of whose writings also came to be translated into Greek (Chapter XV).

It would appear that all these great monastic writers of the seventh and eighth centuries were widely read in the literature available to them in Syriac. Isaac, for example, at one point quotes from the *Life* of the pagan philosopher Secundus, who had taken upon himself a vow of silence.[15] Whereas these writers wear their learning lightly, most Syriac authors of the Arab period (mid-seventh century onwards) follow a trend also to be found in contemporary Greek and Arabic writers, adopting an encyclopaedic approach. This phenomenon culminates in the thirteenth century with the massive summaries of theological, philosophical, and scientific knowledge by the Syrian Orthodox polymath Bar Hebraeus (Gregory Abu'l Faraj; died 1286). Towards the end of his life Gregory turned to writing on topics concerning the spiritual life, producing two works which still serve as handbooks on the subject in the Syrian Orthodox Church, namely the *Ethicon*, with directives for Christian living, both lay and monastic, and the much shorter *Book of the Dove*, a guide specifically intended for monks. In the Church of the East comparable theological compendia were produced by Abdisho (Ebediesus; died 1318).

Although the Mongol invaders of the thirteenth and fourteenth centuries at first favoured the Christian communities in the Middle East, their eventual adoption of Islam inaugurated a bleak period in the history of the oriental Churches, and the flourishing literary activity, characteristic of both the Syriac Churches in the twelfth and thirteenth centuries, was brought to an abrupt end. Contrary to the impression given by some histories of Syriac literature, however, the use of Syriac never died out, and indeed a great deal of writing in both prose and poetry has continued to be produced up to the present day. Most of this, however, remains in manuscript and is largely unexplored. It is thus possible that among these neglected texts lies some masterpiece on the spiritual life, still waiting to be discovered.[16]

SOME FEATURES OF SYRIAC SPIRITUALITY

In order to link the great Syriac saint with the prestigious traditions of Greek theology and Egyptian monasticism, the author of the sixth-century *Life* of St Ephrem introduces two unhistorical episodes in the form of visits to St Basil in Cappadocia and to St Bishoi (Pisoes) in Egypt. Later Syriac tradition went a step further and attributed the introduction of the monastic life into Syria and Mesopotamia to a travelling Egyptian monk, St Awgen (Eugenius) and his seventy disciples, thus obliterating awareness of a native Syrian tradition of the consecrated life which had already been in existence when monasticism inspired by the Egyptian model spread north into Syria in the second half of the fourth and in the fifth century. This native tradition can for convenience be termed 'proto-monasticism'; in the course of the fifth century its distinctive features became absorbed into the main monastic tradition of Egyptian inspiration, and so it is chiefly upon fourth-century writings that we must depend for our knowledge of its character.

One of the most important texts on Syrian proto-monasticism is Aphrahat's sixth *Demonstration*, entitled 'On the *bnay qyāmā*', or 'members' (literally 'sons') 'of the covenant', misleadingly rendered as '*de monachis*' and 'on monks' in the Latin and English translations of this work.[17] The exact connotations of the term *qyāmā* have been much disputed, but it is probably best to associate it with the same word in the Syriac Old Testament, where it translates the Hebrew *brīth*, 'covenant'. It seems to have been understood in the sense of a formal agreement, promise, or vow of an ascetic nature made probably at baptism itself. The *bnay qyāmā*, who included both men and women, lived their dedicated life in small informal groups in the midst of the larger Christian community.

Aphrahat tells us that they consisted of two categories of
people, *bthūlē* or 'virgins' (the term is used for both
sexes), and *qaddīshē*, (literally 'holy ones'), married people who had 'sanctified themselves' in the sense that the
Jewish people at the lawgiving on Mount Sinai had been
commanded to 'sanctify themselves' (cf. Exod 19:10); in
other words, as we learn from verse 15 of the same chapter, 'to abstain from marital intercourse'.

Aphrahat employs a second important term, when he
also refers to the *bnay qyāmā* as the *īḥīdāyē*, a word for
which there is no satisfactory English equivalent. *Īḥīdāyā*
(the singular) has a whole variety of diffirent connotations, notably the following: 'singular, individual, unique;
single-minded, undivided in heart; single, celibate; Only-
Begotten' (in the Syriac Bible *īḥīdāyā* translates the title
monogenēs, John 1:14, 18). It is very likely that the term
monachos in the *Gospel of Thomas* (which has a Syrian
background) represents this Syriac term *īḥīdāyā*. Only in
Syriac texts of the fifth century and later does *īḥīdāyā*
come to be used as an equivalent to the Greek *monachos*
in the sense of 'monk'; more frequently, however, in these
later texts the term *dayrāyā* is used of the cenobitic
monk, while *īḥīdāyā*, in the sense of 'solitary, hermit' is
reserved for monks who spend longer or shorter periods
of solitary life.

It is significant for the understanding of the term
īḥīdāyā within the Syrian proto-monastic tradition that
the word is used of Adam in his pre-fallen state,[18] as well
as of Christ. First Adam—Second Adam typology plays a
very prominent role in early Syriac Christianity; thus
Ephrem describes God the Word as 'putting on the body
of Adam', or even 'putting on Adam', as in the following:

He put on Adam and in him opened up the gate of
Paradise by entering therein (*Hymns against the Here-
sies*, XXVI.2).

The significance of this typology becomes clear when we recall that one of the key conceptual models for the early Syriac Church was that of baptism as the re-entry into Paradise:[19] according to this model the Church should ideally function as Paradise anticipated here on earth. The Second Eve and the Second Adam make possible the restoration of the Fall which had been brought about by the self-will of the First Eve and the First Adam.

Here it is important to realize that we are not just dealing with a return to the state of primordial Paradise; eschatological Paradise, to which the Christian is restored in potential at his or her baptism, is far more glorious than the original Paradise, for Christ, the Second Adam, has reversed the effects of the disobedience of the First Adam. As Ephrem explains, both in his *Commentary on Genesis* and in his *Hymns on Paradise*, God had created Adam and Eve in an intermediary state, neither mortal nor immortal:[20] if they obeyed the commandment God had given him, they would be rewarded with the fruit of the Tree of Life which they had temporarily been forbidden; if they disobeyed and tried to seize the fruit of their own accord, then they would be reduced to the state of mortality, having proved themselves unworthy of the Tree of Life. For Ephrem, Christ himself is the fruit of this Tree of Life, who gives himself to be 'plucked daily' (i.e. in Communion) by the baptized: it is this fruit which confers divine life, providing humanity with the possibility, once again, of attaining that perfect state which had been intended for Adam and Eve, if only they had listened to God's instruction.[21] Now originally, according to Aphrahat, virginity conceived of its own accord and gave birth,[22] and it was only after the Fall that birth-giving as a result of marital intercourse was introduced. In this paradisiacal context the moral and interior aspects of virginity are, of course, of as great importance as the physical or exterior.

This conceptual model of baptism as providing a potential re-entry into Paradise was clearly a very powerful one

in early Syriac Christianity, and it finds expression in all
sorts of different ways, but perhaps above all in the imagery of clothing:[23] thus we repeatedly encounter state-
ments to the effect that at baptism the Christian puts on
the 'robe of glory' (or 'of praise') with which Adam and
Eve had, according to a Jewish tradition taken over by
some early Christian traditions, been clothed in Paradise
before they were stripped naked as a result of their disobedience. Ephrem sums up salvation history by means of
clothing imagery in a single stanza, as follows:

> All these changes did the Merciful One effect,
> stripping off His glory and putting on a body;
> for He had devised a way to reclothe Adam
> in that glory which Adam had stripped off.
> He was wrapped in swaddling clothes,
> corresponding to Adam's leaves,
> He put on clothes instead of Adam's skins;
> He was baptized for Adam's sin,
> He was embalmed for Adam's death,
> He rose and raised up Adam in his glory.
> Blessed is He who descended,
> put on Adam, and ascended.
> (*Hymns on the Nativity*, XXIII.13)

So potent was this idea of baptism as effecting a re-entry
into Paradise (made possible by Christ's own baptism,
death, and resurrection) that some tried to live out the
conceptual model in their actual baptismal life: hence the
promise of 'virginity' or 'holiness' (in its technical sense,
explained above) made at baptism by those who wished to
become *bnay qyāmā*, Christians who sought to attempt
to make a reality here already on earth of this potential to
re-enter Paradise which was conferred upon them at their
baptism.

Far from being the outcome of a dualistic world view
and a negative attitude to the body, these ascetic ideals in

fact imply a very biblical—and positive—attitude towards the human person as body-*cum*-soul, with great value attached to the sanctity of the body, and emphasis laid on the interpenetration of the physical and the spiritual worlds. The life of virginity and 'holiness' (where the spiritual dimensions are just as important, if not even more so, than the physical ones) was an ideal to which only a minority would feel called; alongside it marriage was equally seen as a state whose truly sacred character was something which wife and husband should also constantly strive to establish. Moreover, it is important to remember that those who chose the life of virginity here on earth were by no means rejecting marriage as something inferior, but only postponing it to the eschaton when the wedding feast with Christ the Bridegroom would take place,[24] for at baptism the soul had been betrothed to Christ. Thus, in order to remain faithful to the Only-Begotten (*īḥīdāyā*) Bridegroom, the heart too must be 'single' (*īḥīdāyā*), single-minded in its loyalty to Christ. For the *bnay qyāmā* this 'singleness' was to be lived out to the full.

Yet another conceptual model offered support for the ideal of the celibate life for the *bnay qyāmā* and *īḥīdāyē* (plural of *īḥīdāyā*). This was provided by the connotations for Syriac readers of the spiritual ideal of wakefulness and vigilance, commended on many occasions in the Gospels (e.g. Matt 25:13, the parable of the virgins). Following the usage found in the Book of Daniel, the early Syriac Church called angelic beings 'Wakers' or 'Watchers', and in Ephrem we find Christ himself described as 'the Wakeful One who came to make us Wakers here on earth' (*Hymns on the Nativity*, XXI.4). The angelic life of 'wakefulness' is thus put forward as a model for the ascetic life, and one of the features of the life of angels was its marriageless character (cf. Luke 20:35–36).[25]

Ephrem speaks of both the body and the heart as the bridal-chamber for Christ the Bridegroom. Syriac tradition inherits the biblical understanding of the heart as the spiritual centre of the human person: it is the focal point of the intellect as well as of the feelings;[26] accordingly there is no dichotomy between the heart and the mind, such as we often encounter in other Christian traditions. From the fifth century onwards, when Syriac spirituality came under the increasingly strong influence of its Greek counterpart, most Syriac writers treat the *nous*, or 'spiritual intellect', as identical with the heart. A few writers adhered strictly to the older terminology, but most came to prefer the newer; many in fact employed both terms, more or less synonymously.

One of the aspects of the heart is its interior liturgical role: it is the altar inside the sanctuary of the temple constituted by the body (1 Cor 6:19), and on this altar the interior offering of prayer should continuously be made. Such an idea of prayer as an offering was already familiar from the Old Testament (e.g. Ps 141:2), while in the Syriac Bible (Sir 39:5) it is specifically stated that the heart is where prayer should take place. In the passages from Aphrahat and Ephrem translated in Chapters I–II we find that the location where the offering of prayer should be made is likewise identified as the heart, on the basis of Matthew 6:6, 'Pray to your Father in secret, with the door shut', following an exegesis of the passage also found in Origen and Ambrose.[27] In the *Book of Steps* the 'altar of the heart' features prominently (Chapter III (1)): in this work we have the concept of a three-dimensional liturgy which should take place simultaneously in the visible church on earth, in the church of the heart of the individual christian, and in the heavenly church. In the passage from Martyrius (Chapter XI) the imagery is further developed and given prominent eucharistic overtones.

The parallels between interior prayer of the heart and the Eucharist have important connotations in the close associations regularly seen in the Syriac (and most Eastern Christian) tradition between the Eucharist and the Incarnation:[28] just as the overshadowing of the Spirit on Mary effects the Incarnation, so the overshadowing of the Spirit on the Bread and Wine at the eucharistic epiclesis brings about their transformation into the Body and Blood of Christ. When this analogy is extended to the prayer of the heart we can readily understand how this came to be described in the dynamic language of birth-giving. Two quotations will illustrate this aspect of interior prayer. The first is taken from a work by Simeon the Graceful (Shem-ʿōn d-ṭaybūteh),[29] a contemporary of Isaac of Nineveh:

> Prayer in which the body does not toil by means of the heart, and the heart by means of the mind, together with the intellect and the intelligence, all gathered together in deep-felt groaning, but where instead prayer is just allowed to float across the heart, such prayer you should realize is just a miscarriage, for while you are praying, your mind is drawing you away to some other business that you are going to see to after praying. In such a case you have not yet managed to pray in a unified manner.

The second quotation comes from the prayer before Communion by Joseph the Visionary, translated in full in the Appendix:

> May I receive You, not into the stomach which belongs to the body's limbs, but into the womb of my mind, so that You may be conceived there, as in the womb of the Virgin.

These links between Incarnation and Eucharist gave rise to a technical term for a certain mystical experience, *maggnānūtā*.[30] Once again one is hard put to find a suitable English equivalent for the Syriac term, since it has overtones both of 'overshadowing' (Luke 1:35) and 'tabernacling, indwelling' (John 1:14).[31] Isaac has an entire

section on the term,[32] in which he explains that it has two
basically different senses. Sometimes it refers to God's
continuous protection, of which the saints alone are fully
aware: 'It is a spiritual power which protects and hovers
over someone continuously, driving from him anything
harmful which may happen to approach his body or soul.
This is something which is not perceived by the mind in
any visible way, but it is manifestly evident to the eye of
faith'. But the word can also refer to a gift from God full
of mystery: it is 'a sanctification which is received through
divine grace, when, through the operation of the Holy
Spirit, someone is sanctified in his body and soul'. Only
Mary, Isaac explains, has experienced this fully, but it may
be experienced partially by other holy men and women.
He goes on: 'When someone is held worthy of this overshadowing, the mind is seized and dilated with a sense of
wonder, in a kind of divine revelation. As long as this
divine activity overshadows the mind, that person is
raised above the stirring brought about by the thoughts of
his soul, thanks to the participation of the Holy Spirit'.

Many of the excerpts translated below speak of 'pure
prayer', a phrase absent from the Hebrew and Greek Bibles, but familiar to readers of the Syriac Bible from 1 Chr
16:42: 'These holy men [who were ministering before the
Ark] gave praise, not with musical instruments of
praise. . . but with a joyful mouth and with pure and
perfect prayer'. The precondition for 'pure prayer' is, as
Aphrahat point out, ' purity of heart'. Other writers often
use a slightly different term, *shafyūt lebbā*, 'limpidity,
lucidity, luminosity, clarity, purity, transparency, serenity
or sincerity of heart' (no single English word is adequate
to cover all the connotations of Syriac *shafyūtā* satisfacto-
rily). The noun *shafyūtā* and the adjective *shafyā* are
recurrent in Syriac writers on the spiritual life, and they
constitute a distinctive aspect of the vocabulary of Syriac
spirituality. The words have two particular biblical connotations: Is 26:7, 'Straight and clear (*shafyā*) is the way of

the righteous', and especially Luke 8:15, 'The seed in the good ground refers to those who hear the Word with a luminous (*shafyā*) and good heart' (the Greek has 'an excellent and good heart').[33] Probably the background to this phraseology is to be found in Jewish Aramaic, for at Gen 22:6, where the Hebrew says that Abraham and Isaac proceeded up the mountain on their momentous journey 'together', the Palestinian Targum interprets 'together' by 'with a luminous heart' (Philo similarly paraphrased, with the words 'in unanimity').

A luminous heart is thus the fertile soil upon which the seed of the Word must fall if it is to sprout up and bear fruit. As John the Elder said, 'One thing really pleases God: that the heart should be utterly luminous'.[34] A 'luminous heart' is also needed in order to be able to see things with a 'luminous eye'.[35] This is a term to be met with a number of times in Ephrem's writings; for example, he describes Eve and Mary as the two spiritual eyes of the world, and the second person of the Trinity as the light by which these eyes can function.[36] Eve's eye has become darkened and no longer receives into itself the light, thus losing its power of vision; as a result, when the world relies on her eye, it gropes around after error. Mary's eye, on the other hand, has been preserved luminous, and so 'she is the land which receives the source of light: through her it has illumined the whole world with its inhabitants, which had grown dark through Eve'.

There is yet another important context in which this terminology of 'luminosity' and 'clarity' is employed; this concerns mirrors, which, being made of metal in antiquity and not of glass, had constantly to be kept in a state of high polish if they were to function effectively. Such a highly polished mirror possesses this quality of *shafyūtā* or clarity. The possibilities of this imagery for describing all sorts of aspects of the spiritual life are obvious, but it is important in particular to note the theophanic aspect of prayer which is brought out by means of the use of this image; thus Ephrem, addressing Christ, writes:[37]

Let our prayer be a mirror, Lord, placed before Your face, then Your fair beauty will be imprinted on its luminous surface.

The more polished and luminous this interior mirror becomes, the more possible will it be for the 'luminous in heart' to behold God—in whose image they are created—reflected in it.

The author of the *Book of Steps* bids his reader to 'run after uprightness of heart and of body, and after limpidity (*shafyūtā*), humbleness, and peace of heart and body'.[38] It was 'from grace of heart and limpidity of mind', he explains elsewhere, that 'Adam had rebelled, thus acquiring a heart which knows evil through his own self-will.[39] From this we can see that *shafyūtā*, or limpidity, luminosity, is one of the attributes of the paradisiacal state,[40] and so its attainment is part of the continual quest in the life of the christian to effect the reality of the re-entry into Paradise, granted in potential at baptism.

Many writers in the later East Syrian mystical tradition likewise speak of the 'sphere', or 'place of limpidity' as a goal of the spiritual life.[41] It is Joseph the Visionary above all who gives extensive descriptions of this exalted 'place of limpidity', to which entry is only rarely granted, and then purely through God's grace.[42] In Joseph's threefold schema of the stages of the body, of the soul, and of the spirit, the 'place of limpidity' is situated at the borders between the stage of the soul (*nafshānūtā*) and the stage of the spirit (*rūḥānūtā*; also termed the stage of perfection, *gmīrūtā*). The 'place of purity' belongs in this scheme to the stage of the soul, and it represents the state of humanity before the Fall. Beyond it, and at the very borders between the possibilities provided by the First

Creation and those of the eschatological 'New World' stands this 'place of limpidity' or 'serenity'.

Although Isaac of Nineveh does not use quite the same terminology,[43] he nevertheless offers an analogous schema in his *Discourse* XXII (translated below, Ch. XII (2)). There he is anxious to distinguish between 'purity of prayer' or 'pure prayer', on the one hand, and 'spiritual prayer' or 'contemplation (*theōria*)' on the other. When contemplation is reached, according to Isaac, prayer actually ceases,[44] and 'spiritual prayer' really consists in a momentary revelation and realization of the 'New World' which will only fully be experienced at the Resurrection. 'Spiritual prayer', Isaac emphasizes, is granted only by grace, and solely to those who possess 'limpidity of soul'.

In this supreme state the 'movement of prayer' is stilled, and utter wonder takes over.[45] Here again we meet an idea which is very characteristic of the Syriac tradition, and in particular of the writings of Ephrem, for whom 'wonder' and praise are the responses of the person whose luminous eye is able to perceive the richness of all the types and symbols latent in the created world and in Scripture, all pointing towards the mysteries of the Godhead.

In order for someone to attain to these exalted stages in the spiritual life Isaac and the other East Syrian writers repeatedly stress the necessity for utter and complete humility. Among the signs which Joseph the Visionary lists as indications that the Spirit 'whom you received from baptism is operating within you' is 'a love of God burning like fire in the heart'. Out of this there 'are born in the heart self-emptying and true humility'.[46] This term 'self-emptying' (*msarrqūtā*) likewise has a long ancestry in Syriac tradition. The noun, which is first encountered in the *Book of Steps*, is based on Phil 2:7, 'Christ. . . emptied himself, taking the form of a servant', and so conveys with it the idea of self-emptying in imitation of Christ's own self-emptying: divine *kenōsis* needs to be met by human *kenōsis*. 'Let us abandon everything and

proceed with our Lord's humility and with his self-emptying', says the author of the *Book of Steps* at the very
opening of his work.[47] In *Discourse* XII (translated below,
Ch. III (1)), he speaks of 'the hidden self-emptying of the
heart'. The term once again turns out to belong to the
context of First Adam/Second Adam typology: the Evil
One had urged Adam and Eve, 'cast from yourselves abstinence, self-emptying, the holy state, and humility'.[48] It
was precisely in response to this wish of Adam 'to grab so
that he might become an equal of God in exaltation, and
not in humility' that, in the paraphrased words of Paul,
'Christ did not want to become an equal of God by grab-
bing, as did Adam, but instead he emptied himself'; and
this included emptying himself 'of wanting to become
God amid earthly riches; instead He took the likeness of a
servant while He was in the likeness of that created First
Man, in His obedience, love and humility, in order to
show us how someone becomes a brother, son, heir and
neighbour'.[49] The author goes on to quote Matt 23:12 in
an expanded form: 'Whoever exalts himself, like Adam,
shall be abased; whoever abases himself, like Jesus, shall
be exalted, just as He was exalted'.

These then, are some of the more prominent features
characteristic of the Syriac tradition. In this brief survey it
has been necessary to pass over in silence many others,
also of considerable importance, such as the imagery of
fire and light, and the language of 'mingling' and 'inter-
mixing'.[50] It is striking how often one can discern a clear
thread of continuity between early and late writers as one
moves forward in time from the Semitic pole to the Hellenic pole of Syriac Christianity. With this continuity, of
course, comes development, as the later writers absorb
and adapt in an eclectic way the various strands of the
Greek tradition of spirituality made available to them in
Syriac translation.
In looking back over the Syriac tradition we need to

observe how, time and time again, the starting point for distinctive developments is to be located in the biblical text itself, in the wording of the Syriac Bible (sometimes a little different from that of the Hebrew, Greek and Latin Bibles, and thus from the English translations made from those languages).

Early Syriac Christianity can justly be described as the product of a creative and fruitful meditation upon Scripture. With the fusing, in the fifth and following centuries, of the native Syrian proto-monastic tradition with that of Egyptian monasticism and the spirituality of the desert, and with the increasing prestige, among Syriac writers, of Greek monastic literature, the character of Syriac spirituality was bound to change. What we find in writers of the fifth century onwards is an intermingling, in varying proportions, of the various traditions upon which each individual author happened to draw. Invariably the native Syriac tradition constitutes one component; another is provided, more often than not, by Evagrius.[51] Sufficient has been said to indicate that Syriac Christianity offers a discrete tradition of its own, quite distinct from that of the Greek and Latin Churches and their various descendants today. Thus to the familiar pair of Greek East and Latin West we should add a third component of Christian tradition, which might for convenience here be termed the Syriac Orient. But none of these three traditions is isolated from the others, for not only do they have common roots in the Gospel message, but throughout their existence they have always interacted with one another, directly and indirectly, and often in unexpected ways. As far as Western tradition is concerned, the Greek elements incorporated into the later Syriac tradition provide an obvious common link with that tradition, seeing that the Latin world of Late Antiquity and the Middle Ages inherited many of the same Greek patristic writings which had also found their way into Syriac. Subsequently, during the seventeenth, eighteenth, and nineteenth, centuries several classics of Western spirituality, both Catholic and Protestant, came to be translated into Syriac.[52] But the movement has by no means always been one way, and several Syriac writings on the spiritual life have had a delightfully disconcerting way of crossing difficult linguistic, cultural, and ecclesiastical boundaries, to play an ecumenical role already long before the age of ecumenism. The 'monophysite' Philoxenus' _Letter to Patricius_ was read in Greek Orthodox circles in a Greek translation under the name of the 'nestorian' Isaac.[53] Isaac himself kept his own name in Greek, but offending authors whom he cited, such as Theodore of Mopsuestia, were tacitly given the names of respectable writers such as John Chrysostom. The case of Isaac is particularly instructive, for over the centuries he has had far more influence on the monastic (and non-monastic) tradition in other Churches than on that of his own Church of the East. Many of his works are transmitted in Syriac by Syrian Orthodox scribes, while in Greek, Latin, Arabic, Russian, English, French, and other translations he has reached a very much wider audience belonging to a whole variety of different Churches.[54] Isaac remains today a favourite author on Mount Athos, and it was the inspiration afforded by his writings that lay behind the recent monastic revival in the Coptic Orthodox Church.[55] With the recent appearance of an excellent new English translation[56] Isaac's wisdom has now become more readily accessible to the English-reading world; only the future will indicate what seeds this may sow.

Notes to General Introduction

1. The term 'Monophysite', often applied to them, is misleading and should be avoided; all these Churches reject the teaching of Eutyches, whose 'monophysite' views were condemned at the Council of Chalcedon.

2. The other Oriental Orthodox Churches are the Armenian, Coptic, and Ethiopian Orthodox Churches.

3. The common appellation of this Church as 'Nestorian' is likewise misleading.

4. The Eastern Rite Syrian Catholics and Chaldeans (the branches of the Syrian Orthodox Church and the Church of the East which have entered into communion with Rome), of course, also accept the Council of Chalcedon.

5. Awareness among Maronites in North America of the importance of this Syriac heritage is given expression, for example, in *The Maronites: A Living Icon* Brooklyn NY, Diocese of St Maron, 1985).

6. English translation of the former, by J. A. Emerton, in H. F. D. Sparks, ed., *The Apocryphal Old Testament* (Oxford, 1984) 683–731; and in J. H. Charlesworth, *The Odes of Solomon* (Missoula, 1977); of the latter in A. F. J. Klijn, *The Acts of Thomas* (Leiden, 1962).

7. English translation by R. M. Price, *Theodoret of Cyrrhus: A History of the Monks of Syria*, Cistercian Studies Series, 88; (1985).

8. Cf. H. J. W. Drijvers in S. Hackel, ed., *The Byzantine Saint* (London, 1981) 26–8, reprinted in his *East of Antioch* (London, 1984) ch. IV.

9. Narsai's liturgical homilies are of considerable importance for liturgical studies; see R. H. Connolly, *The Liturgical Homilies of Narsai* Texts and Studies 8/1, (1909). An English translation of one of Jacob's most famous homilies, on the Veil of Moses, can be found in *Sobornost/Eastern Churches Review* 3:1 (1981) 70–85.

10. English translation by E. W. Brooks in *Patrologia Orientalis* 17–19 (1923–5); a more recent translation of the lives of three women from this collection is given in S. P. Brock and S. A. Harvey, *Holy Women of the Syrian Orient* (Berkeley, 1987), ch. 5.

11. An English translation of the Syriac version of many of these is available in E. A. W. Budge, *The Wit and Wisdom of the Christian Fathers of Egypt: The Syrian Version of the Apophthegmata Patrum by ʿAnan Ishoᶜ of Beth ʿAbhe* (Oxford, 1934). The early Syriac translation of the Life of Antony (ed. R. Draguet in CSCO 417–8 [1980,] with French translation) raises interesting questions about the Greek original of the work: see T. Barnes, 'Angel of Light or Mystic Initiate? The Problem of the Life of Antony', *Journal of Theological Studies* 37 (1986) 353–68.

12. A masterly study of this is given by A. Guillaumont in his *Les 'Kephalaia Gnostica' d'Évagre le Pontique et l'histoire de l'origénisme chez les grecs et chez les syriens* (Paris, 1962).

13. The relevant passage is translated in Brock and Harvey, *Holy Women of the Syrian Orient*, ch. 8.

14. Evidence for their presence is provided by inscriptions from Kamed (in the Beqa plain, Lebanon), from near Jericho, and from near Beersheba. For the Second Part of Isaac's works, see the Introduction to Chapter XII.

15. *Discourse* LXVII (tr. Wensinck, p. 271); cf. my 'Secundus the Silent Philosopher: some notes on the Syr-

iac tradition', *Rheinisches Museum für Philologie* 121 (1978) 94–100.

16. One such discovery of an earlier writer has been announced by A. Vööbus, 'Important discoveries for the history of Syrian mysticism: new manuscript sources for Athanasius abu Ghalib', *Journal of Near Eastern Studies* 35 (1976) 269–70.

17. By Parisot and Gwynn (for titles, see Bibliography to Chapter I). On the *bnay qyāmā*, see especially G. Nedungatt, 'The Covenanters of the early Syriac-speaking Church', *OCP* 39 (1973) 191–215, 419–44.

18. Wis 10:1. The Jewish Palestinian Targum at Gen 3:22 has 'Behold, the first Adam whom I created is single (*iḥiday*) in the world, just as I am single in heaven'. For the prehistory of the monastic sense of the word *monachos*, see F. E. Morard, 'Monachos, moine: histoire du terme grec jusqu'au IVe siècle', *Freiburger Zeitschrift für Philosophie und Theologie* 20 (1973) 332–411.

19. See my *The Holy Spirit in the Syrian Baptismal Tradition*, Syrian Churches Series, 9 (Poona, 1979) 49–51.

20. The same idea is found in Theophilus of Antioch, *To Autolycus*, II.27. An English translation of Ephrem's *Hymns on Paradise*, together with the relevant sections of his *Commentary on Genesis*, is forthcoming in my *St Ephrem: Hymns on Paradise*.

21. For this Semitic conception of *theosis* in Ephrem, see *The Luminous Eye: The Spiritual World Vision of St Ephrem* (Rome, 1985) 123–8.

22. *Demonstration* VIII.6: 'without conceiving, the earth gave birth in its virginity'. In Ephrem and in subsequent liturgical poetry typological parallels are regularly seen between the virgin births of Adam from the Earth, of Eve from Adam, and of Christ from Mary.

23. For further details, see *The Luminous Eye*, Ch. 5, and 'Clothing metaphors as a means of theological expression in Syriac tradition', in M. Schmidt, ed., *Typus, Symbol, Allegorie bei den östlichen Vätern und ihren*

Parallelen im Mittelalter, Eichstätter Beiträge 4 (1982) 11–40.

24. For Christ as Bridegroom see especially Matthew 9:15, 25:10 and John 3:29. This is a recurrent theme in early Syriac Christianity: see my *The Luminous Eye,* Ch. 7.

25. Compare, for example, Aphrahat, *Demonstration* VI.19: 'love virginity as a heavenly portion, an intermingling with the Watchers of heaven'. The monastic life as the angelic life is also very familiar in Greek and Latin writers, cf. S. Frank, *Angelikos Bios* (Münster, 1964).

26. See my 'The prayer of the heart in Syriac tradition', *Sobornost/Eastern Churches Review* 4:2 (1982) 131–42.

27. Origen, *On Prayer,* XX.2; Ambrose, *On the Sacraments,* VI.12–13. Among later Syriac writers see Anonymous I (p. 169) and Martyrius (p. 202), below.

28. See my 'Mary and the Eucharist: an oriental perspective', *Sobornost/Eastern Churches Review* 1:2 (1979) 50–59.

29. Ed. A. Mingana, *Early Christian Mystics,* Woodbrooke Studies 7, (1934) p. 58 (translation), p. 313 (text); the translation here is mine. Compare Isaac of Nineveh's words in *Discourse* XVIII, translated below, p. 250.

30. Further details can be found in my '*Maggnānūtā*: a technical term in East Syrian spirituality and its background', forthcoming in the *Festschrift* for A. Guillaumont; see also my 'Passover, Annunciation and Epiclesis', *Novum Testamentum* 24 (1982) 222–33.

31. In the Syriac Bible the same Syriac verb (from which the noun discussed here is derived) is employed in both passages.

32. Chapter LIV in Wensinck's translation (this chapter is absent from the Greek).

33. In 2 Peter 3:1 *shafyā* refers to the mind (2 Peter, however, was not translated into Syriac until *c.* AD 500, since it did not form part of the New Testament canon of the early Syriac-speaking Church).

34. Letter 51, 1 (PO 39, fasc. 3, p. 228).

35. The phrase occurs at Matthew 6:22 in the early seventh-century revision of the Syriac New Testament known as the Harklean (Greek 'if your eye is sound', lit. 'simple, sincere').

36. *Hymns on the Church*, XXXVII; see my *The Luminous Eye*, pp. 52–60.

37. *Hymns on the Church*, XXIX.9.

38. *Book of Steps*, X.4.

39. *Book of Steps*, XXII.5.

40. Ephrem calls the mountain of Paradise 'the luminous (*shafyā*) height' (*Hymns on Paradise*, V.5); likewise Philoxenus speaks of Adam's original *shafyūtā* (*Discourse* IX, tr. Budge, p. 303). It is intriguing to find that in Jewish Aramaic *shafyūtā* is given an eschatological context in the Palestinian Targum's paraphrase of Genesis 3:15.

41. On this see especially G. Bunge, 'Le lieu de limpidité: un apophthegme syriaque', *Irénikon* 55 (1982) 7–18. The term *atrā shafyā*, 'luminous sphere', already occurs in Ephrem (*Hymns on Faith*, XXXVII.7) and John of Apamea (*Letters*, ed. Rignell, pp. 57–9).

42. See especially the discourse 'On the prayer which comes to the mind in the sphere of limpidity', translated by Mingana, *Early Christian Mystics*, pp. 151–62 (Mingana translates the phrase by 'sphere of serenity').

43. I have not noticed the phrase 'sphere', or 'place of limpidity' in the text of Isaac published by Bedjan; compare 'the vale of limpidity' in *Discourse* LIII (p. 384). The noun is rather rare in Isaac.

44. For this feature see Chapter XII, note 12.

45. The Syriac words for 'wonder' are *tehrā* and *temhā*; Wensinck usually translates by 'ecstasy'. Both terms are already of great importance in Ephrem and John of Apamea.

46. In Mingana, *Early Christian Mystics*, pp. 165–6 (Mingana translates *msarrqūtā* by 'complete renunciation').

47. *Book of Steps* I.2.

48. This and the following quotations are from the *Book of Steps* XXI.9.

49. In other words, the New Testament terms of the relationship between humanity and God.

50. For fire, see my *The Holy Spirit in the Syrian Baptismal Tradition*, pp. 11–14. Metaphors of mixing are prominent in Ephrem to describe the coming together of God and Creation effected by the Incarnation. Subsequently the imagery fell under a cloud owing to the misunderstandings it potentially posed in the christological controversies. Outside that particular context, however, it still remained popular in the later Syriac writers: see G. G. Blum, 'Vereinigung und Vermischung. Zwei Grundmotive christlich-orientalischer Mystike', *Oriens Christianus* 63 (1979) 41–60.

51. It will be recalled that Evagrius' influence reached the west by way of the works of his pupil Cassian; in Greek tradition it is clear that he exerted an unacknowledged influence on many later writers, notably Maximus the Confessor.

52. Notably 'Thomas à Kempis', *Imitation of Christ*, and John Bunyan's *Pilgrim's Progress*, both of which were published in Modern Syriac translation in the nineteenth century.

53. Letter 4 in the Greek edition (Spetsieris, pp. 366–95); the Greek text is also to be found in A. Mai, *Nova Patrum Bibliotheca* 8 (1871) pp. 157–87. The Syriac original was published, with French translation, in PO 30, fasc. 5 (1963).

54. A Latin translation of some works, entitled *De contemptu mundi*, was first published in 1506 (reprinted in PG 86: cols 811–86). Theophane the Recluse incorporated some texts from Isaac in the Russian edition of the Philokalia (English translation in E. Kadloubovsky and G. E. H. Palmer, *Early Fathers from the Philokalia* (London, 1954) 181–280). On Isaac's influence, see I. Hausherr,

'Dogme et spiritualité orientale', *RAM* 23 (1947) 12–24, reprinted in his *Études de spiritualité* OCA 183 (1969) 154–66.

55. Cf. O. Meinardus, 'Recent developments in Coptic monasticism', *Oriens Christianus* 49 (1965) 79–89.

56. [Dana Miller], *The Ascetical Homilies of St Isaac the Syrian* (Boston, 1984). It is quite likely that Isaac and other East Syrian mystics may have had some influence on early Sufism in Islam; cf. M. Molé, *Les mystiques musulmans* (Paris, 1965) Ch. 1.

Select Bibliography and Sources

The bibliographies to the individual chapters are divided into two sections: A gives details of the source(s) from which the translation has been made; B lists the more important secondary literature on the author concerned, and provides some references to further translations, where available, of his works. For fuller bibliographical information the following should be consulted: C. Moss, *Catalogue of Syriac Printed Books and Related Literature in the British Museum* (London, 1962), supplemented by the classified bibliographies for 1960-1970 and 1971-1980 in *Parole de l'Orient* 3 (1973) and 10 (1981/2). A short bibliographical introduction to Syriac studies as a whole can be found in J. H. Eaton, ed., *Horizons in Semitic Studies*, Department of Theology, University of Birmingham, (1980) 1-33.

GENERAL STUDIES

A. Baker, 'Early Syrian asceticism', *Downside Review* 88 (1970) 393-409.

S. J. Beggiani, *Early Syriac Theology* (Lanham, 1983).

S. P. Brock, 'Early Syrian asceticism', *Numen* 20 (1973) 1-19, reprinted in *Syriac Perspectives on Late Antiquity* (London, 1984) Ch. I.

—, 'World and Sacrament in the Writings of the Syrian Fathers', *Sobornost* 6:10 (1974) 685-96.

—, 'The Prayer of the Heart in Syriac tradition', *Sobornost/Eastern Churches Review* 4:2 (1982) 131-42.

—, 'Syriac spirituality', in E. J. Yarnold *et al.,* edd., *The Study of Spirituality* (London, 1986) 199-215.

B. Colless, 'The Place of Syrian Mysticism in Religious History', *Journal of Religious History* 5 (1968) 1-15.

A. Guillaumont, *Aux origines du monachisme chrétien,* Spiritualité orientale, 30 (1979).

I. Hausherr, *Noms du Christ et voies d'oraison,* OCA 157 (1960); English translation *The Name of Jesus,* CS 44 (1978).

—, *Hesychasme et prière,* OCA 176 (1966), Ch. 3, 4, 7, 8, 13, 15.

—, *Études de spiritualité orientale,* OCA 183 (1969), Ch. 1, 7, 10, 11, 15.

R. Murray, *Symbols of Church and Kingdom. A Study in Early Syriac Tradition* (Cambridge, 1975).

—, 'The features of the earliest Christian asceticism', in *Christian Spirituality: Essays in Honour of E. G. Rupp* (London, 1975) 65-77.

—, 'The characteristics of the earliest Syriac Christianity', in N. G. Garsoian, T. F. Mathews and R. W. Thomson, edd., *East of Byzantium: Syria and Armenia in the Formative Period* (Washington DC, 1982) 3-16.

M. Smith, *Studies in Early Mysticism in the Near and Middle East* (London, 1931).

A. Vööbus, *History of Asceticism in the Syrian Orient,* I-II, CSCO 184 and 197, Subsidia 14 and 17 (1958, 1960).

Chapter I

Aphrahat
Mid 4th Century

INTRODUCTION

A PHRAHAT, or 'the Persian Sage' as he is sometimes called, is the first major Syriac writer whose works survive. Nothing is known of the circumstances of his life; later tradition anachronistically made him into an abbot of the famous monastery of Mar Mattai, near Mosul in north Iraq. He was evidently a prominent figure in the Christian Church in the Persian Empire, and he witnessed the beginnings of the persecution of church leaders by the Sasanian King Shapur II in the early 340s, a consequence of the outbreak of war with the Roman Empire whose rulers had newly become Christian.

Aphrahat has left twenty-three homilies, entitled *Demonstrations*. These for the most part deal either with the Christian life, or with the threat posed to the Church by Judaizing tendencies among Christians. To the former category belong homilies on Faith, Love, Fasting, Prayer (translated here), the 'Members of the *qyāmā*, or Covenant', the Penitent, and Humility.

Aphrahat's *Demonstration IV* has the distinction of being the earliest extant Christian treatise on prayer which is not primarily concerned with the Lord's Prayer, as is the case with the well-known works on Prayer by Tertullian, Origen, and Cyprian. The *Demonstration*, which is characteristically packed with biblical examples, is concerned primarily to emphasize the need for purity of heart if prayer is to be acceptable to God. Throughout, the idea of prayer as an interiorized offering or sacrifice is very prominent, and in section 2 this leads Aphrahat to introduce an intriguing exegetical tradition in order to explain how Abel knew that his sacrifice has been accepted and Cain that his had been rejected: fire from heaven descended on Abel's, but refused to touch Cain's. The motif is clearly borrowed from such passages as 1 Chr 21:26 (David's sacrifice) and 2 Chr 7:1 (Solomon's sacrifice), where the biblical text specifically mentions the descent of fire. The application of this motif to Gen 4, however, also has an exegetical basis: in verse 4 the Hebrew text *wayyīshaᶜ*, is usually rendered by both ancient and modern translators as 'And the Lord looked with favour on. . .'. The Jewish reviser of the Septuagint called Theodotion, however, linked the Hebrew verb with *'ēsh*, 'fire', and translated 'And the Lord *burnt up with fire*. . .'. Nor is this the only link with Jewish tradition in the homily, for the whole concept of prayer as a replacement for the Temple sacrifices was widespread in Judaism after the destruction of the Second Temple in AD 70.

Like Origen before him (*On Prayer*, XX.2), Aphrahat understands the 'inner chamber' (Matt 6:6) where prayer should take place as the heart, and this is an interpretation which we shall meet again in Ephrem, *Hymns on Faith*, XX (stanza 6). Great emphasis is laid on the importance of interior attitude (in particular, forgiveness) as a prerequisite for prayer. Prayer, however, is by no means just an interior matter: it also involves perfecting 'the rest of' God' (Is 28:12), in the form of works of mercy. Aphrahat offers two practical examples to illustrate how these sometimes need to take precedence over more conventional forms of prayer.

Throughout the homily Aphrahat shows himself to be an early witness to the rich eastern tradition of the spirituality of the heart, anticipating various themes and ideas which were later to become prominent.

It is evident that Aphrahat exerted a continuing influence on Syriac spirituality, especially during the sixth to eighth centuries, for his homilies are tacitly quoted by a number of writers. His works were translated at an early date into Armenian, where they circulated under the name of his contemporary, St James (Jacob) of Nisibis. Individual *Demonstrations* also found their way into Arabic (attributed to Ephrem), Georgian, and Ethiopic.

APHRAHAT,
Demonstration IV, on Prayer

PURITY OF HEART constitutes prayer more than do all the prayers that are uttered out aloud, and silence united to a mind that is sincere[1] is better than the loud voice of someone crying out.

My beloved, give me now your heart and your thought, and hear about the power of pure prayer; see how our righteous forefathers excelled in their prayer before God, and how it served them as a *pure offering.** Mal 1:11 For it was through prayer that offerings were accepted, and it was prayer again that averted the Flood from Noah; prayer has healed barrenness, prayer has overthrown armies, prayer has revealed mysteries, prayer has divided the sea, prayer made a passage through the Jordan, it held back the sun, it made the moon stand still, it destroyed the unclean, it caused fire to descend. Prayer closed up the heaven, prayer raised up from the pit, rescued from the fire, and saved from the sea.[2] The power of

5

prayer, like the power of pure fasting, is very great; and, just as I explained and told you in the previous chapter about fasting, I shall not refrain from telling you here about prayer.

2. First of all, it was through Abel's purity of heart that his offering was acceptable before God, while that of Cain was rejected.* And how do we know that Abel's offering was accepted, while Cain's was rejected? How was Abel aware that his offering had been accepted, and how did Cain realize that his had been rejected? I will try to explain to you about this as well as I can.

Gen 4:4

You are aware, my beloved, that an offering that was acceptable before God was distinguished by the fact that the fire would descend from heaven and the offering would be consumed by it. Now when Abel and Cain offered up their offerings both together, living fire that was doing service before God* came down and devoured Abel's pure sacrifice, but did not touch Cain's because it was impure.³ It was from this that Abel knew that his offering had been accepted, and Cain that his had been rejected. And the fruits of Cain's heart later testified and showed that he was full of deceit, when he killed his brother: for what his mind had conceived, his hands brought to birth. But Abel's purity of heart constitutes his prayer.

cf Ps 104:4

3. I shall demonstrate to you, my beloved, how fire used to devour all acceptable offerings: when Samson's father Manoah offered up an offering, living fire came down and devoured it,* and in that

Jdg 13:20

same flame the angel who had been speaking with him ascended to heaven. Likewise Abraham, on the occasion when God assured him of the promise that a son would be born to him, was told: *Take a three year old calf, and a goat of the same age, and a pigeon and a young dove;* * and when he had sacrificed them and cut them into pieces, setting them out limb by limb, there fell upon him silence and darkness, and fire came down, passing over the divided pieces, and consumed Abraham's offering. *

Gen 15:9

cf Gen 15:17

Again, in the case of the offerings that were made in the Tabernacle, living fire used to come down to consume them. So too, when Aaron's sons, Nadab and Abihu, despised the administering of the offering, fire came down as usual at the time of the offering and, not finding their offerings made in purity, it refused to touch them. On seeing that their offering had not been consumed, they brought in fire from outside to consume it, so that they should not incur Moses' blame, asking why the offering had not been consumed. The fire introduced from the outside indeed consumed the offering, but fire from heaven consumed them. * By their fate the holiness of the Lord was preserved, in that they had despised his service.

cf Lev 10:2

Likewise, when two hundred and fifty men were divided against Moses, offering up incense without authorization, fire was bidden to come forth from the Lord's presence, and it consumed them. * Thus their

cf Num 16:35

censers were kept sanctified at the expense of their lives.

Again, when Solomon built the sanctuary and offered up sacrifices and whole offerings, he prayed and fire came down from heaven, consuming the fat of the burnt offerings on the altar.* Similarly, when Elijah made an offering, fire came down and consumed it,* and his offering was accepted just as Abel's had been, while that of the worshippers of Baal was rejected, as was Cain's. The purpose of my writing to you all this explanation about fire is that you may be certain that fire consumed Abel's offering.

4. Hear then, my beloved, about this pure prayer, and what powers have been manifest in it. When Abraham prayed, he brought back all those who had been captured by the five kings;* and at his prayer a barren woman gave birth.* Again it was through the power of his prayer that he received the promise that in his seed the nations would receive blessing.* Isaac too demonstrated the power of prayer when he prayed over Rebecca, and she gave birth;* and over Abimelek, with the result that the divine wrath was held back from him.[4]

5.* Our father Jacob too prayed at Bethel and saw the gate of heaven opened, with a ladder going up on high.* This is a symbol of our Saviour that Jacob saw: the gate of heaven is Christ, in accordance with what he said: *I am the gate of life; every one who enters by me shall live for ever.* David too said: *This is the gate of the Lord, by which the righteous enter.* Again, the ladder

2 Chr 7:1

1 Kgs 18:38

cf Gen 14:16
cf Gen 21:2

cf Gen 22:18

cf Gen 25:21

[Wright 4. cont.]
Gen 28:12

John 10:9

Ps 118:20

which Jacob saw is a symbol of our Saviour, in that by means of him the just ascend from the lower to the upper realm. The ladder is also a symbol of our Saviour's Cross, which was raised up like a ladder, with the Lord standing above it; for above Christ is the Lord of All, just as the blessed Apostle said: *The Head of Christ is God.** *1 Cor 11:3* Now Jacob called that place Bethel;* and *Gen 28:18* Jacob raised up there a pillar of stone as a testimony, and he poured oil over it. Our father Jacob did this too in symbol, anticipating that stones would receive anointing—for the Peoples who have believed in Christ are the stones that are anointed; just as John says of them: *From these stones God is able to raise up children for Abraham.** For in Jacob's prayer the calling of *Lk 3:8* the Nations was symbolized.

6.* See, my beloved, how many symbols *[Wright 5]* are hidden in that vision which Jacob saw: he saw the gate of heaven, which is the Messiah; he saw the ladder, symbol of the Cross; he anointed the stones, a type for the Peoples.[5] He also vowed to give tithes to Levi, and in him are hidden those who give tithes and received firstfruits.* In his *Gen 28:22* loins is Judah, the lion's whelp,* in whom *Heb 7:9-10 &* is hidden the king Messiah; and by him he *Gen 49:9* pointed to baptismal anointing. And the tribes who were still within him vowed tithes to the Levites, and the kings still in his loins swelled his heart, and in him the spirit of the prophets discerned those of his seed who would come into being. *With only his staff he crossed the Jordan:** it was *Gen 32:10* a wondrous symbol he held in his hand in

anticipation—the sign of the Cross of the
cf Gen 29:1 great Prophet.* And he lifted up his feet on
to the land of the people of the East, be-
cause it was from there that *a Light shone
Luke 2:32 out to the Peoples.** He reclined by the well
that had a stone on its mouth which many
men had not been able to lift—for many
shepherds had been unable to lift it and
Gen 29:8, 10 open up the well, until Jacob came* and,
through the power of the Shepherd who
was hidden in his limbs, lifted up the stone
and watered his sheep. Many prophets too
had come without being able to unveil baptism, before the great Prophet came and
opened it up by himself, and was baptized
in it, calling out and proclaiming in a gentle
voice: *Let everyone who thirsts come to me
Jn 7:37 and drink.**

Jacob also prayed when he returned back
from Laban, and he was rescued from the
hands of his brother Esau. He prayed as
follows, confessing and saying: *With my
staff have I crossed this river Jordan, and
Gen 32:10 now I have become two camps.** Wondrous symbol of our Saviour! When our
Lord first came, the staff left the stem of
cf Is 11:1 Jesse,* just like Jacob's staff; and when he
returns from his Father's house at his Sec-
ond Coming, he goes back to him with two
camps, one from the People, the other from
the Peoples—just like Jacob who returned
to his father Isaac with two camps.

Jacob returned with his eleven sons, and
with our Saviour will come his eleven disciples, eleven because Judas will not be with
them. Afterwards Benjamin was born, and
there were twelve sons of Jacob; and after-

wards Tolmai was chosen, making twelve
disciples of our Saviour.⁶

So much for Jacob's prayer.

7. What then are we to say about the
boundless power of Moses' prayer? For his
prayer saved him from the hands of
Pharoah, and it showed him the Shekinah
of his God.* Through his prayer he brought   *cf Ex 3:2*
the ten plagues upon Pharoah,* and it was   *Ex 7–11*
his prayer again that divided the sea, and
made bitter water sweet;* it caused manna   *Ex 14:21, 15:23–5*
to descend, and it brought up the quails;* it *Ex 16, 17:6*
split the rock, and caused water to flow;* it *Ex 17:8–13*
vanquished Amalek, and strengthened
Joshua;* it routed Og and Sihon in war;† it   *Num 21: 21–35*
brought the wicked ones down to Sheol;* it   *†Num 16:31*
averted the wrath of his God from his peo-   **Num 16: 47–50*
ple; it pulverized the Calf of sin;* it   *Ex 32:20*
brought the Tablets of stone down from the
mountain and made Moses' face shine.*   *Ex 34:29*

His prayer takes more telling than does
Jacob's. Joshua, son of Nun, also excelled in
his prayer before his God:* his prayer di-   *Josh 3:13–17*
vided the Jordan;* it also overthrew the   *Josh 6–7*
walls of Jericho and routed Achar; it held
back the sun, and made the moon stand
still;* it destroyed kings and subdued the   *Josh 10:12*
land,* giving it to the Israelites to inherit. *cf Josh 12*

8. Let us now come to the prayer of silence, that Samuel's mother, Hannah,
prayed: how it was pleasing before God,
and opened up her barren womb, removing
her shame, whereupon she gave birth to a
Nazirite and a priest.*   *1 Sam 1*

Samuel also prayed before his God,
showing the Israelites a sign, when he told
them of their sins in that they had asked for

a king: Samuel offered up a whole sacrifice on the altar* and rain came down—at the time of the wheat harvest.

*1 Sam 12:
17–18*

David too prayed before his God, and he was saved from the hands of Saul.* He also prayed after he had numbered the people, and wrath and anger were averted from them,* when the destroyer had been given authority over them.

1 Sam 19–20

2 Sam 24:25

Asa also prayed and his prayer manifested great power: when Zerah the Indian [Ethiopian] went out against him with an army of 1,000,000 with him, Asa then prayed saying: 'By this shall your power be known, O our God, when you finish off a vast people by means of a small people'. God heard his prayer and sent His angel to rout them.* Thus the vast army was defeated by the power of Asa's prayer.

*2 Chr 14:
10–15*

Joshaphat, his son, also destroyed the enemy's army* by his prayer, which thus defeated them. Hezekiah too prayed, and his prayer overthrew 185,000 men, by means of an angel who served as leader of the army.* Jonah also prayed before his God from the depths of the sea,* and he was heard and answered, and was delivered without suffering any harm; for his prayer pierced the depths, conquered the waves and overpowered tempests; it pierced the cloud, flew through the air,* opened the heavens, and approached the throne of majesty by means of Gabriel who brings prayers before God.[7] As a result the depths vomited up the prophetic man, and the fish brought Jonah safely to dry land.

*2 Chr
20:3–30*

*1 Kgs 19:15,
35*

Jon 2

cf Sir 35:17

Likewise in the case of Ananiah, Azariah

and Mishael, their prayer conquered the
flames and tamed the strength of the fire,
altering its natural attribute of burning. It
subdued the king's wrath, and saved these
just men.*   *Dan 3*

9. Daniel too prayed, and his prayer shut
the mouth of the lions:* the devouring   *Dan 6*
mouth was closed before the flesh and the
bones of the just man. The lions stretched
out their paws and caught Daniel so that he
would not fall on to the ground; they em-
braced him in their arms and kissed his
feet.[8] When Daniel stood up in the pit to
pray he stretched out his hands to heaven,
and the lions followed Daniel's example.
He who receives prayers came down to
them and shut the lions' mouths. For
Daniel told Darius: *My God sent his angel
and he shut the mouths of the lions, and so
they did not harm me.** For the pit was   *Dan 6:22*
covered and sealed, and light shone out inside it, whereat the lions were happy, in
that they had seen the light because of
Daniel. When Daniel dozed off and wanted
to sleep, the lions lowered themselves so
that he might sleep lying on them, and not
on the ground. That pit was more illumined
than the upper room with its many win-
dows;* and he uttered more prayers there   *cf Dan 6:10*
than he had in his upper room, where he
prayed only three times a day. When Daniel
went up victorious, his accusers fell into
the pit in his place and the lions' mouths
were opened, and they devoured them,
grinding up their bones.

His prayer also caused the Captivity to

Dan 9:23

return from Babylon, once seventy years had been completed.*

Thus each one of our righteous fore-fathers took up the armour of prayer⁹ whenever affliction met them, and through it they were saved from affliction.

10. Likewise our Saviour taught the following kind of prayer: 'You should pray in secret to him who is hidden, but who sees all'. For he said: *Enter the chamber and pray to your Father in secret, and the Father who sees in secret will reward you.**

Matt 6:6

Why, my beloved, did our Saviour teach us saying: 'Pray to your Father in secret, with the door shut'? I will show you, as far as I am capable. He said 'Pray to your Father with the door closed'. Our Lord's words thus tell us 'pray in secret in your heart, and shut the door'. What is the door He says we must shut, if not your mouth? For here is the temple in which Christ dwells, just as the Apostle said: *You are the temple of the Lord** for Him to enter into your inner person, into this house, to cleanse it from everything that is unclean, while the door—that is to say, your mouth—is closed.¹⁰ If this were not the case, how would you understand the passage? Suppose you happened to be in the desert where there was no house and no door, would you be unable to pray in secret? Or if you happened to be on top of a mountain, would you not be able to pray? Our Saviour also indicated how God knows the will of the heart and the thought—just as our Lord wrote, saying: *Your Father knows what you require before you ask*

1 Cor 3:16

*Him.** It is also written in the prophet   *Matt 6:8*
Isaiah: *I will hear those whom I have cho-*
sen before they call, and I will answer
*them before they make appeal.** Again   *Is 65:24*
Isaiah said concerning the wicked: *Even if*
you multiply your prayers, I will not lis-
*ten.** He also said: *Let them cry in my hear-*   *Is 1:15*
ing with a loud voice, yet I shall not hear
*them.** He said this about deceitful prayer,   *Ez 8:18*
that is, not acceptable. Listen to every word
with discerning, and catch hold of its
meaning.

11. Our Saviour says something else
there, and it is to be listened to with discerning;* for He said: *Where two or three*   *[Wright 6]*
are gathered in my name, I am among
*them.** And how should this be understood   *Mt 18:20*
by you, my beloved? For our Saviour said:
Where two or three are gathered in my
name, I am there among them; does this
mean, if you are alone Christ is not with
you? It is written concerning those who
believe in Christ, that Christ dwells in
them;* by this He showed that even before   *cf Jn 6:56–7*
there are two or three, even then Christ is
with them. I will further show you that
there is a place where, instead of two or
three, there are more than a thousand gathered in the name of Christ, but Christ is not
with them. At the same time there is a man
who is all by himself, and Christ is with
him.

This saying which our Saviour uttered is
fair and beautiful to those who hear it, for
He said: *Where two or three are gathered*
*in my name, I am there among them.**   *Mt 18:20*
When a man sweeps clean his soul in the

name of Christ, Christ dwells in him, and
God dwells in Christ: henceforth that man
becomes one of three persons—himself,
Christ who dwells in him, and God who
dwells in Christ. As our Lord said: *I am in*

Jn 14:10–11   *my Father, and my Father is in me.** He
also said that *I and my Father are one*, and

John 10:30,   again *You are in me and I am in you.**
14:20   Likewise he spoke through the prophet: *I*

2 Cor 6:16   *shall dwell in them and walk in them.** It
(Ez 43:9)   is in this sense that you can understand this
saying which our Saviour uttered.

12. And I will show you, my beloved,
how God was in each one of our righteous
ancestors who prayed. When Moses prayed
on the mountain he was alone, and God
was with him, and it was certainly not the
case that he was not heard because he was
alone. No, Moses' prayer was very much
heard, and it appeased the wrath of God.

Elijah too was alone on top of the mount
Carmel, and his prayer manifested amazing
powers; for through his prayer the heavens
were closed up, and it was through his
prayer again that their bonds were loosed.
His prayer seized people from the hands of
death and removed them from Sheol; his
prayer, too, uprooted uncleanness from
Israel; his prayer brought fire on three different occasions—once on the altar, and
twice on the nobles; and fire performed
vengeance for him when it came down at
his prayer. He knelt down on his knees and
prayed, and was answered at once, while
the four hundred and fifty who cried out at
the top of their voices were not heard, because they were invoking the name of Baal.

And Elijah, although alone, was all the more heard.

Likewise when the prophet Jonah prayed from lowest Sheol he was heard.[11] Although he was all alone, he was heard and was answered at once.

Elisha too prayed, and brought someone back from Sheol, and he was rescued from the hands of the wicked who encircled him. Although on appearances he was alone, yet a great army surrounded him; for he said to his disciple: *Those who are with us are more numerous than those who are with them.** Though they were alone, they were really not alone.

From these examples I have given you, you will be able to understand our Lord's saying: *Where two or three are gathered in my name, I am there among them.**

13.* As I urged you above, the moment you start praying, raise your heart upwards, and lower your eyes downwards;[12] enter inside your inner person and pray in secret to your Father who is in heaven. All this have I written to you on the subject of prayer— how it is heard when it is pure, and not heard when it is not pure—because there are amongst us people who multiply prayers and make long supplications, doubling themselves up and spreading out their hands, while the true task of prayer is far from them; for they pray the prayer our Saviour taught: *Forgive us our debts, as we too will forgive our debtors**—[but fail to keep their part]. You who pray should remember that you are making an offering before God: let not Gabriel who presents

2 Kgs 6:16

Mt 18:20

[Wright 7]

Mt 6:12

the prayers be ashamed by an offering that has a blemish. When you pray to be forgiven, and acknowledge that you yourself forgive, consider first in your mind whether you really do forgive, and only then acknowledge 'I forgive'. You must not act deceitfully with God and say 'I forgive' when you do not really forgive; for God is not like you, a mortal, whom you can deceive.* *When one man sins against another, he can beseech the Lord, but when someone has wronged God, who then can he beseech?** Do not bring condemnation upon yourself through your prayer.

cf Num 23:19

1 Sam 2:25

Listen once more to what our Lord said: *When you bring an offering and remember you have some grudge against your brother, leave your offering in front of the altar, and go and be reconciled with your brother; then come back and make your offering**—so that when you have already started to pray, you do not then remember that you have some resentment against your brother. In such a case you should consider in your mind that your prayer has been left in front of the altar, and Gabriel, who presents prayers, does not want to take it from earth because, on inspection, he has found a blemish in your offering. Whereas, if it is pure, he raises it up before God. And if he finds in your prayer the words 'forgive me, and I forgive others', then Gabriel, who raises prayers up, says to the person praying: 'First of all forgive your debtor, and then I will raise up your prayer to him to whom you are in debt. Forgive the hundred denarii* in your poor condition, and

Mt 5:23–4

cf Mt 18:23–5

your creditor will forgive you the ten thousand talents in accordance with his own munificence, and he will not ask you for any repayment or interest. If you are willing to forgive, then Gabriel who offers up prayers will receive your offering and raise it up; but if you do not forgive, then he will say to you: 'I will not bring your unclean offering before the sacred throne'. Instead, you will go there to give an account to your Creditor, taking your offering with you, while Gabriel will leave your offering and go off.

Listen to what the prophet says: *Cursed is he who has a fine ram in his flock, yet vows and sacrifices a sickly one to the Lord.** For he said: *Offer it to your overlord, and see if he is pleased with you and will give you preferential treatment.** Thus you must forgive your debtor before your prayer; only after that, pray: when you pray, your prayer will thus go up before God on high, and it is not left on earth.

14.* Now it says in the prophet: *This is my rest; give rest to the tired.** Therefore effect this 'rest' of God, o man, and you will have no need to say 'forgive me'. Give rest to the weary, visit the sick, make provision for the poor: this is indeed prayer, as I shall explain to you, my beloved. All the time that someone effects the 'rest' of God, that is prayer; for it is written: *When Zimri committed fornication with the Midianite woman, Phinhas, the son of Eleazar, saw him, entered into the chamber and slew the two of them.** And his killing was con-

Mal 1:14

Mal 1:8

[Wright 8]
Is 28:12

Num 25:6–8

sidered prayer, for David says of him, *Phinhas rose up and prayed, and it was considered a merit for him, for eternal ages.** Because he killed them for the sake of his God, it was reckoned as prayer for him.

Ps 106:30–31

Watch out, my beloved, lest, when some opportunity of 'giving rest' to the will of God meets you, you say 'the time for prayer is at hand. I will pray and then act'. And while you are seeking to complete your prayer, that opportunity for 'giving rest' will escape from you: you will be incapacitated from doing the will and 'rest' of God, and it will be through your prayer that you will be guilty of sin. Rather, effect the 'rest' of God, and that will constitute prayer.

15. Listen to what the Apostle has to say: *If we were to judge ourselves, we would not be judged.** Judge in yourself what I am going to tell you: suppose you happen to go on a long journey and, parched with thirst in the heat, you chance upon one of the brethren; you say to him, 'refresh me in my exhaustion from thirst', and he replies, 'It is the time for prayer; I will pray, and then I will come to your aid'; and while he is praying, before coming to you, you die of thirst. What seems to you the better, that he should go and pray, or alleviate your exhaustion? Or again, suppose you go on a journey during the winter and you meet rain and snow and get exhausted from cold. If once again you run into a friend of yours at the time of prayer and he answers you in the same way, and you die of cold, what

1 Cor 11:31

profit will his prayer have, seeing that he has not alleviated someone in trouble?

For our Lord, in his description of the time of judgement when he separated out those who were to stand on his right and on his left, said to those on his right: *I was hungry and you gave me to eat, I was thirsty and you gave me to drink, I was sick and you visited me, I was a stranger and you welcomed me in.** He spoke in the same sort of way to those on his left, and because they had done none of these things, He sent them into torment, while those on the right He sent into the kingdom.

Mt 25:35

16. Prayer is beautiful, and its works are fair; prayer is accepted when it provides alleviation, prayer is heard when forgiveness is to be found it in, prayer is beloved when it is pure of every guile, prayer is powerful when the power of God is made effective in it.

*I have written to you, my beloved, to the effect that a person should do the will of God, and that constitutes prayer. That is how prayer seems to me to excel. Nevertheless, just because I have said this to you, do not neglect prayer; rather, be all the more eager for prayer, and do not weary in it—as it is written that our Lord said: *Pray and do not weary.** You should be eager in wakefulness, and remove far from yourself drowsiness and sleep; you should be watchful both by day and by night, and do not be disheartened.

[Wright 9]

Lk 18:1

17. Now I shall show you the different occasions for prayer. There is petition,

thanksgiving, and praise. In petition one
asks for mercy for one's sins, in
thanksgiving you give thanks to your Father who is in heaven, while in praise you
praise him for his works. At a time when
you are in trouble, offer up petition, and
when you are well supplied with good
things, you should give thanks to the Giver,
and when your mind rejoices, offer up
praise. Make all these prayers of yours with
discernment to God. See how David was
always saying: *I have risen to give thanks*
Ps 119:62 *to you for your judgments, O Just One.**
And in another psalm he said: *Praise the*
Ps 148:1 *Lord in heaven, praise him in the heights.**
Again he says: *I will bless the Lord at all*
times, and at all times his praises are in
Ps 34:1 *my mouth.** Do not pray using only one
kind of prayer, but all separately.

18. I am convinced, my beloved, that
everything that people ask in diligence,
God will grant them. But He takes no pleasure in the person who offers up prayer in
mockery. As it is written:[13] *This is required*
of the person who prays, offering up
prayer: that he turn over and inspect his
offering well, lest some blemish be found
cf Mt 5:23–4 *on it; only then should he offer it*—so
that your offering does not remain on
earth. What is this 'offering', if not prayer,
as I wrote to you above. For David says:
Make a sacrifice of thanksgiving to the
Lord, and fulfil your vows to the Most
Ps 50:14 *High.** Of all offerings pure prayer is the
best.

Be eager, then, my beloved, for prayer
which speaks with God on your behalf. As

it is written in the prophet Isaiah, when he informed the Israelites of their sins and called them *rulers of Sodom,** instead of *children whom I have brought up and raised.** For they had exchanged their honour for disgrace. Above Isaiah had said of them *children whom I brought up and raised,** but lower down he says *rulers of Sodom and people of Gomorrah.** And when they did not listen to the prophet's message to them saying *their land is desolate and their towns burnt with fire,** he then called them *rulers of Sodom and people of Gomorrah.* It was then that they brought along their offerings so that they might be forgiven, but their offerings were not accepted, because their wickedness was so great, as was the case with the House of Eli the priest; for it says in Scripture that *the wickedness of the House of Eli will not be forgiven by means of sacrifices and offerings.** The Israelites received the same sentence, for Isaiah told them: *What is this multitude of your sacrifices to me? says the Lord. I have had my fill of whole offerings of rams and the fat of fattened calves and the blood of bulls; nor do I require any offerings of goats. Who requested all these at your hands?** And they said to him: 'Why did you ask for them, and why are our offerings not acceptable?' The prophet replied to them: *Because your hands are full of blood.** They say to him, 'What can we do?', and he says: *Wash and be clean, remove the evils of your works from my sight; cease from evil and learn how to do good. Seek out judgment and do*

Is 1:10

Is 1:2

Is 1:2
Is 1:10

Is 1:7

1 Sam 3:14

Is 1:11–12

Is 1:15

good to the afflicted. *Judge the case of the*
Is 1:16–17 *orphans and widows.* * They say to the
prophet: 'When we have done this, what
will happen to us?' He tells them: *Thus says*
the Lord, when you have done these things,
Is 1:18 *come and we will speak with each other.* *
And how do men speak with God, except
in prayer which is without a blemish? For
prayer that has a blemish does not converse
with God; as it is written, He said in reply:
Even though you multiply [your] prayers, I
will not listen, for your hands are full of
Is 1:15 *blood.* * And he told them: 'When you have
washed and we have spoken together,
though your sins are like scarlet, I will
whiten them like snow; though they be red
as crimson, they shall be like wool. And if
you obey and listen to me, you shall eat
the good things of the earth; whereas if you
disobey and are contentious, you shall be
destroyed by the sword. The mouth of the
Is 1:18–20 *Lord has spoken.* *

19. What glorious mysteries Isaiah foresaw! For he told them: *Your hands are full*
Is 1:15 *of blood.* * What is this blood that Isaiah
foresaw, if not the Messiah's, which they
took upon themselves and their children,
and the blood of the prophets whom they
slew? This is the blood that was red as scar-
cf Is 1:16 let and crimson, and it marked them. *
They can only be cleansed by 'washing' in
the water of baptism, and partaking of the
Body and Blood of Christ. Blood is washed
off by the Blood, and body is cleansed by
the Body. Sins are washed away in water,
and prayer converses with God's majesty.
See, my beloved, how sacrifices and offer-

ings have been rejected, and prayer chosen in their place. From now on love pure prayer, and labour at petition. At the beginning of all your prayers you should pray the prayer of your Lord. Be eager in all that I have written to you about, and every time you pray, remember your dear friend.

BIBLIOGRAPHY AND NOTES

A. *Demonstration* IV, On Prayer, is translated from the edition by J. Parisot in *Patrologia Syriaca* 1 (1894) cols. 137–82. (The other edition, by W. Wright, published in 1869, has different section numbers: these are given in square brackets where they differ from Parisot's). The present translation, accompanied by an introduction and commentary, is to appear in a long delayed number of the *Annual of the Leeds University Oriental Society* (ed. R. Y. Ebied) devoted to Syriac topics.
B. On Aphrahat good introductions will be found by Irenée Hausherr in *DSpir* 1 (1937) cols. 746–52, and by Robert Murray (forthcoming in a volume of *Aufstieg und Niedergang der römischen Welt*, ed. W. Haase and H. Temporini).

English translations of some other *Demonstrations* can be found in: J. Gwynn, *A Select Library of Nicene and Post-Nicene Fathers* II.13 (Oxford, 1898) with *Dem*. I, V, VI, VIII, XVII, XXI, XXII; and J. Neusner, *Aphrahat and Judaism* (Leiden, 1971) with *Dem*. XI–XIX, XXI and parts of XXIII.

1. The Syriac word is *shafyā*, for whose connotations see the General Introduction, pp. xxviii–xxix.
2. Aphrahat is very fond of such lists of biblical examples; here he refers to Gen 4:4 (Abel), 8:20–22 (Noah), 1 Sam 1–2 (Hannah; or Gen 18, Sarah), Josh 12, Ex 3:2 (or

Dan 8:16), Ex 14, Josh 4, 10:12, Lev 10:2 or Num 16:35, 1 Kgs 18:38 (or 2 Kgs 1:10), 1 Kgs 17:1, Dan 6, Dan 3 and Jon 2. Many of these are taken up again in sections 4–9, 12.

3. For this exegetical tradition, common in Syriac writers, see the Introduction to this chapter; and for further details, my 'Jewish traditions in Syriac sources', *Journal of Jewish Studies* 30 (1979) 225–6. Aphrahat goes on to extend the idea of the descent of fire to the sacrifices of Manoah and Abraham (in neither case does the biblical text speak of fire descending).

4. No prayer by Isaac for Abimelek is mentioned in Gen 26:6–11; Aphrahat has fused the passage with Gen 20:17, where Abraham does pray for him.

5. In early Syriac writers the 'People' are the Jews and the 'Peoples' the Gentiles.

6. Tolmai is the name found in early Syriac tradition for the disciple who replaced Judas; in the Greek text of Acts 1:26 he is named Matthias.

7. The idea that Gabriel is the special recipient and transmitter of prayers is perhaps based on Dan 9:21.

8. This delightful embellishment on the biblical narrative has its nearest parallel in the medieval Hebrew work known as Josippon.

9. The phrase 'armour of prayer' is perhaps derived from Wis 18:21. It becomes a commonplace in Syriac writers.

10. For this interpretation see also Ephrem, *Hymns on Faith*, XX.6 (p. 33), and General Introduction, with note 27.

11. The positioning of Jonah between Elijah and Elisha here perhaps suggests that Aphrahat knew the tradition that Jonah was the widow's son whom Elijah raised (1 Kgs 17:24).

12. This corresponds almost exactly to the words of the third-century Rabbi Jose, recorded in the Babylonian Tal-

mud (*Yebamot* 105b): 'he who prays should have his eyes directed downwards but his heart upwards'.

13. For this uncanonical form of the quotation see A. Resch, *Agrapha*. *Aussercanonische Schriftfragmente*, Texte und Untersuchungen 30,3/4 (1906) 192.

Chapter II

Ephrem
d. 373

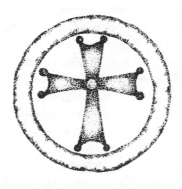

INTRODUCTION

As both poet and theologian St Ephrem is unsurpassed among Syriac writers and he has justly been acclaimed as 'the greatest poet of the patristic age and perhaps the only theologian-poet to rank beside Dante'.[1]

The sixth-century *Life* of St Ephrem is unfortunately filled with legendary episodes, such as visits to St Bishoi (Pisoes) in Egypt and to St Basil at Caesarea, and when these are all removed little firm historical fact is left. On internal evidence his parents seem to have been Christian (the *Life* portrays his father as a pagan priest who threw his son out of the house for consorting with Christians), and most of his lifetime was spent as a deacon, serving the catechetical school at Nisibis, on the easternmost border of the Roman Empire. A baptistry whose erection Ephrem must have witnessed still stands as a church and can be visited in modern Nuseybin today.

In his late fifties Ephrem was forced to leave Nisibis, for in 363 the town was handed over to the Persian Empire in the peace treaty which followed the emperor Julian's death during a disastrous incursion into the heart of the Persian Empire. Ephrem moved some hundred miles west to Edessa, whose king Abgar had, according to a legend already circulating in Eusebius' day (*Ecclesiastical History*, I.13), corresponded with Jesus. There he passed the last ten years of his life. An early biographical source (Palladius, *Lausiac History*, 40) records how, during a famine shortly before his death, Ephrem organized relief for the destitute of Edessa.

Ephrem's extensive writings fall into four categories: (1) prose works; these include fine commentaries on Genesis and on the *Diatessaron* (Gospel Harmony), as well as a number of controversial writings against the followers of Marcion, Bardaisan of Edessa, and Mani; (2) works in artistic prose, notably the *Discourse on our Lord* and the *Letter to Publius* which takes the form of a meditation on the Last Judgement; (3) verse homilies (*mēmrē*), the most important of which is a collection of six, on Faith; and (4) hymns (*madrāshē*), of which at least five hundred survive. It is upon the hymns, collected together into separate cycles in the early fifth century, that Ephrem's reputation as a theologian and poet primarily rests. Interestingly enough, many of them were specifically written for women's choirs.

The hymns, which are soaked in Scripture, cover a very wide range of topics. Particularly fine are a group of fifteen on Paradise (envisaged as a mountain); in these Ephrem explores the significance of the Genesis narrative and at the same time considers some of Paradise's eschatological aspects.

Owing to his immense reputation as a poet a great many works have been attributed to Ephrem which are certainly not by him. Among the extensive corpus of works that go under his name in Greek only a small number of texts are to be found which are certainly by Ephrem. Of the two hymns translated here which deal specifically with prayer, the first, from the large cycle of hymns on Faith, is definitely genuine, but an element of doubt attaches to the second, known only from an Armenian translation of a collection of hymns which are no longer extant in Syriac.

In *Hymns on Faith*, no. XX, Ephrem sees Prayer and Faith as things to which the Christian needs to give birth: the voice is to give birth to the utterance of Faith, the heart is to give birth in silence to Prayer. Failure to do so will result in death, as can be learnt from observation of what happens in the natural world. In order that Faith and Prayer, and the related pair, Truth and Love, may function together in harmony, the heart must be undivided: it needs to remain 'single' for the 'Single One' (*īḥīdāyā*, the Only-Begotten).

The hymn preserved only in Armenian approaches the subject in a much more direct manner and largely consists in an enumeration of the biblical examples of the potency of prayer; this paradigmatic treatment results in many parallels with Aphrahat's *Demonstration on Prayer*. It will be noticed that the theme of singlemindedness, with which *Hymns on Faith*, no. XX, ended, reappears in stanza three.

1. EPHREM,
Hymns on Faith, no. XX

T o You, Lord, do I offer up my faith with my voice, for prayer and petition can both be conceived in the mind and brought to birth in silence, without using the voice.[2]

Refrain: Blessed is Your birth, for Your Father alone is aware of it.

2. If the womb holds back the child, then both mother and child will die; may my mouth, Lord, not hold back my faith with the result that the one perish and the other be quenched, the two of them perishing, each because of the other.

3. The tree that holds back its buds withers up and the birth of the green bud miscarries; but if fruit buds appear from the womb of the tree full of sap, then let my faith rejoice!

4. The seed, swollen with moisture, bursts asunder its covering of soil and out peers the blade of wheat, full of symbols.

So faith, whose bosom is filled with goodly fruits, is a blade bearing praise.

5. Fish are both conceived and born in the sea; if they dive deep, they escape those who would catch them. In luminous silence within the mind let prayer recollect itself, so as not to stray.

6. Petition that has been refined is the virgin of *the inner chamber*:* if she passes the *door* of the mouth, she is like one astray.³ Truth is her bridal chamber, love her crown, stillness and silence are the trusty eunuchs at her door.

Mt 6:6

7. She is betrothed to the King's Son: let her not come wantonly out, but let Faith, who is publicly the bride, be escorted in the streets on the back of the voice, carried from the mouth to the bridal chamber of the ear.

8. For it is written that there were many who believed in our Lord, but out of fear their voices dishonoured Faith; although their hearts confessed, yet He considered those who kept silence along with those who denied.

9. Jonah prayed a prayer that had no sound:* the herald was put to silence in the fish's belly; out of the dumb creature did his prayer creep forth, and God on high heard, for his silence served as a cry.

Jon 2

10. In a single body are both Prayer and Faith to be found, the one hidden, the other revealed; the one for the Hidden One, the other to be seen. Hidden prayer is for the hidden ear of God, while faith is for the visible ear of humanity.

11. Our prayer has become like a hidden

taste within our body, but let it richly give forth the fragrance of our faith: fragrance acts as a herald for the taste in the case of that person who has acquired the furnace which tests all scents.

12. Truth and Love are wings that cannot be separated, for Truth cannot fly without Love, nor can Love soar aloft without Truth; their yoke is one of amity.

13. The eye's two pupils see and move together; although the nose separates them, they are not divided, for not even the slightest blink of one eye can escape the other's attention.

14. Nor were the feet ever divided so as to travel in two different directions; but the heart that travels on two paths at once is divided: on the two roads of darkness and of light it travels in contrary directions of its own choosing.

15. A man's feet and eyes reprove him for being thus divided; the heart is like a toiling ox, equally divided, for it has divided itself up between two yokes, the righteous yoke, and that of injustice.

16. Such a person has subjected his will to the accursed husbandman: under a heavy yoke he draws out error and tills, sowing thorns in the place of wheat, while the goad of sin urges him on.

17. Let prayer wipe clean the murky thoughts, let faith wipe clean the senses outwardly; and let one such man who is divided collect himself and become one before You.[4]

2. EPHREM,
Hymns Preserved in Armenian, no. I

1. Open up the treasury door for us, Lord, at the prayers of our supplications; let our prayers serve as our ambassador, reconciling us with Your Divinity. Listen, all who are wise,* pay attention, all who are learned, acquire understanding and knowledge, seeing that you are instructed and wise, I will relate before you the accomplishments of holy prayer.

Prov 4:5

2. Prayer divided the Red Sea,* allowing the People to cross though its midst; by the same prayer the sea was reunited once more, swallowing up Pharoah, the rebellious and impious.* Prayer brought down manna from heaven, prayer brought the quails from the sea,* prayer struck the rock in the desert, causing water to gush forth for the thirsty.*

Ex 14:22

Ex 14:28

Ex 16

Ex 17:1-7

3. Blessed is the person who has consented to become the close friend of faith and of prayer: he lives in singlemindedness and makes prayer and faith stop by with him. Prayer that rises up in someone's heart serves to open up for us the door of heaven: that person stands in converse with the Divinity and gives pleasure to the Son of God. Prayer makes peace with the Lord's anger and with the vehemence of his wrath. In this way too, tears that well up in the eyes can open the door of compassion.

4. Come, let us look at those warriors who conquered, who excelled in both faith

and prayer. Prayer caused the sun to stop in
its course at Gibeon and the moon at the
field of Ayyalon;* it overturned the sevenfold walls of Jericho that mighty city;* it
brought devastation to Amalek with its
king,* it slew Sisera along with Madon,
Sihon, Og and all their princess,* giving
their land as an inheritance to Israel, the
People of God.*

Josh 10:12–13

Josh 6

Ex 17:8–13

Jdg 4,
Josh 11: 1

Num 21:21–35

5. I will show you, my brethren, what
faith and prayer have effected: the prayer
which held back the sun at Gibeon can
hold back evil from us: He who held back
the moon at the field of Ayyalon, who overthrew the sevenfold walls of Jericho that
mighty city, who drove off Amalek along
with its king, will drive off and break into
picces the might of Satan.

6. Prayer gave manna to the people, and
by the same prayer the just are nourished.
The prayer that bound the heavens* released them too, just as it had first bound
them.* Prayer brought down from heaven
the fire* that devoured the sacrifice and
licked up the water; prayer seized and fin-
ished off the four hundred and fifty priests
of Baal.*

1 Kgs 17:1

18:41–5

18:38

18:40

7. For forty days prayer accompanied
the prophet in the recesses of his cave on
Horeb;* he openly conversed with the De-
ity.* Fiery charious were harnessed and descended,* they took him up, ascending
with him to the God whom he loved. The
Watchers on high rejoiced at the ascent of
the prophet to heaven in his body.

1 Kgs 19:3–8

19:9–13

2 Kgs 2:11

8. Prayer shut up and fettered the
mouths of lions inside the pit, so that the

Dan 6

Dan 3

1 Sam 1: 19–20

just Daniel was not harmed.* Prayer preserved the Three Children in the Furnace of
fire.* Prayer opened up the wombs of barren women,* providing them with heirs.
Such are the wonders that prayer and faith
have continuously brought about—and
there are others even greater than these!

BIBLIOGRAPHY AND NOTES

A. Hymns on Faith, *XX*, is translated from Dom F. Beck's edition, *Des heiligen Ephraem des Syrers Hymnen de Fide*, CSCO 154, Scr. Syri 73 (1955). Armenian Hymns, I, is translated from the edition by L. Mariès and C. Mercier, *Hymnes de saint Ephrem conservées en version arménienne*, PO 30, fasc. 1 (1961). B. There are good encyclopaedia articles on Ephrem and his works by E. Beck in *DSpir* 4 (1960) cols. 788–800; by L. Leloir in *Dictionnaire d'Histoire et de Géographie Ecclésiastique* 15 (1963) cols. 590–7; and by R. Murray in *Theologische Realenzyklopädie* 9 (1982) pp. 755–62. An introduction to Ephrem's spirituality is to be found in S. P. Brock, *The Luminous Eye: The Spiritual World Vision of St Ephrem*, Centre for Indian and Inter-Religious Studies (Rome, 1985), with bibliography. cf. also P. Yousif, *L'Eucharistie chez S. Éphrem de Nisibe*, OCA 224, 1984. Recent English translations of other Hymns by Ephrem include: S. P. Brock, *The Harp of the Spirit: 18 Poems of St Ephrem*, Supplements to Sobornost 4 (2nd ed. London, 1983); *idem, St Ephrem, Hymns on Paradise* (Crestwood, forthcoming); K. McVey, (a volume of translations forthcoming in Classics of Western Spirituality). For details of other translations of individual hymns in *Eastern Churches Review* and *Sobornost*, and of older English translations, see the bibliography to my *The Luminous Eye*. Another translation of Hymns on Faith XX, by R. Murray, appears in *Parole de L'Orient* 6/7 (1975-6) 19–20.

1. Robert Murray, *Catholic Dictionary of Theology*, ed. J. H. Crehan (London, 1967) II:222

2. For prayer and faith in Ephrem see E. Beck, 'Glaube und Gebet bei Ephrem', *Oriens Christianus* 66 (1982) 15–50.

3. For this interpretation compare Aphrahat, *Demonstration* IV.10 (p. 14 above).

4. Ephrem not infrequently provides such self-deprecating endings to his poems; for this purpose he often makes use of Matt 15:27 (and parallels), 'the crumbs for the dogs'.

Chapter III

The Book of Steps

Late 4th Century

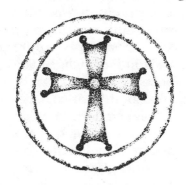

INTRODUCTION

THE ANONYMOUS *Book of Steps*, or *Ascents* (*Liber Graduum*) consists of thirty homilies or discourses and constitutes the earliest corpus of Syriac writings which specifically deal with the more advanced stages of growth in the spiritual life. A passing reference to the River Zab, which flows into the River Tigris, indicates that the author was, like Aphrahat, a representative of Persian Christianity, living outside the Roman Empire. It seems probable that his *floruit* was round the turn of the fourth/fifth century, or slightly earlier.

The *Book of Steps*, has a number of features in common with the Macarian Homilies, whose Mesopotamian background is now generally accepted; there are, however, no direct literary links. Both works have been claimed as Messalian by certain modern scholars (including M. Kmosko, the editor of the Syriac text of the *Book of Steps*) but none of the distinctively heretical Messalian teachings are to be found in either collection, and it seems preferable to see these texts as the product of charismatic communities out of which Messalian tendencies were liable at times to emerge. The distance of the *Book of Steps* from Messalian aberrations can be seen particularly clearly in *Discourse* XII, translated below. Here great stress is laid on the importance of 'the visible Church' and her sacraments—in complete contrast to the Messalian tendency to play down the significance of the sacraments of this 'visible Church'.

A theme running throughout the *Book of Steps* is the distinction between two different kinds of commandments given in the Gospels: first there are the 'small commandments', summed up in the Golden Rule, that 'one should not do to anyone else what is hateful to oneself; and what one wishes others to do to oneself, one should do to those whom one meets' (*Discourse* I.4; cf. Matt 7:12, Luke 6:31). These 'small commandments' concern the life of active charity, and people who observe them are called 'the upright'. Those, however, who seek to become 'perfect' (Matt 19:21) and to receive the plenitude of the Spirit (identified as the baptism of fire and Spirit, Matt 3:11 and Luke 3:16) must also keep the 'great commandments', and this involves the complete renunciation of family, marriage, and property. Such self-emptying (*msarrqūtā*) is in imitation of Christ's own self-emptying (*Discourse* I.2; cf. Phil. 2:7). The 'small commandments' are the 'milk' (Heb 5:13; cf. Rom 14:2), whereas the 'great commandments' constitute the 'solid food of the full-grown, or perfect' (Heb 5:14).

Discourse XII, 'On the ministry of the hidden and the manifest Church', provides an example of the difference between 'milk' and 'solid food'. Baptism in the visible and manifest Church 'gives birth to men and women as children, and they suck her milk until they are weaned'; with growth, however, 'they make their bodies temples and their hearts altars; they consume 'solid food', superior to 'milk', until they become perfect (or, full grown) and consume our Lord himself in truth' (XII.3). Christian growth is seen as a growth in awareness, and the discovery, made possible by the functioning of the visible Church, of the hidden church of the heart. This discovery then leads to an awareness of the heavenly Church upon which the visible Church had been modelled by Christ and his apostles. Awareness of the existence and functioning of the heavenly Church in turn results in a deepened perception of the significance and reality of the sacraments of the visible Church which had been the starting point in this process of growth. Those who have thus become full grown, or perfect, 'consume our Lord himself in truth', that is to say, with a full awareness of what this really means.

The second excerpt translated here, *Discourse* XVIII, is entitled 'On the tears of prayer'. This is concerned with the therapeutic and purifying role of tears in the process of turning away from sin, with its concomitant sense of distance from God. The movement is through tears of sorrow, which stem from the awareness of having separated oneself from God, to tears of joy, the result of drawing close once again to God—'just like the person who sees his dear friend whom he had not expected to see, and he falls on his neck, weeping over him with sobs and tears of joy' (XVIII.2).

1. BOOK OF STEPS,
Discourse XII: ON THE MINISTRY OF THE HIDDEN AND THE MANIFEST CHURCH

BRETHREN, since we believe that there is a hidden self-emptying[1] of the heart when it leaves the earth and is raised up to heaven, it is right that we should empty ourselves in the body too of our possessions and inheritance. Then we shall be keeping the commandments of him who gives life to all, and we shall realize that the person who is bound up in our Lord and ponders on him continuously possesses hidden prayer of the heart. Let us pray with our body as well as with our heart, just as Jesus blessed and prayed in body and in spirit; and so too did the apostles and prophets pray. We should not be fools who fail to listen to their parents: we should not lose our spiritual parents and acquire false parents who belong to the flesh, who will cause us to stray from the truth of our Lord and those who preach Him.

And since we know that there is a hidden
fasting of the heart, fasting from evil
thoughts, we should also fast openly, just as
our Lord fasted and as did those who have
preached him, of old and more recently.
Since we also know that the body is become a hidden temple and the heart a hidden altar for ministry in the spirit, we
should show our eagerness at this visible
altar and in this visible temple, so that, as
we labour in these, we may have rest for
ever in that church in heaven which is free
and magnificent, and at that altar which is
adorned and exalted in the spirit, before
which the angels and all the saints minister,
while Jesus acts as priest and effects sanctification[2] before them, above them, and on
every side of them.

And since we know that the 'perfect' are
baptized in Jesus Christ and purified in a
hidden way, we should firmly believe in
this visible baptism, that it is of the Spirit,
effecting forgiveness and remitting sins in
the case of everyone who has faith in it, is
baptized, and does good works.

2. It was not without purpose that our
Lord and his preachers, of old and in more
recent times, established this church, altar
and baptism which can be seen by the
body's eyes. The reason was this: by starting from these visible things, and provided
our bodies become temples and our hearts
altars, we might find ourselves in their
heavenly counterparts which cannot be
seen by eyes of flesh, migrating there and
entering in while we are still in this visible
church with its priesthood and its ministry

acting as fair examples for all those who imitate there the vigils, fasting and endurance of our Lord and of those who have preached him. Let us both do and teach this; then, once we have attained to humility and have shown honour to everyone, great and small, the heavenly church and the spiritual altar will be revealed to us, and on the altar we shall make a sacrifice of thanksgiving in the prayer of our hearts and in the supplication of our bodies, believing all the time in this visible altar, and assured in this priesthood ministering there; for everything that exists in this church has been established in the likeness of that hidden church.

If, however, we should have doubts and despise this visible church, with its visible altar and visible priesthood, and this baptism that brings forgiveness, then our body will not become a temple, neither will our heart become an altar or a well-spring of praise. Nor shall we have revealed to us that church on high with its altar, its light and its priesthood, where are gathered all the saints who are pure in heart, who dwell in its glory, exulting in its light, seeing that they do not despise this blessed nurse who daily gives birth and brings up fair wards whom she sends on to that great church on high.

This visible church can be seen by everyone: its altar, baptism and priesthood were instituted by our Lord; for in it our Lord prayed, and his apostles were both baptized[3] in it and they sacrificed his Body and his Blood in it, truly serving as priests. It is the church in truth, and the blessed mother who brings up everyone as children. Likewise that body and heart in which our Lord dwells—also because the Spirit resides there—is in truth a temple and an altar, seeing that our Lord resides there, as it is written: *Your bodies are temples of the Lord and Christ dwells in your inner person.* *

1 Cor 6:19

As for the church in heaven, all that is good takes its beginning from there, and from there light has shone out upon us in all directions. After its likeness the church on earth came into being, along with its priests and its altar; according to the pattern of its ministry the body ministers outwardly, while the heart acts as priest⁴ inwardly. Those who are diligent in this visible church become like that heavenly church as they follow after it. This is why the visible church is supremely important, being the mother of all those who are baptized; but in particular it is because the face of our Lord shines upon her and illuminates her.

3. This church, with its altar and baptism, gives birth to men and women as children, and they suck her milk until they are weaned. Then they come to growth and to knowledge that belongs both to the body and to the heart, whereupon they make their bodies temples and their hearts altars; they consume solid food, superior to milk, until they become perfect and consume our Lord Himself in truth, just as He himself said, 'Whoever shall consume me shall be alive because of me'. * Once they have eaten the true food—as the Apostle said,

Jn 6:58

'*The true food belongs to the perfect who
are trained** in strength to know *what is
the height, depth, length and breadth'** —
then they attain to that church on high
which makes them perfect, and they enter
the city of Jesus our King. There they worship in that great and perfect palace which
is the mother of all the living and the
perfect.

Accordingly we should not despise the
visible church which brings up everyone as
children. Nor should we despise this
church of the heart, seeing that she
strengthens all who are sick. And we
should yearn for the church on high, for
she makes perfect all the saints.

4. These three churches and their minis-
tries possess Life, but *one glory is greater
than another.** Someone who passes away
from the ministry of this church without
attaining to the church of the heart or to
that on high, still departs from this world
without sins; he is virtuous and his good
works accompany him. But the person who
passes away from the church of the heart is
even better; and as for the person who attains in his heart to the church on high and
then passes away, blessed is his spirit! He
will become perfect and will go to see our
Lord face to face. By striving in this visible
church a person will find himself in the
church of the heart and in the church on
high: just as when someone is baptized in
visible water, he receives from it baptism in
fire and in the Spirit,* neither of which is
seen; or, just as, once someone has had
faith, he will come to love, and once he has

Heb 5:14

Eph 3:18

1 Cor 15:14

cf Mt 3:11,
Lk 3:16

loved he will be made perfect, and once he is made perfect he will reign.[5] Without this visible baptism no one is baptized in fire and in Spirit, and without this visible church no one will be in either the church of the heart or in the church on high. For if someone is separated from the visible church, and 'ministers in the mountain',[6] then he has either proved guilty or gone astray. But wherever he is, it should have been assured for him that Life exists in her, and he should not break his covenant.

5. Just as a nurse who brings up a child teaches it to eat bread as something superior to milk, so does this visible church teach her children to eat something better, and far greater, whereby they can grow up. It is not the case that the nurse who brings up a child does not have other food, but it is the child who is too feeble for food, and so milk is appropriate for it. Nor is the Spirit who ministers in the visible church weaker than the Spirit who ministers in the heart or on high, for one and the same Spirit ministers to all three. But the children of Adam are very feeble, and unless the church brings them up like children, they will not be able to take solid food.

But what nursing mother who has many children, some thirty years old, others only thirty days old, is going to be able to set before them all one and the same food? If she were to set before them just solid food alone, then her thirty day old child would die, whereas the thirty year old would grow; but if she provided only milk, then the thirty day old one would live and grow plump, whereas the thirty year old one would die in agony. This is the reason why our Lord and his preachers, who serve as leaders for everyone, instruct the thirty day old child as follows: *'Do not* eat with adulterers or *mix with prostitutes,* drunkards and accursed people, or with any whose actions are evil'; but to the thirty year old they say, *'Take on the sickness of the sick, and be all things to all men;* * do not call anyone* a pagan *or unclean* * or evil, even though he may be so. Hold everyone *to be better than* * yourself, and in this way you will grow in stature.

cf 1 Cor 5:9, 9:22
Acts 10:28

Phil 2:3

6. Thus they instructed everyone in accordance with what was appropriate for him. If someone thirty days old were to go off to the house of evil men, he would perish; but if a thirty year old goes to the house of evil men, he may convert them; and if they are not converted, he himself will not perish, for he has become a fully grown man in the spirit.

Likewise they instruct a person whose nature is youthful and inexperienced* to work and then to eat, until he recovers his strength. It was not that the Apostle was worried about the food: he was afraid that when such a person stopped his visible work, not knowing how to undertake hidden work he might learn about foolishness, deceit and slander, and thus fall into old wives tales, joking, laughter and distasteful story-telling,* forgetting that he is a Christian. On the other hand, to the person who is grown up in mind and experienced in heart, who knows how to undertake invisi-

cf 2 Thess 3:12

cf 1 Tim 4:7 & Eph 5:4

ble work, our Lord and those who preach
Him say, *'Do not worry about your body,*

Mt 6:25 &
Lk 12:22

*what you are going to wear,** or about
how you are going to sustain yourself;
rather, you should *seek for what is above,*

Col 3:1-2

and *ponder on what is above'.** For anyone like this is able to admonish, pacify,
exhort and teach people to act pleasingly to
Him who gives life to all; such a person will
stop people from distasteful story-telling,
joking, inappropriate laughter, bad language and evil actions. Because such conduct is so useful, our Lord does not allow
someone who is of such assistance to all to
toil on the land, for he says to him as he did
to Simon, *'If you love me, shepherd my*

Jn 21:15-17

*flock, my sheep, my ewes and my lambs'.**
Now the person who shepherds the flock
of Christ cannot go off and work with a
plough or labour on the visible land; he
will be gathering in, shepherding, and paci-
fying the sheep entrusted to him. He shall
stand with unabashed face on that final day
before Him who bade him *'Shepherd my
flock, my ewes and my lambs'.*

7. Blessed is the person who has entered
that church in heaven, in which our Lord
shines out openly in the same way that the
visible sun does over this visible church
and over these temples consisting of our
bodies. However often the sun may set
from these, from the church above the light
of the countenance of our Lord and our
Saviour Jesus Christ never departs. For even
though our Lord is in every place, he is
only to be seen openly in that church
which is in heaven, and only by those who

have abased themselves and become at
rest[7], gentle towards everyone, people who
have struggled and done battle on their
own with evil spirits, who have purified
their hearts of evil thoughts, just as the
Apostle said, '*Your struggle was not with*   *Eph 6:12*
human beings of *flesh and blood, but with
principalities and powers, with evil spirits*
and with Satan the corruptor'. Those who
have fought with Satan and vanquished him
become worthy of this church which is
above all, in which our Lord shines out
openly, and they receive the glorious light
of his countenance.* For our Lord said,   *cf Ps 4:6*
'*Blessed are those who are pure in heart,
for they shall see God'*.*   *Mt 5:8*

Even though there are other blessings
and other places, for each according to his
works, yet only those who have been purified from all that is evil and from defiled
thoughts are raised up to that great place
and can behold it: they are glorified along
with our Lord Jesus and they receive blessings from his priesthood. *Who will go up
to the mountain of the Lord and who will
dwell in His holy mountain?*—this is the   *Ps 24:3–5*
church which is in heaven: *The person
whose hands are pure and who is chosen
in his heart. This is the one who will receive blessing from the Lord and righteousness from God our Saviour*—who is our
Lord Jesus Christ. Praise to him for eternal
ages, amen!

54

2. BOOK OF STEPS,
Discourse XVIII: ON THE TEARS OF PRAYER

Jn 16:20

2 Cor 7:10

Ps 118:24–5

Ps 100:1

1. Grasp what I am going to say, my child. There are tears that arise from sorrow and there are tears that arise from joy, just as our Lord said: '*You shall weep, lament and sorrow, but the world will rejoice; but after a time your tears will be turned to joy*'.* Someone may weep because of his sins—and he does well to do so, as is written: *Sorrow that is because of God is compunction which turns one to salvation.** Others may have conquered sin and moved away from sinful acts to perform good deeds: they weep in joy, out of their love for their Lord who has performed a great act of grace for them, delivering them from the slavery of death, and making them free; for these people have humbled themselves and kept His commandments, just as David said: *This is the day that the Lord has made; come, let us dance with joy at it. O Lord, deliver us; rescue us!** Let us dance with joy on this day of our salvation!

When someone has been delivered from servitude to death, he serves the Lord in joy, and not in sorrow, as David explained: *Serve the Lord in joy and enter his presence with praise*;* and again he said *Serve the Lord in awe and take hold of him with trepidation. Kiss the Son lest he be angry and you all perish from his way; for shortly his wrath will burn, and all the*

*wicked will be burnt up. However, blessed
are those who trust him** from this world: *Ps 2:11*
He will deliver them and then they shall
leave it and be made perfect in the love of
our Lord Jesus; they will be glorified with
Him on the great and awesome day.

2. On the subject of tears, which I mentioned: a person may weep for his friend,
because he loves him and he is distant from
him. If, then, someone far away weeps for
his friend, it may be either out of his love,
or out of his sorrow; but once he actually
sees his dear friend, he will also weep
when they meet face to face, and his tears
will pour out over his friend's neck, in the
sight of anyone who happens to be nearby.
It is obvious to everyone that these are tears
of joy; for when such a person sees this
dear friend whom he had not been expecting to see, he will weep and sob with an
abundance of tears.

It is the same with people who sin and so
are distanced from our Lord and his righteousness: they weep with sorrow, just as
someone weeps when he is far from his
friend and feels sorrow concerning him.
Such people feel sorrow for their sins, since
they fear the judgement of our Lord, and
they weep so that God may have compassion on them and forgive them.

If they then turn away from their sins and
are justified, they can draw close to our
Lord and their tears turn to ones of joy.
And when they become without sins and
are delivered from sin, they weep with joy
as they encounter our Lord, just like the
person who sees his dear friend whom he

had not expected to see, and he falls on his neck, weeping over him with sobs and tears of joy.

Accordingly, in our case we should be eager to try to become without any sins, asking our Lord to deliver us from sin, just as Paul said: *What a wretched person I am! Who can save me from this body of death, apart from the grace of God which is in* Rom 7:24–5 *our Lord Jesus Christ?**

3. Let us therefore leave behind everything that is visible, seeing that it is transient, and pass over from external sins. Then, once we have cut off those of our sins that are visible, we can take our place in the struggle against the sin that dwells right inside us—those evil thoughts which sin forges in our heart; and we can run towards the contest which awaits us, engaging in it in prayer, just as our Lord did before us: for [Paul] showed us that Jesus *offered supplication with a mighty groan and many tears to Him who delivers him from death*; and he was heard *and he was* Heb 5:7, 9 *made perfect.**

Our Lord teaches us the same thing: when we have come to the state where we are without any outward sins, we should approach the contest of prayer, just as our Lord both said and did.

Paul said to the brethren in the Lord: *Epaphras performs a contest for your* Col 4:12 *sakes in his prayer.** This is the prayer which our Lord gasped out forcefully when *he was in anguish in prayer, and his sweat* Lk 22:43 *was like drops of blood,** and he shed many tears—in order to show us that when we no longer have any external sins and outward faults we should offer up supplication and prayer. For until we find ourselves in anguish in prayer, just as he did, and we too shed tears just as he shed them, groaning forcefully just as he groaned,—not until then will we be delivered from the sin which dwells in the heart, or from the evil thoughts which it devises from within us.

Thus it is appropriate for men who are in Christ to *raise up their hands everywhere and in every place, without anger and without any evil thoughts;** they should shed tears in their love and yearning for our Lord, waiting for when they shall come and see him face to face, as is written: *Blessed are the pure in heart, for they shall see God** in this world, as Paul said, *as though in a mirror, in the eyes of our hearts we behold our Lord; but in that world, face to face.**

1 Tim 2:8

Mt 5:8

1 Cor 13:12

4. The heart does not become pure, then, unless hidden sin has disappeared from it, and any evil thoughts that had been hidden away in it through the strength of the sin that dwells there have come to a complete end. Neither will this sin be eradicated from our heart, nor will the evil thoughts and the sin's other fruits disappear unless we pray just as our Lord and all who preached him prayed.

Then, once we have prayed to the Lord in our heart, we shall be full of joy from our lips inwards. For we will rejoice inwardly when our heart no longer reproves us of sin, and when we have become open-faced in the presence of our Lord, having kept all

His commandments. We will rejoice in the way that David described: *My heart will rejoice in you, Lord, and in those who reverence your name. I will give thanks to you, my Lord and my God, with all my heart; and I will praise your name for ever, for your grace has been abundant upon me, and you have rescued my soul* *Ps 86:11–13* *from lowest Sheol.**

You can see how God delivered our fathers from the grasp of Sheol, and how their hearts rejoiced in the Lord and in those who reverence his name, just as Mary said: *My soul magnifies the Lord, and my spirit has rejoiced in God my Saviour, for he has looked upon the lowliness of his* *Lk 1:46–8* *maidservant.** You can see how she was rejoicing in her spirit inwardly, and exulting in her mind, having found grace and mercy in the presence of the Lord.

5. Let it be a law for ourselves, then, that we should run after perfection. Once we have heard the word of truth and of mercy, *Mt 13:8* let us be *the good soil** for it, and let it put forth in us rootlets, striking root in our souls, and sprouting so as to *give fruit, thirty-fold, sixty-fold and a hundred-* *Mt 13:23* *fold.** Do not let us prove to be *thorny* *Mt 13:22* *ground,** choking the seed of truth, with the result that we ourselves are choked of life on that day of judgement of our Lord. Nor let us be the poor earth on the roadway which does not allow anyone to hide the good seed, but the birds come along and peck it up, so that it never sprouts. Thus we should not be the hard ground, otherwise the word of life will not enter us and strike

root in us, but instead the evil one will snatch the good seed from our earth. Nor should our minds be far distant from awareness, and we be like the thin soil in which seed withers and does not sprout, owing to the rays of the sun.

Let us, rather, be diligent in providing fruit lest, when there spring up children who perform the acceptable and perfect will of our Lord, we ourselves actually wither under the new *Sun of Justice*, that Sun of mercy *on whose wings is healing.** *Mal 4:2*

So once we have heard the Word which summons us to the way of life of our Lord and of his heralds, let us come and allow ourselves to be made perfect; let us set as a law for ourselves their imitation, saying Why do we not become like them, seeing that they themselves were like us? Let us listen to Paul who says I have despised all that is visible, *and I consider as dung all* the gain that will remain behind* (*sc.* when *Phil 3:8* I die), and not accompany me to that world of truth and of glory. *Become like me,* for I too was like you.* *Phil 3:17*

You see that, if we want, we shall become like Paul.

BIBLIOGRAPHY AND NOTES

A. The translation is made from M. Kmosko's edition, *Patrologia Syriaca* 3 (1926) cols. 285–304 and 433–44. B. Good orientations on this work are provided by A. Guillaumont in *DSpir* 9 (1976) cols. 749–54, and in his 'Situation et signification du *Liber Graduum* dans la spiritualité syriaque', *OCA* 197 (1974) 331–22. Kmosko's edition contains a Latin translation; an English translation by M. Parmentier and R. A. Kitchen is in preparation (a duplicated translation of Homilies I—VI, by M. Parmentier, has been already published by Dutch Interchurch Aid, Utrecht, 1984). Another translation of the short Homily XII can be found in R. Murray, *Symbols of Church and Kingdom* (Cambridge, 1975) 264–8.

1. For 'self-emptying' (*msarrqūtā*) and its connotations of Phil 2:7, see the General Introduction, pp. xxxi-xxxii.

2. The Syriac term is *mraḥḥef*, often used of the sanctifying action of the Spirit; cf. Gen 1:2, where the word is used of the action of the Spirit of God over the primordial waters. See further my 'The epiclesis in the Antiochene baptismal ordines', *OCA* 197 (1974) 208–9.

3. R. Murray translates the verb as an active, which presupposes an easy emendation of the Syriac text.

4. The Syriac has *mkahhen*, a verb derived from *kāhnā* 'priest'; it is used of Jesus in Section 1 and of the apostles in Section 2.

5. Compare the *Gospel of Thomas* 2 for this series.

6. It has been suggested that this is a reference to Juda-izers (probably based on Jn 4:21); the passage remains obscure.

7. Perhaps an allusion to Mt 11:28, 'I will give you rest'. The concept of 'rest' and of Christ as 'the restful one' (so the Syriac at Matt 11:29; Greek *praus*) is important in early Syriac Christianity: see G. Winkler in *Le Muséon* 96 (1983) 267–326.

Chapter IV

Evagrius

d. 399

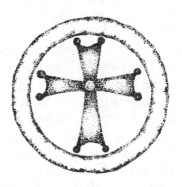

INTRODUCTION

E VAGRIUS is one of the most important eastern writers on the spiritual life. Although he wrote in Greek an excerpt is included here for two reasons: first, many of his writings (including the text translated here) survive only in Syriac, for reasons elucidated below; and secondly, because he is regularly acknowledged by Syriac writers as a great authority on the spiritual life.

Evagrius was born in Pontus about 345. He was ordained reader by St Basil and deacon by St Gregory Nazianzus, whom he always regarded as his intellectual mentor. A brilliant career at Constantinople was cut short by an affair, as a result of which he had to flee the capital. This traumatic experience was the occasion for his conversion to the ascetic life, into which he was initially guided by Melania the Elder and Rufinus at Jerusalem. About 383 he moved on to Egypt, where he spent the last sixteen years of his life, first in the Nitrian desert (for two years), and then in the desert of the Cellulae (cells)—both between Cairo and Alexandria. His disciple Palladius devoted a chapter (38) to him in his *Lausiac History*. Evagrius also features in some of the *Apophthegmata* literature, and several elements of his teaching are reflected in the works of Cassian.

Although Evagrius was one of the most prolific and influential of Greek writers on the interior life, only a few of his works survive in Greek, and then usually under some other name. This was largely a consequence of the

64

condemnation of his more speculative teaching at the Fifth Council (553), in Constantinople. By that time, however, many of his works had already been translated into Syriac and Armenian, and so it is in these languages, unaffected by the decisions of the Fifth Council, that most of his works survive. Through the Syriac translations Evagrius exercised a profound influence on many later Syriac writers, including St Isaac of Nineveh, for whom Evagrius was one of the great masters of spiritual knowledge. His influence likewise travelled west, by way of Cassian's writings, while in the Byzantine world it has left its mark on a number of writers, notably St Maximus the Confessor.

Among the best known of Evagrius' many works are his 'Hundred Chapters [*Kephalaia, i.e.* Headings, or Texts] on Prayer', whose Greek original survives, attributed to St Nilus. Much less accessible is the text translated below. Unlike some of Evagrius' other works, where the theoretical or speculative element predominates, this short work is essentially very practical in the advice it offers. It survives only in Syriac, and is regularly accredited as belonging to Evagrius in the six earliest manuscripts (the oldest belongs to the sixth or seventh century); in the East Syrian tradition, however, it eventually came to be incorporated among the works of Abraham of Nathpar (on whom see chapter X, below). Its influence on later writers can be directly observed in the anonymous text on prayer translated in Chapter VIII, below, for here a whole paragraph from this text by Evagrius has been tacitly incorporated.

EVAGRIUS,
Admonition on Prayer

YOU KNOW VERY WELL, my brother, that someone who wants to set out on a long journey will first of all examine himself, and then he will attach himself to other travellers with whom he is able and willing to keep up; otherwise he may get left behind by his companions on the journey and come to harm. It is exactly the same with a person who wants to travel on the road to righteousness. First of all let him look into himself and see how strong he is, then let him choose a way of life that is appropriate to himself. It is better to begin from one's feeble state and end up strong, to progress from small things to big, than to set your heart from the very first on the perfect way of life, only to have to abandon it later,—or keep to it solely out of habit, because of what others will think—in which case all this labour will be in vain.

It is the same with people who travel: if

they tire themselves out on the very first day by rushing along, they will end up wasting many days as a result of sickness. But if they start out walking at a gentle pace until they have got accustomed to walking, in the end they will not get tired, even though they walk great distances.

Likewise anyone who wishes to embark on the labours of the virtuous life should train himself gently, until he finally reaches the perfect state. Do not be perplexed by the many paths trodden by our Fathers of old, each different from the other; do not zealously try to imitate them all: this would only upset your way of life. Rather, choose a way of life that suits your feeble state; travel on that, and you will live, for your Lord is merciful and he will receive you, not because of your achievements, but because of your intention, just as he received the destitute woman's gift.* *Mk 12:43 & Lk 21:3*

If you are thinking of adding to your labours, do not be in a hurry. Be patient. Then, if the idea remains with you, urging you on to yearn for something more ambitious, you may know that this is to your advantage, and you can carry out your intention in confidence, for it is of God. But if the idea should come to you only once or twice, and not again, then you should consider it to be of Satan who cunningly wants to hold you back. It is the same with all one's thoughts: as the Fathers have said, 'Do we not discern between them'?

A person who embarks on this way of life needs to be both astute and simple, both wise and foolish, both cunning and guile-

cf Mt 10:16 less:* in each case, the former with respect
to anything good, and the latter with respect to all that is bad. Let us be wise in
keeping a good watch over our way of life,
not letting the demons lead us astray; but
let us be guileless and not think anything ill
of our companions, and let us not harbour
resentment against our fellow.

Above everything else, choose for yourself humility. Set an example and foundation by means of all your good words. Bend
down as you worship, let your speech be
lowly, so that you may be loved by both
God and other men and women.

Allow the Spirit of God to dwell within
you; then in his love he will come and make
a habitation with you; he will reside in you
and live in you. If your heart is pure you
will see him and he will sow in you the
good seed of reflection upon his actions and
wonder at his majesty. This will happen if
you take the trouble to weed out from your
soul the undergrowth of desires, along with
Mt 13:22, Mk
4:18, Lk 8:14 the thorns and tares of bad habits.*

A sinner who begins to show concern
over his soul and who becomes penitent is
like a kitchen utensil which is full of filth
and blackened; yet once washed and
scrubbed it glistens. Again, he resembles a
piece of charcoal that was dark-coloured
and cold, but when it is put in the fire it
becomes hot and glows. Or he is like gold
or silver vessels which were badly dis-
coloured, but were then polished up. You
could also compare him to a corpse into
which the soul is breathed, to a dead person who has come to life, to someone lost

who has been found,* to a stray lamb that   *cf Lk 15:6, 24*
has returned, to a sick person who has recovered, to someone poverty-stricken who
has become rich, to a person mourning
who now rejoices, to someone starving
who has got enough to eat, to a royal portrait that has been renovated, to a ruined
house into which a king has entered and
taken up residence after having restored it.

Have a love for penitence, then; put your
neck under its yoke. Give pleasure to your
Lord by changing from bad actions to good.
*Be reconciled** readily, while there is still   *Lk 12:58*
time, while you still have authority over
your soul. Carry out whatever you are capable of doing, and then after it is all done
reckon yourself as *a useless servant,** for   *Lk 17:10*
you have not been able to repay anything of
what you owe. Say to yourself, 'I am a hired
labourer; why am I slow in wanting to perform my work? I have received an invitation,
so why do I delay to join my companions? I
owe a great sum, when shall I repay it? I have
a long journey ahead, when shall I reach its
end, and how much shall I need by way of
provisions? My Lord has sent for me and is
wanting me, when shall I reach him? I need
to run, so why am I carrying all this weight
of earthly things around? I am tied down by
the bonds of love of the world. My companions are awake, should I then sleep? My companions are struggling, should I then be
defeated? My companions are weeping,
should I then be laughing? My companions
are in grief, should I then be merry? My companions are silent, should I then talk? My
companions have their thoughts on their

Lord, his Kingdom and his glory, should I
still be thinking about the very things I
promised to leave behind?'

And when you want to get up to pray
during the night and your body is feeling
sluggish, ponder all these things and recall
to your mind how many others are standing
in prayer on their feet, or are bowed, or
kneeling; how many are weeping and gasping amid groans, how many are lamenting
at the body's sluggishness, how many are
drunk with love and have forgotten their
own natures, how many are singing in their
hearts to the Lord.

If you think about all this, then you will
find relief from all your sluggishness and
weariness, and you will offer up your
prayer eagerly and with many tears. Then
recollect how many are awake and at their
work, how many are travelling on journeys,
are ploughing, or carrying out various
crafts; remember the shepherds, the night
watchmen, those guarding their treasures.
If all these take such trouble over things
that are transient, how much more should I
take trouble over my Lord.

When you stand up for prayer, do not
begin in a slovenly way, lest you perform all
your prayer in a slack or slovenly and wearied way. Rather, when you stand up, sign
yourself with the sign of the cross, gather
together your thoughts, be in a state of recollection and readiness, gaze upon him to
whom you are praying, and then com-
mence. Force yourself, so that right at the
beginning of your prayer tears may flow

and you feel suffering in yourself, so that your whole prayer may prove beneficial.

When you do not have thoughts which hinder you, it is not necessary to make space between one group of psalms and the next. But if your thoughts are in turmoil, you should spend more time in prayers and tears, than in the recitation of the psalms. Drive the thoughts away by whatever means you have tested out, whether by varying the words[1] or by some other means. Take in what I am telling you. If you should then have some beneficial thought, let it take the place of the psalms for you: do not push away from yourself what is the gift of God just in order to fulfil your prescribed portion of psalms.

Prayer that does not have mingled into it the thought of God and interior vision is a weariness of the flesh. Do not rejoice over saying a great quantity of psalms when a veil is thrown over your heart: a single word said with an attentive mind is better than a thousand when the mind is far away.

At the time of prayer be straightforward and simple, an astute child, and then you will behold the glory of God. Remove from yourself all crooked and evil thoughts; make yourself like a weaned child with its mother.

Blessed are you if you have to struggle hard in prayer. Say your words, offer up your complaint, seek out your Judge.* Reply to your adversary Satan with anger, until he is defeated. Then your Lord will see your vigilance and will adjudicate your case with righteousness, condemning your enemy so that he will no longer be found,

cf Lk 18:1–7

while at the same time giving support to your weakness.

If the pleasurable passions should fight against you, seek escape from them from your Lord. And if unclean thoughts should enter your mind, do not be upset; just refuse to consent to them: do not accept them or allow them any place in your mind, then they will leave all of a sudden and run off, like a traveller who turns aside for the night, but then moves off early.

Be careful lest your mind wander during your time of prayer, thinking about empty things. In that case you will stir the Judge to anger, rather than to good will, seeing that he has been insulted by you. Should you be afraid in the presence of ordinary judges but show contempt in the presence of God? How can a person who is not aware of where he is standing and what he is saying imagine of himself that he is offering up prayer? His mind is blinded by passions: he stands on his feet, he is without sleep, he refrains from worldly activities, he is thought by many to be dead to the world and forgetful of such things, yet he is enticed by the thought of matters far away from him, and so none of these other things are of any benefit to him— just as dreams do not bring any advantage to those who see them.

Arouse yourself, wretch; your Lord is speaking with you. Do not wander off. His elect angels surround you, do not be dismayed; the ranks of the demons stand facing you, so do not grow lax.

My brother, realize that just as the angels rejoice when we praise God, following their example, so too the demons are aggrieved when they see us paying attention in prayer. Because they themselves have refused to give praise, they devise ways of preventing us from praising God, seeing that their machinations are foiled by praise, it being a shield and armour against them. Accordingly they are eager to hold us back from our service, and when they see that we are not listening to them, but are always constant in our converse with God, then they act cunningly in order to do us harm by means of thoughts and worries about particular persons, imagining conversations with them—sometimes with friends, sometimes with enemies—in order to exchange our love of God for love of men. The result is that, instead of praying for our enemies, as we are bidden,* we acquire hatred for those who have grieved us, and so our prayer becomes the cause of anger.

Mt 5:44 & Lk 6:28

Beware, then, of the ambushes of the adversaries; guard yourself against those who are intent on adding to their wickedness, erring themselves, and causing others to err.

Set off on the path of prayer with confidence, then swiftly and speedily will you reach the place of peace, which is your stronghold against the place of fear. Thus, while your mind is wide awake and attentive, the offering of your prayer will be accepted as was Abel's offering,* whereas your adversary will be put to shame, and you yourself will prove an object of fear to the demons at your time of prayer, and the words of your mouth will be in accord with the will of God.

Gen 4:4

BIBLIOGRAPHY AND NOTES

A. The *Admonition on Prayer* (*Clavis Patrum Graecorum* II, no 2440 (2)) is translated from the edition of the Syriac version by W. Frankenberg, *Evagrius Ponticus*, Abhandlungen der kgl. Gesellschaft der Wissenschaften zu Göttingen, phil.-hist. Kl. NF XIII, 2 (Berlin, 1912) 558–62 (the Greek text there is Frankenberg's retroversion from Syriac; the original is lost). Frankenberg used the earliest surviving Syriac manuscript, British Library Add. 14578, of 6th/7th century. The *Admonition* is included among the works of Abraham of Nathpar in Br. Libr. Or. 6714 (fol. 88a–89b), of ninth/tenth century, Add. 14614, of tenth century, and elsewhere.

B. An excellent introduction to Evagrius' writings and thought by A. and C. Guillaumont will be found in *DSpir* 4 (1960) cols. 1731–44; there is a more recent article on him, by A. Guillaumont, in *Theologische Realenzyklopädie* 10 (1982) 565–70. Evagrius' influence on Syriac writers is studied by A. Guillaumont in his *Les 'Kephalaia Gnostica' d'Evagre le Pontique et l'histoire de l'Origénisme chez les grecs et les syriens* (Paris, 1962). There are two English translations of Evagrius' 'Hundred Texts on Prayer' (attributed to Nilus in the Greek manuscripts): J. E. Bamberger, *Evagrius Ponticus. The Praktikos, Chapters on Prayer*, Cistercian Studies Series 4, (1970), and G. E. H. Palmer, Philip Sherrard and Kallistos Ware, *The Philokalia* (London/Boston, 1979), 1; 55–71; a valuable commentary, together with a French translation, was provided by I. Hausherr, *Les Leçons d'un Contemplatif: Le Traité de l'Oraison d'Évagre le Pontique* (Paris, 1960). A German translation of the Letters is now available, by G. Bunge, *Evagrios Pontikos, Briefe aus der Wüste* (Trier, 1986), and of the texts on prayer, *Praktikos-Über das Gebet,* Schriften zur Kontemplation (Münsterschwarzach, 1986), translated from the English.

1. Some manuscripts read 'chants'.

Chapter V

John of Apamea

First half of 5th Century

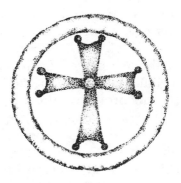

INTRODUCTION

A N IMPRESSIVE NUMBER of works on different aspects of the spiritual life are attributed to an author variously known as John of Apamea, John the Solitary (*īḥīdāyā*), or (erroneously) John of Lykopolis. The identity of this John, who is today beginning to emerge as a major writer of the early Syriac Church, is shrouded in mystery. It is clear from the writings under his name—by no means all of which have yet been published—that their author was a man of considerable education and culture, and several of his discourses make use of the dialogue form, essentially a Greek *genre*. Recent studies suggest that he belongs to the first half of the fifth century, and the title 'of Apamea' links him with the famous city of that name in Syria (it had produced the Greek philosophers Posidonius and Numenius, and for many years the Neoplatonist Iamblichus had taught there). An entry in a tenth-century Lexicon by Bar Bahlul[1] further indicates that his monastery was near Nikertai (in the vicinity of Apamea), the place where Theodoret lived as a monk prior to his being made bishop of Cyrrhus in 423.

Works by John which have so far been published include: three dialogues on the soul, a series of dialogues with a certain Thaumasius, three treatises on baptism and the life of the 'New World', three long letters, and a short work on prayer and silence (a sixth-century adaptation of which, by Abraham of Nathpar, features in Chapter X, below). The *Letter to Hesychius*, translated here, has not

78

yet been published. The identity of Hesychius is not known, but on internal grounds it is clear that he had only recently adopted the monastic life. John's Letter provides him with much practical advice. An indication of how greatly this advice was appreciated by later generations of monks is given by the large number of manuscripts which survive containing the Letter.

John's writings clearly exerted a strong influence on later Syriac monastic literature; in particular his threefold scheme of the spiritual life, divided into the levels of the body, of the soul, and of the spirit, was adopted by many Syriac writers, including Isaac of Nineveh and Joseph the Visionary. For John the aim of the Christian life is the actualization, as far as is possible, in this life of the resurrection life in Christ, the hope and pledge of which has been given to each Christian at baptism.

Growth in the Christian life is seen by John as a gradual process of liberation from the evil passions, and in this process the three levels simply represent three main successive states in what is really a continuum. At the level of the body (*pagrānūtā*) there still exists enslavement to sin and subjection to the body's cravings; any love that may be present is both unstable and interested. At the level of the soul (*nafshānūtā*) there is a turning away from the body's desires and an increasing awareness and cultivation of the virtues of the soul. It is at this level that repentance occurs and prayer is one of the principal accompaniments of the state; this prayer, however, is subject to distraction, and is not yet either pure or continuous. Progress takes place as a result of a process of 'self-emptying' (a term he perhaps borrows from the *Book of Steps*); this leads ultimately to 'purity of soul', which stands at the dividing point between the level of the soul and that of the spirit (*rūḥānūtā*). 'Purity of soul' makes possible 'luminosity, or transparency, of soul' (*shafyūt nafshā*), which is a condition of receptivity to the light of the revelation of divine mysteries. Only here is the meaning of 'true love' realized.

This is the point at which entry is made into the life of the New Person (cf. Eph 2:15, 4:24) in the New World. Such a state may be glimpsed at during mortal life, and serves as the constant object of hope, but it can only be fully realized after the resurrection.

The following quotation from the *Dialogue on the Soul* provides a good illustration of John's teaching on the subject:

Eusebius: What is the beginning of the way of life of the inner person?

The Solitary: Self-emptying of love of money. After self-emptying of the love of money it is absolutely necessary that one empty oneself of the passion of love of praise. Then afterwards such a person has the possibility of existing in excellence of mind, in humility and forbearance, in serenity and in mental awareness, in joy at the hope of this, in wakefulness and concern for what is beautiful and good, in perfect love of God and of human beings. For it is by these things that a person approaches purity of soul, which is the sum of the entire way of life which God bade human beings to follow during this life. For all his commandments bring a person as far as transparency of soul. Now once he has done battle and overcome all the evil passions, and stands in purity of mind, a person leaves the entire way of life commanded by God in this life, and henceforth he begins to enter in from transparency of soul to the way of life of the New Person. No longer is he a servant subject to a law, but a beloved son who has been liberated from everything that belongs to this world. He begins to become a sharer in the mystery of God. *Dialogue on the Soul*, ed. S. Dedering, *Johannes von Lykopolis. Ein Dialog über die Seele und die Affekte des Menschen* (Uppsala, 1936) pp.6–7.

JOHN THE SOLITARY,
Letter to Hesychius

YOU ARE WELL AWARE, my brother, that the separation of one limb causes pain to the other limbs; even though their painful suffering may not be manifest, this suffering, you realize, is expressed through the tongue, and the pain is indicated through tears in the eyes. Suffering finds expression out of its inner silence by means of the tongue, the key to the body's store-house which opens and closes the door of words,[2] and from within the heart—perception's treasury—it provides for its beloved friends with an utterance from its treasures. For the tongue acts as the mouthpiece of the intellect, giving expression to the mind; it serves as an advocate on behalf of the mind's hidden silence, it is the medium by which the mind's instructions are carried out. Whatever the tongue is told by the heart—the sovereign of all knowledge—it passes on in words to its listeners. Thus by means of the tongue, the

81

key of the intellect, the door to the heart is opened: without it, this door cannot be opened, nor can audible sound be emitted. Nevertheless the intellect does have the power to make known what is hidden within it without making use of any sound, employing instead silent words in the form of writing; in this way its silence finds expression in stillness. But however much the mind ministers to what lies hidden within it by means of silence, it still needs the tongue to expound its secrets to the faculty of hearing which is attentive to every sound.

2. By this analogy you can understand the pain caused by your separation from us. But since your life is lived in that equilibrium which our Lord manifested, there is consolation to be found in our sorrow, and you are no longer far away, since your way of life is infused with the love of Christ; for those who are in love are one in their closeness together. Just as his love is not divided up between them, so they are not separated from one another. For those who carry out the will of the Lord of all are bonded together in a single body, in that they have a single will.

3. Thus, my brother, from the moment I heard of your life in Christ, I have not ceased to remember you in my feeble prayers, as I beg of God's mercy that he may grant that your way of life be established in whatever manner is pleasing to his majesty. Nor do I hesitate to seek from you admonition in the form of instructive discourse.

4. Be on the watch throughout the whole course of your life, my brother; fix in your mind the thought of your Lord's Passion, for he is the spiritual fortress of our souls, the place of refuge for righteousness wherein the labour of good works is kept safe.

5. Beware, my brother, of cunning snares, of hidden traps and secret nets: do not grow weary of asking our Lord by night and by day to guard your steps, lest you be caught in Satan's cunning traps. If you are persistent in making this request, God will not hesitate to listen to your wish.

6. Hold fast, brother, to that spiritual glory of which our Lord's passion has made you worthy. Be vigilant so as to guard your thoughts from tempests; beware lest the glorious things you have in Christ undergo change due to some indication of pride. Now it is only when your mind is wrapped in meditation on the incarnation of Christ our Lord—at whose good will and pleasure you have been held worthy to perform good works—that pride will not be sown within you. For without his self-abasement, we should have been far too low down for those beautiful qualities of his, and not even a distant recollection of them would have entered our minds. For this reason his grace has granted to us that he should of his own will listen to us, and that he will bring us close to his Father. What is required of us is to give him thanks unceasingly—not indeed to the full extent that befits his gift, for no one is capable of giving him thanks as would be appropriate, for his grace is far

greater than the thanksgiving of all peoples; it is enough for us to realize that we have not the ability either to repay him, or even to thank him sufficiently—and in the case of a person who has such an understanding of God's grace, it could almost be said of him that by grace he has repaid it.

7. Be careful of this precious labour which you now undertake; for you will not have the same trouble losing it as you had in struggling to attain it. It is much easier to lose than to find. It is put together with great labour, but is lost in a single moment. *At the time when the master of the house does not expect it, the thief comes and breaks into his home.** For this reason it is essential that our mind should be awake at all times—like a wakeful pilot in charge of a ship. You know very well that it is through labour, vigilance, toil, and all sorts of vexations that a ship is constructed and completed, but it can be wrecked in only a short moment. Similarly the likeness of a human person can be well depicted in a portrait only by means of careful skill and the proper mixture of colours and paints, yet it can be destroyed in just a brief moment: it does not take to destroy it the labour that it took to make it. Destruction is much easier than construction, pulling down than building up.

Mt 24:43, Lk 12:39

8. Meditate on what Christ your teacher has caused to be written down for you: find strength in what he has transmitted to you in his Gospel.

9. Eschew idle conversation: words are

not always profitable to you, for converse of words bring distraction to the mind.

10. Be tranquil and serene in your monastery [*or* abode]: do not answer back concerning anything you are instructed to do; rather, be gently obedient, so that many shall love you.

11. Greet everyone, and you should be the first in greeting people, just as our Lord taught the apostles how, whenever they entered, they should be the first to make the greeting.* You only need a word, and you will thereby gladden someone's mind.

cf Mt 10:12

12. Do not pay attention to all the other people who have not yet learnt why they became disciples, because they have not even bothered to ask what this way of life is, and why this exemplar ever appeared in the world; rather, they consider themselves wise, and imagine that their knowledge is sufficient to teach them.

13. From now on be despised by the world so that you may be chosen by God. Be despicable before men so that you may progress before your Lord. Be like a simple person, so that his wisdom may dwell in you. Be guileless towards your brethren, but cunning towards the Enemy.*

cf Mt 10:16

14. Let everyone be important in your eyes, and do not despise those whose knowledge is less than yours.

15. Do not seek for honour in anything, but meet everyone on his own level. Do not be angry with a brother who exalts himself over you. Recognize that his knowledge is deficient; it is as a result of a lack of knowl-

edge that a brother exalts himself above another.

16. Let your outward actions testify to your inward ones: not in a pretence before other people, but in truth before the Lord of all.

17. Imagine that there is nothing else in front of your eyes—as though you were not among mankind—because you are seeing nothing else but God, for God is the entire reason for your way of life.

18. Think about people in a way that will profit you, so that you sorrow for the lost, feel pain for those gone astray, suffer for those in pain, pray for sinners, and in the case of the good, entreat God to preserve them.

19. As long as you are in this world, let such be your thought. But a New World is coming when we will not have our present understanding, since then it will not call to mind or think of anything apart from awe at the majestic glory of the Lord of all.

20. Let those who are older than you in the monastery be held in special honour; consider them in your mind as fathers. Let your manner of life be that of a person who genuinely considers himself to be inferior to everyone else. Live in stillness among your brethren like a dead person who has no voice. For this constitutes the love of God; whoever has this in mind need not think of anything else; for thus you will not grow angry—and after anger, hatred get the better of you.

21. The evil man who is distant from you is still your brother, and he should be

drawn by you: will you tear him to pieces with the words of your lips? Cast all this, therefore, from your thoughts, and let your mind be occupied with our Lord and not with man.

22. Do not impose upon yourself a labour that is beyond your strength, otherwise you will enslave yourself to the need to please others.

23. Live in concord with your brethren, for you are a source of tranquillity in the monastery. The interior labour is sufficient for you: choose vigilance, even in preference to fasting, for vigilance makes the understanding luminous, it keeps the intellect awake, it makes the body still, it is more beneficial than all other labours. Nevertheless those who labour in fasting are also in converse with the Lord, and fasting chases away cravings, ensuring that they do not become enslaved to sin.

24. Pay attention to the reading of the words of Scripture, in order to learn from them how to be with God. Do not choose for yourself just standing in prayer and neglect reading, for it is not required of you that just your body should be at labour, while your mind is idle. Intersperse your way of life with various kinds of occupations: a time for reading, a time for prayer. In this way you will be illumined in prayer as a result of your reading. For the Lord of all does not require of us an outward stance, but a mind that is wise in its hope for him, and which knows how to draw close to perfection.

25. Be both a servant, and free: a servant

in that you are subject to God, but free in that you are not enslaved to anything—either to empty praise or to any of the passions.

26. Release your soul from the bonds of sin; abide in liberty, for Christ has liberated you;* acquire the freedom of the New World during this temporal life of yours. Do not be enslaved to love of money or to the praise resulting from pleasing people.

cf Gal 5:1

27. Do not lay down a law for yourself, otherwise you may become enslaved to these laws of yours. Be a free person, one who is in a position to do what he likes. Do not become like those who have their own law, and are unable to turn aside from it, either out of fear in their own minds, or because of the wish to please others; in this way they have enslaved themselves to the coercion of their law, with their necks yoked to their own law, seeing that they have decreed for themselves their own special law—just when Christ had released them from the yoke of the Law!

28. Do not make hard and fast decisions over anything in the future, for you are a created being and your will is subject to changes. Decide in whatever matters you have to reach a decision, but without fixing in your mind that you will not be moved to other things. For it is not by small changes in what you eat that your faithfulness is altered: your service to the Lord of all is performed in the mind, in your inner person; that is where the ministry to Christ takes place.

29. Do not be tied down to anything, or

let anything enslave you. Release yourself from the yoke of the world by means of the freedom of the new life. There are ninety-nine commandments which have been dissolved and annulled by God, and do you want to establish your own law? There are many people who are more careful not to let their own law be broken, rather than all other laws.

30. Be free, therefore, and free yourself from every kind of destructive slavery. For unless you become free, you cannot be a worker for Christ; for that kingdom in the heavenly Jerusalem which is free does not accept children of slavery. The children of a free mother are themselves free,* and are not enslaved to the world in anything.*   *cf Rom 8:15*
cf Gal 4:23

31. Be fully aware in all your activities. As you walk, do not let your eyes wander this way and that; rather, your eyes should look modestly straight ahead.

32. Be modest and chaste in your clothing; let your gaze be downwards, but your mind directed upwards towards your Lord.[3] As far as possible you should not sate your eyes on the faces of other people; rather, let your gaze be modest, and do not stare at anything in a domineering way, but, like a pure virgin, guard yourself for Christ.

33. Be friendly to everyone, but do not seek for attachment to your loved ones [i.e. family], for your way of life does not require that. You are a solitary, and you should not be tied down by anything. In your mind you should hold in special love those who give you helpful advice, or the person who rebukes you for a good pur-

pose. Do not be annoyed in such cases, otherwise you may become a hater of the word of God.

34. Let your soul be vigilant in divine worship. If possible, do not be aware of who is standing next to you, so that your mind may be fully concentrated on your Lord. It is not up to you to make investigations; you have not been put in a position of authority or leadership. You are someone who is given orders, and you do not even have authority over yourself.

35. Do not look at those whose attention wanders to their companions, otherwise your mind will be disturbed by anger, and so your own part in the service will be without profit.

36. Do not press for your own needs in anything, for your discipleship was not of the kind that your needs should richly be met in everything. No, your discipleship was to a state of need, to poverty in Christ. If your needs are made good, then consider this as something extra. If you consider the meeting of your needs in this light, then you will give thanks, and you will not complain about your state of need.

37. Be constant in the reading of the prophets. From them you will learn about God's greatness, about his kindness, about justice and grace.

38. Ponder on the sufferings of the martyrs so that you may become aware of how great is the love for God.

39. Concern yourself with the teachings of the wise; whatever teaching you find helpful to yourself, persevere in reading

this. Do not take delight in the outward sounds, as children do, but like a wise person discern those words in which power is hidden—for it is by means of words of power* that our Saviour's Gospel has been proclaimed to us.

cf 1Th 1:5

40. Do not be like those who love to hear descriptions of various things; rather be eager for the words spoken by the perfect, which will show what is the way of life of the perfect.

41. Be attentive to the thoughts of the mind. If some evil thought passes through you, do not get upset, for it is not the transient thoughts of your mind that the knowledge of the Lord of all observes, rather, he looks at the depths of mind to see if you take pleasure in that evil thought which resides there; for hateful thoughts float over the surface of the mind, but it is the senses that are lower down which can chase away hateful thoughts, which the Lord of all examines. He does not judge what just passes over the mind, but rather the thoughts that are lower down than those hateful ones, namely those which appear in the depths of the mind, which can drive them away with its hidden hand. For he does not pardon the thoughts which spring up from the depth of the mind, for it is they which should be chasing away those which pass over the surface of the mind; he judges those thoughts which have a passage into the heart.

42. Even if some hateful thought finds a nest in you and remains in your mind for some time, as long as there is deeper down

some other thought which finds abhorrent, and is at loggerheads with, the thought temporarily abiding in you, then you need not be alarmed, for the evil thought can be rooted out, and you will not suffer judgement for it. Rather, great is your reward in the case of the good thought which springs up in the depths of your mind, seeing that it is the foundation which prevents any evil thought being built upon it.

43. Beware of those evil thoughts to which your mind takes a liking, for which a foundation is already laid there. They are the ones which are placed under God's judgement; punishment is decreed for them all.

44. Toil at reading the Scriptures more than at anything else: for in prayer the mind frequently wanders, but in reading even a wandering mind is recollected.

cf Cant 8:6

45. Let the love of God be stronger than death* in you: if death releases you from the desire for everything, how much more appropriate is it that the love of God should release you from desire for everything.

46. Do not be proud in anything, except in the fact that you are not proud. Do not boast in anything, except in the fact that you do not boast. He who is proud in this way is right to be proud, provided that he is not really proud; he who can boast in this way is right to be boastful, provided that he does not really boast. He who rejoices in this is right to rejoice, provided he rejoices in God. He who exults in this is right to exult, provided he does not exult in the things of the world.

47. You should not be contentious in anything, except against sin.

48. Do not hate evils in others when they exist in yourself; rather, show hatred for the evils in your own person.

49. Sing the praise of good deeds by your actions rather than by words.

50. Rebuke hatred by your deeds rather than by your words. When you see anyone rebuked for some wrongdoing, do not pay attention to his wrong, but consider whether you yourself have done anything worthy of rebuke.

51. Honour peace more than anything else. But strive first of all to be at peace in yourself: in this way you will find it easy to be at peace with others. How can someone whose eyes are blind heal others?

52. You should not imagine that any cause is good which hinders peacefulness; for one good does not annul another. Get rid of any causes that undo your sense of peace, for the sake of the establishment of peacefulness.

53. Let respect be infused on your face— not as something purely exterior, but as stemming from your interior self.

54. Consider that your true wealth lies in truth; for truth consists in the love of God, the awareness of his wisdom, and the fulfilling of his will. These things should be established inside you, and not in an exterior way.

55. Everything that lies outside your good volition, hold in contempt.

56. Be a proclaimer of the Gospel at all times. You will become a proclaimer of the

Gospel when you lay upon yourself the Gospel's way of life.

57. Show to the world that the other world exists. You will show that the other world exists when you despise this world.

58. My brother Hesychius, we should realize that we live in a world of deception. If we recognize that we are going astray, error will not surreptitiously get the better of us. It is like the case of those who see a dream: if they realize in their dream that they are just seeing a dream and not reality, then they will not be led astray by what they see. The same applies to the person who is held worthy to be aware that he lives in this world in a state of deception. Such a person is not perturbed by love of material objects.

59. So, my beloved, let us perfect ourselves before we depart from the body. Each day of our lives we should imagine to be our last day. Like someone who is seeking for the merchandise of salvation you should daily take stock of your own merchandise, to see wherein there lies loss for you, and wherein profit.

60. When evening comes, collect your thoughts and ponder over the entire course of the day: observe God's providential care for you; consider the grace he has wrought in you throughout the whole span of the day; consider the rising of the moon, the joy of daylight, all the hours and moments, the divisions of time, the sight of different colours, the beautiful adornment of creation, the course of the sun, the growth of your own stature, how your own person has been protected; consider the blowing

of the winds, the ripe and varied fruits, how the elements minister to your comfort, how you have been preserved from accidents, and all the other activities of grace. When you have pondered on all this, wonder of God's love towards you will well up within you, and gratitude for his acts of grace will bubble up inside you.

61. Take thought too, in case you have done something that is contrary to these acts of grace: say to yourself 'Have I done anything to anger God today? Have I said or thought anything that does not befit that will which created me?' And if you become aware that you have done something to displease him, stand up for a short while in prayer and give thanks for the graces you have received throughout the entire day's ministry, and make supplication for what you have done wrong. In this way you will sleep peacefully and without sin.

62. If, in the case of one human being who has done wrong to another, God in his grace has commanded that we should be forgiving to the offender *seventy times seven*,* how much more will God forgive the person who offers up supplication for his sins?

Mt 18:22

63. It is folly that, when someone who is more important than us is angry with us, we sleep in fear and sorrow, whereas we go to sleep untroubled by any thought of regret for the fact that we have provoked God all day long in our ingratitude for all his goodness.

64. Such, then, should be your daily aim throughout life: each morning you should

look back on your service during the night,
each evening look back on your service
during the day. Complete your ways thus in
purity, in accordance with the will of God.

65. When you stand in prayer before
God, take care that your mind is recollected. Push aside any distracting thoughts.
Feel in your soul the true weightiness of
God. Purify the movements of your
thoughts; if you have to struggle with
them, be persistent in your struggle and do
not give up. When God sees your persis-
tence, then all of a sudden grace will dawn
in you, and your mind will find strength as
your heart burns with fervour and your
soul's thoughts shine out. It may even be
that wonderful intuitions of God's majesty
will burst forth in you: this comes as a result of such supplication and luminous understanding; for just as we do not put
choice perfumes in a foul-smelling
container, neither does God stir up intuitions of his true majesty in minds that are
still ugly.

66. At the beginning of your prayer have
it in mind to say in God's presence, 'Holy,
holy, holy, Lord almighty, with whose glory
cf Is 6:3   both heaven and earth are filled.'*⁴ Then
be mindful of whatever is appropriate in
your prayer, which should always include
remembering God's Church, petitions for
the weak and afflicted, entreaty for those
who have gone astray, compassion for sinners, forgiveness of those who have done
wrong.

67. Make supplication before God that in
the thoughts of your soul you may continu-

ously say the following: 'O God, make me worthy in your grace of that greatness which you will give in the world to come in return for labours, and may your justice not judge me on the great day of your coming. O God, in your compassion make me worthy of true knowledge of you, and of participation in your perfect love.' And when you have come to the end of your supplication, seal your prayer with that prayer which Christ our Lord gave to his disciples. Be assiduous in all this, meditate on it, and thereby you will be able to make prayers before God and men.

68. My brother, you should not be confident that the end of your life will be adorned with the divine beauty that is now depicted in you; such an idea will give rise to relaxing your concentration, resulting in negligence before you have succeeded in bringing this to effect. Just as there is no assurance that a ship's voyage will end up safely in harbour, so with each of us, there is no assurance that our life's journey will end up without stumbling.

69. This is how your life will be preserved in good works: by constantly having before your eyes the picture of your death; for when someone does not live in expectation of the next day, then fear induced by having just the present day acts as his guide. For what sins or laxity will a person let himself get involved in, when he considers that his life will last but a single day, and he does not rely on the morrow.

70. Insofar as you are able to understand, and insofar as it is appropriate to

your way of life, I have written down these few things, urged on by your love, for your wisdom in Christ, thanks to the peace we have between us. And may our Lord who has made you worthy of such an exalted state of glory grant that you may indeed obtain this and be possessed by him, through that mercy which guards your life. And may you be firm in the faith of Life right to the day when our Saviour is revealed. And I beg and beseech you to beg Christ's mercy for me, that he may have compassion on me too at the judgement.

BIBLIOGRAPHY AND NOTES

A. The letter to Hesychius is translated from my forth-coming edition (whose section numbers are used here). At least nineteen manuscripts are known, of which the oldest is dated AD 587.
B. A general introduction to John of Apamea's writings is given by B. Bradley in *DSpir* 8 (1974) cols. 764–74. An English translation of John's short treatise on Prayer was published in my 'John the Solitary, On Prayer', *Journal of Theological Studies* ns 30 (1979) 84–101, and is reprinted in *The Ascetical Homilies of St Isaac the Syrian* (Boston, 1984) 466–8 (the slightly expanded form of this work, recycled by Abraham of Nathpar, is translated in Chapter X). An English translation of John's first 'Tractate', on still-ness, is given by D. Miller in *The Ascetical Homilies of St Isaac the Syrian*, 461–6. French translations of several other works are available: I. Hausherr, *Jean la Solitaire. Dialogue sur l'âme et les passions de l'homme*, OCA 120; (1939); R. Lavenant, *Jean d'Apamée. Dialogues et traités,* Sources chrétiennes 311; (1984), which translates the texts published, with German translation, by W. Strothmann in 1972. German translations of some further texts will be found in L. G. Rignell, *Briefe von Johannes dem Ein-siedler* (Lund, 1941), and *Drei Traktate von Johannes dem Einsiedler*, Lunds Universitets Årsskrift 54/4; (1960). Important general studies include: A. de Halleux, 'La christologie de Jean le Solitaire', *Le Muséon* 94 (1981) 5–36, and 'Le milieu historique de Jean le Solitaire', *OCA*

221 (1983) 299–305; P. Harb, 'Doctrine spirituelle de Jean le Solitaire', *Parole de l'Orient* 2 (1971) 225–60; I. Hausherr, 'Un grand auteur spirituel retrouvé: Jean d'Apamée', *OCP* 14 (1948) 3–42 = *Études*, OCA 183 (1969) 181–216; R. Lavenant, 'Le probléme de Jean d'Apamée', *OCP* 46 (1980) 367–90.

Notes to Chapter V

1. *Lexicon Syriacum auctore Hassano bar Bahlule*, ed. R. Duval (Paris, 1888–1901) col. 1275.

2. John is perhaps reflecting Ephrem, *Hymns on Faith*, XIII.7 or XXV.2.

3. Compare Aphrahat, *Demonstration* IV.13, with note 13 there.

4. John quotes the liturgical form, which includes 'heaven'.

Chapter VI

Philoxenus of Mabbug

d. 523

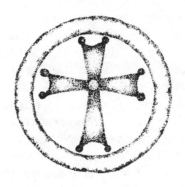

INTRODUCTION

P HILOXENUS is a major Syriac writer and theologian of
the fifth/sixth century. He happens to be best
known as an ardent opponent of the christological
definition of faith laid down at the Council of Chalcedon
(he considered that its wording obscured, in a dangerous
way, the full reality of the incarnation). But Philoxenus
was not just a fiery and zealous controversialist, taking a
front-line position in the ecclesiastical politics of his time;
he was also a creative theologian of considerable stature,
fusing together in a remarkable way elements drawn from
both his native Syriac and from Greek tradition.

Philoxenus was born outside the Roman Empire, somewhere in the vicinity of modern Kirkuk (Iraq), and studied
at the famous theological school in Edessa known as the
'Persian School'. In the doctrinal controversies of the mid-
fifth century the teachers of the School followed the Antiochene theological tradition, in particular that of Theodore of Mopsuestia, but it is clear that some students,
Philoxenus among them, reacted against this and sided
with the Alexandrine tradition of Cyril. According to
some sources it was this that led to his expulsion. Be-
friended by Peter the Fuller, Patriarch of Antioch, Philoxenus soon became a prominent figure in ecclesiastical
circles in Syria and in 485 he was appointed bishop of
Mabbug (to the north-east of Antioch). Among his many
activities as bishop he sponsored a revision of the Syriac
translation of the New Testament, bringing it closer into

line with the current Greek text. After the death of the emperor Anastasius in 518, his successor Justin introduced a change in imperial religious policy and enforced on all bishops acceptance of the Council of Chalcedon and its controversial Definition of Faith; Philoxenus' refusal to do so resulted in his deposition and exile. He died five years later in Paphlagonia.

Philoxenus' writings fall into three main categories: exegetical, dogmatic, and ascetic. From the first two categories his extensive *Commentary on the Prologue of John* (only recently published) and the *Three Tractates on the Trinity and the Incarnation* (also known as the *Book of Sentences*) deserve to be singled out for special mention. The third category of works shows up a quite different aspect of Philoxenus' character, pointing to his deep concern for, and interest in, the religious life. Best known, and long available in an English translation by E. A. W. Budge, are his thirteen *Discourses*. Their range of topics is best indicated by listing their titles: prologue (1), the first commandment that a person should seize upon (2), faith (3–4), serenity (*shafyūtā*; 5), the fear of God (6–7), self-emptying (*msarrqūtā*; 8), greed (9), abstinence (10), fornication (of the mind; 12–13). Among the various letters which fall into the third category is the first text translated here, on the indwelling of the Holy Spirit, and the long letter to a solitary, Patricius of Edessa. This second letter, on the passions of the soul and the commandments of Christ, somehow came to be translated into Greek where, most remarkably, it is published among the works of Isaac of Nineveh.

Fundamental to Philoxenus' way of thinking is the concept of a dual mode of existence which characterizes, in complementary fashion, both the life of Christ and that of the Christian. These two modes of existence he designates the mode of the body (*pagrānūtā*) and the mode of the spirit (*rūḥānūtā*). Before the incarnation the Logos exists, by nature, in the mode of the spirit; but after the incarnation he also exists, by miracle, in the mode of the body. Conversely, the Christian before baptism exists, by nature, in the mode of the body; but after baptism he or she also exists, by miracle, in the mode of the spirit. Such a pattern gives great prominence to the place of baptism in the life of the Christian, and at the same time it brings out the parallelism between the incarnate life of Christ and the baptized life of the Christian, a parallelism which has important implications for an understanding of what is involved in any 'imitation of Christ'.

Philoxenus was evidently borrowing from the *Book of Steps* when he speaks of two ways of life open to the baptized Christian, the way of righteousness and the way of perfection. The way of righteousness he sees as corresponding to the time in Christ's life before his baptism, when he was fulfilling all the requirements of righteousness (i.e. the Law); by contrast, the way of perfection is seen as corresponding to Christ's life after his baptism. Elsewhere Philoxenus compares the way of righteousness to the growth of an embryo in the womb; birth, on this model, corresponds to entry into the way of perfection. This second spiritual birth which takes place subsequently to baptism is called by Philoxenus 'the apperception of our first birth' i.e. baptism; (*Letter to Patricius*, 97). In another place he even speaks of 'two baptisms', the first being 'that of Grace, from the Font, and the second that of your own will, when you are baptized out of the world in the love of God' (*Discourse* IX).

In the baptized life, whether the Christian is following the way of righteousness or has chosen to advance on to the way of perfection, the presence and activity of the Holy Spirit is of course of prime importance. At baptism the Christian 'puts on the spirit', and the Spirit becomes 'the soul of his soul', indwelling permanently in the Christian. The problem of what effect post-baptismal sin has on the presence of the Holy Spirit in the baptized was one which Aphrahat had already discussed in his Sixth *Dem-*

onstration. The same question was posed by a correspondent to Philoxenus, who asked whether the Spirit actually departs when a baptized person sins. Philoxenus' interesting letter of reply—in the negative: the Holy Spirit departs only on apostasy—is to be found in the first of the four texts translated below. The other three are short pieces specifically on prayer which had been excerpted at an early date from longer works which cannot now be identified.

1. PHILOXENUS,
On the indwelling of the Holy Spirit

A Memra by The Blessed Mar Philoxenus In Answer
To Someone Who Asked Him Whether The Holy
Spirit Departs From a Man When He Sins And
Returns To Him Again When He Repents

W E SHOULD MAKE ANSWER to enqui-
ries of this sort, relying not on
our own opinion, but rather on
the teaching of the holy Scriptures, for
there will be found the solution of every
problem that is posed in real faith. Further
we may not ask and put to each other [just]
any question that arises, but only those that
it is proper to ask, and which are profitably
posed. For what is the purpose of a disciple
asking this question: 'Does the Holy Spirit
depart from a man during the time that he
sins, and return to him at the moment of his
repentance?', if it is not to ask and enquire
how one cannot sin, or if one happens to
sin, how one can most quickly feel revul-
sion for that sin, and turn to penitence.

Now there are many subtle questions one can ask on the subject of how not to sin, and there are just as many subtle traps laid by the devil who causes us to sin—whose first objective is to ensnare us, and once he has done this he devises means of preventing us from escaping from our bonds. And just as the idea of our being caught, and then our not being released once we are caught, are both the objectives of our Enemy, so too the idea of our not sinning, and of repenting after we have sinned, are both the helpful promptings of grace.

I turn then briefly to the question of whether or not the Holy Spirit departs from us during the time that we commit sin, for the benefit of those who have discussed the point, or of any others who need to learn about it.

At the time of our baptism through God's grace we received the Holy Spirit from the baptismal waters, but the purpose of our receiving him was not that he should sometimes remain with us and sometimes leave us, but that we should be temples for him, and that he should dwell within us continually; as Paul said: *You are the temple of God, and the Spirit of God dwells within you*;* and again, *Do you not recognize that your bodies are the temples of the Holy Spirit who dwells within you, whom you received from God? For you were bought for a great price, and consequently you should be praising God with your bodies and with your spirit, which all belong to God.* *

1 Cor 3:16

1 Cor 6:19–20

If then you are temples and shrines of

God by reason of the Spirit of God dwelling within us, then no sin, whether it be by deed or by thought, can destroy the temple of God. For sin that is committed by some action is quite different from the denial of God. If then we sin through something we do, our faith in God remains unshaken, and we do not thereby lose our sonship to God, just as in the case of a natural son, however much he wrongs and sins against his father, the fact of his having sinned against his father does not stop him being called his son; for however much a son sins and does wrong, he does not destroy his honourable title of 'son', provided his father does not want to disinherit him.

It was the same with the younger son who squandered his property and dissipated his father's property living among prostitutes:* despite all this he did not lose the honourable title of son that was his. Rather, while he was still in the land of captivity, having rejected his father, he recalled to himself *how many hired servants there are at this moment in my father's house who have more than enough bread, whereas here am I perishing from hunger.** And while he was still a sinner, and though he had sinned to such a great extent that he had thrown to the winds with his misdeeds the entire inheritance he had received from his father, even so he still called God his 'father'. And this indicates that the grace of the Spirit, which authorizes him to call God 'Father', did not depart from him.

Indeed we are quite unable to employ this term of address and call God 'Father',

Lk 15:1

Lk 15:17

except through the authority of the Holy
Spirit who is within us, for it is well known
that those who have not yet become God's
children by the holy rebirth of baptism are
not authorized to use this term, and they
are not permitted to say 'Our Father, who
art in heaven, hallowed by thy name'[1]. The
manifest reason for this is that the Holy
Spirit is not yet within them, to give them
this authorization, and it is well known to
all that, when they approach the Holy Mysteries, the newly baptized all repeat this
prayer with confidence in accordance with
the tradition handed down by our Lord,
and then they proceed to the Holy Mysteries. It is also obvious that we have all
sinned in some way, be it small or great, in
thought or in deed, and there is no one
among us who is not guilty of sin. If then
we are all guilty of sin, then the Holy Spirit
has departed from us all, and how do we
have the audacity to cry out 'Our Father,
who art in heaven' when we approach the
Holy Mysteries? For if the Holy Spirit has
left us because we have sinned, by what
authority do we call God 'Father'? And if
we do this not having within us the Spirit
of God which permits us to do so, then it is
an enormous crime and rebellion against
God, and we would resemble the men who
built the Tower of Babel* so as to ascend to   *cf Gen 11:9*
heaven, or him who audaciously made him-
self god* and wanted to grab for himself an   *cf Dan 3*
honour that had not been given him; who,
as a result of this, destroyed that honour
which he had.

   But in fact the faithful who call God 'Fa-

ther' at the time of the Mysteries do not do
so of their own accord, but rather the priest
who stands at the head of the people permits them to say this; and not even he
would have authority to call God 'Father',
let alone give permission to others to say
this, if it were established that the Holy
Spirit had left all who sin. For none of us,
whether priest or people, is in a position to
hope that he is completely free from sin, if
what Paul says is true: *There is only one*
high priest, Jesus Christ, who is without
wickedness or stain, who is completely free
Heb 7:26   *from sins, and exalted above the heaven:**
and later he says: *Every high priest who*
stands and makes offerings and sacrifices
for sins should first offer sacrifices for him-
Heb 7:27   *self, and only then for the people,** it being
recognized that it is because he is guilty of
sin that he needs propitiation by means of
offerings.

Just as with the former Law of Moses,
every priest who offered sacrifices to God
first of all offered them for himself, and
only then for the people, so also in the
dispensation of the New Testament, it is
well known that all priests first of all offer a
Rom 12:1   'rational sacrifice'* to God for themselves,
and then for the people: in his prayer the
priest asks in the first place for forgiveness
of his own sins and a cleansing of his own
soul and body from all sinful thoughts and
actions; and each priest offers these prayers
to God in accordance with the measure of
his own purity of soul. And after he has
completed the divine sacrifice, and accomplished the Mysteries with the descent of

the Holy Spirit, he does not distribute the
Sacrament to the others before he himself
has received it, as being in need of it; and
thus he proclaims before the entire church
that he receives the Sacrament first of all so
that he may receive propitiation by it. Only
then does he distribute it to the others, so
that the prayer which was offered earlier,
first for himself and then for the people,
might be put into action. For if he had not
offered prayer for himself first, he would
not be the first to approach communion.
Thus his offering testifies that he is a sinner,
and it is as a sinner that he takes the Sacrament, to receive propitiation by it. And so
he distributes it to every one who is in the
same situation.

For this reason, when he distributes the
Mysteries to them, he cries out 'the Body of
God for the forgiveness of sins, and the
Blood of the Son of God for the propitiation of wrongs', recalling by these words
what our Lord said to his disciples when he
distributed his Mysteries to them: *This is
my body which is broken for you for the
forgiveness of sins, and this is my Blood
which is shed for you for forgiveness.** *Mt 26:26–8*
Thus it is that when we approach the Mysteries of our Saviour, we approach as needy
sinners; for there is no need for medicine
except in the case of an illness, or for healing except when someone is sick. For *it is
not the healthy who are in need of a doc-
tor, but those who are ill.** It is evident, *Mt 9:12*
then, that everyone who approaches the
Mysteries receives them for the forgiveness
of his sins, whether it be the priest or the

people. And if the Holy Spirit is not within us because we are sinners, by what authority does the priest invoke the Spirit, or the people approach the Mysteries?

There is the further point, that if the Holy Spirit is not within us, then neither is baptism effective in us—and how can we approach the Sacrament without being baptized? For it is clear that if the Holy Spirit leaves us whenever we sin, our baptism also departs from us, for our baptism *is* the Holy Spirit. When our Lord said to his disciples *John baptized with water, but you shall be baptized with the Holy Spirit after*

Acts 1:5

*not many days,** he was speaking of the Holy Spirit who came down upon the disciples in the upper room in the form of tongues of fire. This descent of the Holy Spirit he calls 'baptism' because the apostles' baptism then was by the Spirit alone, for they had already been baptized in water by John.

It is the same now with us who are baptized: neither the wetness of the water in which we are baptized, nor the oiliness of the oil with which we are anointed, remain with us after our death, but the Holy Spirit, who is mingled in our souls and bodies through the oil and the water, does remain with us, both in this life and after our death. For he is our true baptism, and for this reason we remain always baptized, for the Holy Spirit is within us always, and no sin can strip us of our baptism—neither adultery, nor theft, nor fornication, nor false testimony nor any action of this sort: only the denial of God and consorting with demons can do this, for in such cases the Holy Spirit really does depart, for he does not consent to remain in a place where Satan dwells. *For what fellowship does Christ have with Satan or the believer with the unbeliever, or God's temple with that of demons?* *

2 Cor 6:14

If then we are permitted to say that the Holy Spirit leaves the soul that has received him at baptism, then it is as a result of these sins that he leaves; that is to say, he departs in the face of this depravity—for it is not right for such things to be called mere 'sins': denial of God is not just a sin; it is open revolt against his dominion; it is a state of hostility that wages open war with him.

However much the citizens of a city, or the inhabitants of a country that is subject to the emperor, do wrong and transgress his laws, whether openly or secretly, provided that his statues are not broken and his portraits are not burnt, it is not a case of rebellion; but if this should take place as the result of disturbances among the populace, then the judges at once remedy the matter, and the instigators are punished by death. And if it so happen that an insurgent tyrant should appear in a city and the people or the district rebel with him, defacing and breaking up all the emperor's statues and portraits—whose visible presence is a symbol of his authority over that district or city—by this action they reject the emperor's authority over the city and show open rebellion against him. Clearly the situation is similar with those who deny God after their baptismal confession of faith, either by sacrificing to demonic beings, or by consorting with people who practice magic. Because they have denied the rule of their former emperor and acknowledged that of an alien tyrant, the Holy Spirit, whom they received at baptism, departs from them—just as the imperial government with its laws disappears from that city in which a rebel tyrant has recently set himself up.

That what we have said is the case can be understood from exactly the opposite point of view. Among the pagans who worship idols and created objects, and among the philosophers who have made a name for themselves among the Greeks, there are various virtues that can be found: in some cases, that of justice, in others of integrity, while other men vanquished the lusts of the body, or scorned the love of money; among others again there was to be found a natural compassion. But all these things that were to be found in them were things rejected by Satan, whom they otherwise served. Now Satan has no desire that any of his servitors should get known for any good virtue, yet these men did not, because of these virtues, become rebels against him, and it cannot be said of them that they denied Satan and acknowledged God, simply because they possessed these virtues. Rather, despite these virtues that were to be found in them, they are still described as pagans and worshippers of demonic beings, because they did not actually deny Satan and acknowledge God.

Today, if an unbaptized pagan or Samaritan approaches Holy Baptism, even if such a person does not repent of his former bad conduct, yet the very fact of his denying Satan and acknowledging Christ numbers him among the righteous, and places him in the realm of Christ's Kingdom. Precisely because he denies Satan and acknowledges God he comes to baptism and receives the Holy Spirit, and not because of any actions of his own. How can this take place, except it be a result of their belief in God alone, seeing that they may previously have conducted themselves in every kind of wickedness? If, then, it is solely as a result of their belief in God and their baptism in his name that they receive the Holy Spirit, then it is clear that it is solely through denial of his name and consorting with demonic powers that the Holy Spirit ever leaves us, for he does not consent to remain in a place where his authority is not effective, that is to say in the person who has denied him. For he does not consent to live as a sojourner in an alien country.

Suppose someone objects and says that the Holy Spirit leaves us as the result of other sins as well, and when we repent of them he returns to us. If he leaves us, who is it then who works in us so that we repent of our sins? Repentance does not take place without the Holy Spirit; it is accompanied by fastings and vigils, by almsgiving and prayer, by continual affliction of soul and continual shedding of tears and inexpressible groans, all of which are the result of the activity of the Spirit, just as Paul said:

We do not know how to pray as is properly fitting, but it is the Spirit of God who prays for us with inexpressible groans. He who searches out hearts knows what is the thought of the Spirit who prays for the

Rom 8:26–7   *saints in accordance with God's will.** You see that all the good promptings that bring us to repentance result from the activity of the Spirit; and pure prayer, which brings all these good promptings to completion, is also stirred up in our soul as the result of the Spirit's activity. He too in a hidden way initially arouses us to groans at the memory of our sins.

If the Spirit did leave us the moment we sin, who is it who arouses such feelings in us? Perhaps you may say that it is our own will. But who is it who stirs up our will to good, and who is it who helps it in the execution of that good? Is it not the Holy Spirit? Do you not hear what Paul says: *God incites within you both the will, and*

Phil 2:13   *the putting into action of your will?** You see that it is he who stirs up our will towards the good, and it is he who accomplishes the carrying out of our will.

You may object that in that case there is no free will. There is indeed free will, for

cf Gen 1:26   by this we are 'the likeness of God'.* But free will is not under any compulsion; I did not say to you that the Spirit compels our soul to do good, he only entices it and allures it. One might ask where is the Spirit when someone sins, seeing that he has not held back the soul from sin. You can now clearly see what I meant when I said that the Spirit does not force the soul towards the good, nor does he use any restraint to hold it back from evil; rather in both cases he gives freedom to our will, acting simply as someone who urges for or against an action.

Neither does Satan lead us towards evil by force, nor does the Spirit of God draw us to good by compulsion. Rather, they are both spectators, each urging us on in the direction our own will inclines. Just as the grace of the Holy Spirit, which we have received from the water, is within us when we sin— and however much a baptized person sins, he is still baptized—this grace does not restrain our will from sin by using any compulsion, but is simply angered against us and secretly rebukes us when it sees that we are inclined towards sin. And if the mind knows how to receive that rebuke, and if our deliberation consents to accept the warning, then it is restrained from sin, and grace immediately shines out and illuminates it, filling the mind straightaway with joy and happiness.

This is what normally happens to those who overcome sin at the time of their struggle with it. But if one's deliberation does not listen to the Spirit within, but brings the sin into effect, immediately the house of the soul becomes dark, and grows murky with the smoke of distress, and is filled with sorrow and compunction, and the soul's face is covered with shame, as it is written: 'and the Holy Spirit is grieved and turns his face from the soul'.* Hermas, *Mandates* x.2.2

Paul has this in mind when he gives the following advice: *Do not grieve the Holy*

*Spirit, with whom you have been sealed in readiness for the day of salvation.** You have heard how Paul instructs us on two matters: the Spirit is still in us when we sin, and is grieved because of our sin. *'Do not grieve the Spirit of God* who is within you', he says. He is within us, then, and warns us not to sin and so grieve him, lest we quench the hidden working of our soul, just as Paul says in another place: *Do not quench the Spirit,** that is to say, do not grieve him by sin, otherwise his light will be quenched from your soul—a light which, when kindled within you, gives you possession of a power that is beyond expression and you will be able to contend *with principalities and powers** and fight against the evil spirits under the heaven, and reject all the world with its pleasures and pains. All these things are effected by the fervour of the Spirit within us, and Paul, who knew the power of the working of the Spirit, warns us in his teaching: *Be fervent in spirit,** and again *those who allow themselves to be guided by the Spirit of God are God's children.**

While, then, the Holy Spirit is always within us—that is to say, in those baptized—he does not forcefully restrain the person who wants to sin, but simply instructs and urges him not to. The Spirit does not run away from the soul in which he is dwelling at the time of sin, returning to it when it repents, as the ignorant say; rather, he remains with us, not being put to use.

What reason is there for him to depart

Eph 4:30

1 Th 5:19

Eph 6:12

Rom 12:11

Rom 8:14

from us when we sin, my good sir? As if our sin could harm him, or as if his sanctity was thereby involved in some stain, or as if he could not prevent himself from getting injury from our sin while within us. In that case he too would be infirm, and subject to injuries just as we are. But this is not the case—far from it!

For the Spirit *is* within our soul, sometimes retracting from it, at others shining forth over it. But when he retracts himself, he does not depart, and when he shines forth, he does not come in from somewhere else.

For just as the natural light with which we are familiar is still inside the pupil of the eye when the eyes are closed, and the eyes do not then see with it because the eyelid is spread over it; but once the eye is opened, it sees with the light that was in it all the time, now joining with the light outside; in like manner the Spirit dwells in our soul, just as light in the pupil of the eye, and if a man overlay him with neglect—just like an eyelid over the pupil of the eye—although the Spirit is still in our soul, we do not see with him. But if we roll back the negligence from our mind's face, and direct the clear gaze of our will towards the spiritual light that is within us, then at once light encounters light, just as in the case of the sun's light and the natural light within the eye, and by the combination of the two the vision is illumined.

It is not right, then, that we should speak of the Spirit departing at the time of sin and then returning with repentance, for we would thereby represent him to be both weak and ill-inclined, and an deserter, standing far off and watching for us to repent from our sin, and then, once we are in a state of justification again, returning to dwell within us. Indeed what benefit would I have if he dwells within me after I have already been justified? For if he is not to be found at the time of my fall, to give me a hand and put me back on my feet, how can I perceive his help? Does a doctor leave a patient the moment he sees that he has fallen into some illness and go off, only returning when he has recovered his health? No, rather when the patient is ill the doctor is assiduously in attendance, but when he has recovered he no longer needs the doctor, who then turns to some other task.

If the foolish opinion of these men were true and the Spirit did leave the soul, then at the time of recovery it would be suitable for him to depart even further than at the time of sickness, since, according to our Lord's testimony, *the healthy have no need of a doctor.**

Lk 5:31

So much for this. A soul, therefore, both in time of sickness and in time of good health needs the close presence of the Spirit; the Spirit whom he put on once and for all from the water, he will never again put off, except through denial alone. For if it is through faith that he puts on the Spirit, it is only through denial that he can put him off, seeing that faith and denial are opposites, like darkness and light.

For the Holy Spirit that we receive from

God is the Soul of our soul.[2] For this reason
he was given to the apostles by means of
anointing, and, through them, to all of us.
For instead of our original soul we have
received the Spirit, with the intention that
he should be a soul to our soul, just as our
soul is a soul to our body. The original
spirit that Adam received came from the
insufflation from God, for it is written: *He
breathed on his face the breath of life, and
Adam became a living being* [*lit.* soul].*   *Gen 2:7*
And in the New Testament it is written
*Jesus breathed on the faces of the disciples
and said 'Receive the Holy Spirit; if you
forgive any man's sins, they shall be forgiven him, and if you retain them, they
shall be retained'.* How is it that the Spirit   *Jn 20:22-3*
who forgives sins—as our Lord says—also
runs away from sins? Thus it is not right to
speak of the Spirit leaving in the face of
sins; rather sins flee away from the Spirit's
presence. For it is not darkness which can
quench light, but it is light which can dissi-
pate darkness. Likewise it is not the Spirit
who runs away from sin, but sin which departs from the Spirit's presence.

If, then, the Holy Spirit is a Soul to our
soul, and for this reason he has been given
us by insufflation—as in the case of that
first soul of Adam—then it is obvious that if
that Spirit leaves us, our soul will at once
die, in the same way as a body dies the
moment the soul that dwells in it departs.
And just as the body, once dead because of
the departure of the soul, is not in need of
medicine, seeing that it is no longer capable of being healed—the diseased eye it

may have will not be healed, nor will a broken leg be bandaged up, nor a crippled hand be put right, nor indeed can any of its limbs that have something wrong with them any longer receive healing and adjustment, since the body has been deprived of life, which alone is capable of receiving healing—it is exactly the same with the soul from which the Holy Spirit departs: it becomes henceforth like the body's corpse, unable any longer to receive healing for any of its sins, since it does not have within itself the vitality of the Holy Spirit. How can a medicine or a bandage be applied to something that has lost all sensory power? Have you ever seen a doctor healing a corpse, or bandaging a limb that has been cut off and separated from the rest of the body? It is the same with the soul: if the vitality of the Holy Spirit, which it received at baptism, departs from it, then it has no opportunity for healing, and cannot acquire penitence for its sins.

Before baptism, one is called the *old person*,* but after baptism *the new person.* Now the Holy Spirit is the abiding Soul of the new person, and he remains, not only during the body's life, but also after its death, and in the case of the saints he performs miracles and works signs. For the bones of the just, that is to say, of the apostles and martyrs and all the saints, while they do not have any natural soul in them— for that left them at their death—still have the Holy Spirit abiding with and in them, and it is He who effects signs and wonders in them; and demonic spirits cry out bit-

Eph 4:22
Eph 4:24

terly at his power within them, for sicknesses are driven off and illnesses chased
away.[3]

At the time of the resurrection, when the
souls return to their bodies they find the
Holy Spirit in them, for he has not departed
from them—and never will do so—from
the time when they received him from the
water. And our resurrection too will take
place by the power of the Holy Spirit who
is within us, and because the Holy Spirit is
in the faithful when they die, their death
cannot be called 'death', but only 'sleep'.
Brethren, I want you to know, says Paul,
*about those who sleep: you must not
grieve, like the rest of humanity, who have
lost all hope.*[*]   *1 Th 4:13*

Thus it is only in pagans and Jews that
there is no Holy Spirit, and for this reason
when they die they really die, and are not
just asleep. This is why no honour is given
to the burial of their bodies, and there are
no psalms or canticles when they are taken
to the grave, seeing that they are truly dead,
and not alive though asleep. Contrast [with
this] the death of the believer who has been
baptized even if he is a sinner, even if he has
done ten thousand wrongs, provided he
dies in faith, and has not undone his baptism by denial, and has not washed away
his sacred baptismal washing by demonic
rites of washing, then, when his soul leaves
his body and he dies nature's death, we take
his body to the grave treating him as alive,
albeit asleep. And the reason for this is
clearly because the Holy Spirit, whom he
received from the rebirth from the womb of

baptism, has not departed from him. For our Lord said: *Unless a man be born again from water and the Spirit, he cannot enter the kingdom of God.** If sinners were without baptism, why should their bodies be escorted to the grave with honour, why would spiritual songs be sung, if the Holy Spirit were not there? Why does Paul call the sinner 'asleep' if he be really dead?

Jn 3:5

If you quote me the words of the prophet: *I do not desire the death of a dead sinner,** and say that this refers to Jewish sinners, and for this reason too Ezekiel was told *I have made you a watchman for the house of Israel,** I would reply that it is indeed clear that the words are addressed to the Jews, since it was to them that the prophet Ezekiel had been sent at that time; and today too, after the coming of our Saviour, the words apply to pagans and to Jews and to those who once believed, but then denied their faith. The prophet's words are applicable to those who sin without perceiving their sin, since a sinner who has received baptism, even though he may be dead towards his soul, because he does not perceive his sin, yet he is alive to God because of the grace of baptism that he possesses, in accordance with the words *God is not of the dead but of the living,** for they are all living in him.

Ez 33:11

Ez 3:17

Lk 20:38

How then should a sinner approach to receive the Holy Mysteries, if he does not have within himself the Holy Spirit who authorizes him to do this? For just as someone who has not been baptized is not permitted to come to the Mysteries, the same

would apply to a sinner if it were true that
the Holy Spirit had left him, which is the
foolish opinion of those who say 'he is not
allowed to approach the Mysteries'. If a sinner cannot approach the Mysteries, who
then may do so? And what about the words
'this is my Body which is broken for you
for the forgiveness of sins', and *'this is my
Blood which is shed for you for the forgiveness of sins?'* Is an unbaptized person allowed to approach the Mysteries? But if the
Spirit departs the moment a man sins, then
his baptism departs too, and if his baptism
has departed and he has become unbaptized, then he is no longer permitted to
approach the Mysteries. And if he does not
approach the Mysteries, how will he receive propitiation, how can there be repentance if there is no forgiveness? And if there
is no repentance from sin, how can the
Holy Spirit ever return, as they say he does?
Our Lord openly refuted this foolish opinion when he said *Everyone who eats my
Body and drinks my Blood shall remain in
me and I in him; I will establish him on
the last day.** Now, in as much as a sinner
receives our Lord's Body and Blood in
faith, he is in our Lord, and our Lord is in
him, as our Lord himself says; and where
the Lord dwells, there is his Spirit too.

Had it been because of any justification
on our own part that we received the Holy
Spirit from the water, then the Spirit would
simply be acting in justice, departing from
us because of our sin. But if it is by grace
that the Spirit has been given us, then his
remaining with us is also a gift of grace.

cf Mt 26:26–8

Jn 6:54

And inasmuch as we received him from the water in faith, and immediately he granted us forgiveness of sins, and justified us with sonship to God, so too, now, as long as we believe that he is within us, we receive admonition against sin, and if it so happen that we do sin, then we quickly repent, thanks to the help of his power.

For we were not given a grace that is taken away or altered, as was the case with the Jews, and what was said to them has no bearing on us, namely *I have said 'You are gods, and all of you are children of the Most High; but henceforth you shall die as men, and fall as one of the warriors'.* *

Ps 82:6-7

The reason is that they received the grace of servitude [to God], while we received that of sonship, which is unalterable; as Paul teaches: *You have not received the spirit of servitude to fear any longer, but you have received the Spirit of children, which cries out 'Abba, our Father'.* * You

Rom 8:15

see the fact that we cry out to God 'Our Father who art in heaven' at the time of the Holy Mysteries is due to the permission given us by the Spirit; we have received, as Paul says, *the Spirit of sonship, which cries out 'Abba, our Father',* * for it is the Spirit

Rom 8:15

who authorizes us to cry out 'Our Father' to God at that moment; and those who cry out 'Our Father' then and expect to receive the Mysteries are all sinners. Because of the sins we have committed since baptism, we receive the Mysteries assiduously and we, who are sinners, call God 'our Father' at that time, and it is clear that it is because

the Spirit is within us that he has given us
authority to do this.

Thus it is manifest from every point of
view that the Spirit of God does not depart
from the baptized whenever they sin;
rather, he remains with them even in their
sinning, showing his grace in this way too,
so that the end may be like the beginning,
and Paul's words fulfilled: *We have not received this as a result of any works, in
order that no one might be proud.* *   *Eph 2:9*

I have written all this briefly to refute
those who hold an inept view of the workings of the grace of the Holy Spirit, and
hold that he is weak and of no aid to men.
But do you, O disciple, believe that the
Holy Spirit whom you received from the
baptismal water is within you, and will
never depart from you. The recalling of his
presence will provide you with warning,
and so flee from all the devices of sin, lest it
insinuate itself into your thoughts and
come to fruition by your committing it.
Should sleep come upon you, arouse yourself at once, and if you lapse into fault,
hastily right yourself from your fall, crying
out to him who let fall this word of the
prophet: *Satan, the Lord rebuke thee.* *   *Zech 3:2*
who justifies is close at hand, namely the
Holy Spirit who has been given to me by
my Lord once and for all for the preservation of my life. To Him be praise, along
with the Father and Son, now and always,
Amen.

2. PHILOXENUS,
Excerpt on prayer

ANYONE WHO PRAYS should pray having his heart in touch with his mouth and his mind with his lips. If, however, he bows down and stretches out his hands in prayer while his heart is daydreaming somewhere else, then he is like the cedars which storms bend down and flatten out. Or if his lips are eagerly murmuring but his mind is somewhere outside the monastery, then this resembles the case of doors being buffetted by the winds, which no one can open or shut.

For anyone who stands in prayer a discerning compassion is required. Tears of compunction are also beneficial. He also requires a recollected mind. If he has any grudge against any of his fellows, he should wash this away from his heart. And he should pray in silence, his lips murmuring with awareness. And when he puts the seal on his prayer, let him stop and remain still in silence. He should not occupy himself with empty talk or with unedifying chatter; rather, he should remain in silence and awareness. Then his prayer will be fully accepted by him who receives prayers and pure thoughts.

3. PHILOXENUS,
Excerpt on prayer

PURE PRAYER such as is worthy of God, O disciple of God, is not uttered by means of composite words. Prayer which is worthy of God consists in this: that one gather in one's mind from the entire world, and not let it be secretly bound to anything; that one place it entirely at God's disposal and forget, during the time of prayer, everything that is material, including one's own self and the place where one is standing. One should be secretly swallowed up in the spirit in God, and one should clothe oneself in God at the time of prayer both outwardly and inwardly, set on fire with ardent love for him, and entirely engulfed in all of him, entirely commingled in all of him, with the movements of one's thoughts suffused with wondrous recollection of God, while the soul has gone out in love to seek him whom she loves, just as David said, *My soul has gone out after you.** Ps 63:9

It is with these inner movements that one should pray to God. But since vowels [*lit.* movements] have words as their shadow, I am indicating the shadow of these things for the disciple's instruction, so that he may grasp the shadow and walk in it, thus arriving at the body [which casts the shadow].

4. PHILOXENUS,
Excerpt on prayer

THE SOUL'S STRENGTH consists in continuous prayer; this clothes the mind in the might which comes from the vision of God. One should read Scripture until the mind has become recollected from wandering thoughts; then, on perceiving in the mind that it has returned to its proper place, having come back to itself from the distraction which is outside it, immediately one should put down the Book and revert to prayer. In this way the reading of Scripture will be for the purpose of prayer, and fasting for the purpose of purity of prayer, and the emptying of thoughts of all riches will be for the very purpose of prayer. In other words, let the mind do everything requisite in order that it may become worthy to speak with God in prayer.

The converse of the Holy Spirit [which dwells within us] with God is the aim of all ascetic labours, and the end of the path of righteousness: this is the ministry of the company of Gabriel and Michael.[4] For prayer, I would say, is not psalmody consisting of verses, or songs and hymns: these just serve as the letters and syllables for prayer's authoritative form of reading. Until we become aware that within us there lives the 'spiritual person',* along with all his

1 Cor 2:15

limbs—that is to say, what we become in baptism—battle against that 'old person', whom Christ put to death on his Cross, will not be stilled within us. *

cf Eph 4:22 & Col 3:9

BIBLIOGRAPHY AND NOTES

A. Text 1 is translated from the edition by A. Tanghe, '*Memra* de Philoxène de Mabboug sur l'inhabitation du Saint Esprit', *Le Muséon* 73 (1960) 39–71. Text 2 is translated from British Library, Add. 14582, fol. 181b–182a, dated AD 815/16. Texts 3 and 4 are translated from the edition by P. Bettiolo, in *Le Muséon* 94 (1981) 76–7. Although texts 2–4 are attributed to Philoxenus, there must be an element of doubt about the correctness of the attribution since adjacent texts, also attributed to Philoxenus, can be shown to be by other writers; thus texts 3 and 4 are followed in the manuscript by a third text which is in fact John of Apamea's short treatise on Prayer (translated in an expanded form in Chapter X).

B. A good summary survey of Philoxenus' life and works is given by F. Graffin in *DSpir* 12 (1984) cols. 1392–7. The fundamental work is A. de Halleux, *Philoxène de Mabbog, sa vie, ses écrits, sa théologie* (Louvain, 1963). On his christology: R. C. Chesnut, *Three Monophysite Christologies* (Oxford, 1976) part II. Among the various articles on his spirituality one might cite: I. Hausherr, 'Contemplation et sainteté. Une remarkable mise au point par Philoxène de Mabboug', *RAM* 14(1933), 171–95 = *Hésychasme et priére*, OCA 176 (1966). Chapter 4. P. Harb, 'Le role exercé par Philoxène de Mabbug sur l'évolution de la morale dans l'église syrienne', *Parole de l'Orient* 1 (1970) 27–48; A. Grillmeier, 'Die Taufe Christi und die Taufe der Christen: zur Tauftheologie des Philoxenus von Mabbug und ihre Bedeutung für die christliche Spiritualität', in *Fides Sacramenti, Sacramentum Fidei: Studies in Honour of P. Smulders* (Assen, 1981) 137–75. There is an English translation of the Discourses by E. A. W. Budge, *The Discourses of Philoxenus* (London, 1894) vol. II (French translation by E. Lemoine in *Sources chrétiennes 44*, 1956). There is a French translation of the *Letter to Patricius* by R. Lavenant in PO 30, fasc 5 (1963).

1. The Fathers consistently taught that only the baptized, who had become children of God by adoption (Rom 8:15), could address God as Father and so use the Lord's Prayer.

2. This anticipates Theophane the Recluse: cf. T. Spidlik, *La spiritualité de l'Orient Chrétien*, OCA 206 (1978), 33 [ET, *The Spirituality of the Christian East,* CS 79, (1986) 32].

3. Philoxenus here provides an interesting rationale for the veneration of relics.

4. Abraham of Nathpar employs the same phrase in his adaptation of John of Apamea's short text on prayer (p. 191).

Chapter VII

Babai

Early 6th Century?

INTRODUCTION

T HE TITLE provided in the four medieval Syrian Orthodox manuscripts which contain this work iden-
tify the author as 'Babai whom the wicked
Barsauma slew', in other words, with the patriarch of
Seleucia-Ctesiphon more often called Baboway, who was
put to death by the Persian king Peroz in 484 at the insti-
gation—so later Syrian Orthodox tradition claimed—of
Barsauma, the metropolitan of Nisibis who propagated the
teaching of Theodore of Mopsuestia (castigated as 'Nestorian' by his opponents) in the Church of the East at the
end of the fifth century. This identification cannot, however, be an early one, and so must remain very uncertain;
all that can be said with assurance is that the *Letter* must
emanate from the milieu of Persian Christianity, since the
contents suggest that Cyriacus, to whom it was addressed,
was a convert to Christianity from a noble Zoroastrian
family. Such converts were evidently not infrequent, especially in the sixth century, and on general grounds it
seems likely that the *Letter to Cyriacus* belongs approximately to that period, and perhaps to the first, rather than
to the second, half of that century. Thus in its general
tone and in its very practical advice it stands much closer
to John of Apamea's *Letter to Hesychius*, some of whose
phraseology it may indeed echo here and there, than it
does to the works of the East Syrian monastic tradition of
the late sixth to the eighth centuries. The author is definitely not to be confused with the well-known theologian

of the Church of the East, Babai the Great (died 628); nor is the *Letter* likely to be the lost work on monastic life by Babai the Great's contemporary, Babai of Nisibis.

A very distinctive feature of the Letter is the use of exempla. Thus, for example, someone who fancies that he is in a state of virtue and has a high opinion of himself 'is like the man who chases after gazelles while riding on a donkey: he fatigues his body, but fails to catch the gazelles' (#14). Curiously enough, there are very few good parallels to these particular exempla elsewhere in Syriac literature. In some ways the *Letter* could be described as a late offshoot of the Wisdom literature of the Ancient Near East.

BABAI,
Letter to Cyriacus

THE LETTER OF THE HOLY MAR BABAI WHOM THE WICKED
BARSAUMA SLEW; TO THE PRIEST CYRIACUS ON THE
SOLITARY LIFE AND ON COMPLETE AND DIVINE
RENUNCIATION. MAY HIS PRAYER BE WITH US.

THE PERFECT AND COMPLETE activity is
the worship performed by angels. It
demands the following: purity of
heart, true love of God, wariness over
thoughts, reflection on Christ, prayer without ceasing, assiduous fasting consisting of
an eager struggle against unclean thoughts,
continuous conflict with the body, abstinence from luxurious foods, rest of soul,
true joy, a delight that does not fall within
the means of what the tongue can express,
the spectacle of virtue, a deadness with regard to all that is given or taken, refusal of
everything attractive, cessation of all cares,
escape from all evils, abstinence from the
sight of people's faces,[1] an uninterrupted
course night and day, a wakeful mind un-

mingled with worldly cares, a scanty diet, the arena of the diligent, the tree of self-effacement.

2. O penitent, who drinks the sweat of the body, who grows up on the blood shed by the soul; without these, sir, it is useless for someone to afflict his life by living in the wilderness; these, O penitent, are the daughters of light, and this is what they effect. Use your discernment and choose the course which takes you farthest away from the deadening activities of the stifling world, and brings you close to God; direct your footsteps towards Bethlehem like the blessed Magi* your fellow companions,[2] *cf Mt 2:1–12* until you reach the appointed place of that blessed star which shone from Jacob. You have no need of an actual star to guide you, as did the Magi, for at that time there was no path or road, whereas now many are the roads, paths, and staging posts.

3. *An attendant admonition.* You, who travel on the road of virtue, should be mindful of your departure from your parental home, and know how to acquire your salvation [*lit.* life] with due precaution; for your temporal life is dissipated as a result of neglect during *the days of your empty existence,** and everything which is *Qo 7:15, 9:9* done neglectfully by the discerning during their lifetime brings them to be questioned once they have shaken off dust and corruption, and woken up from the sleep of mortality.

4. Therefore do not make a pretext of the weakness of nature, and do not go astray because of the strength of the body's

passions. You should realize that our entire race is sinful while he [God] is entirely just, and everyone who is close to God has only reached this state aided by grace. On this point let the upright persuade you, people who have completely given themselves over to God, both men and women. Accordingly you should strive to get rid of anything that is a hindrance to you, which enslaves you to neglectfulness. Do not rely on tomorrow: your business belongs to today,* for our time is not a time for just words or for acquiring property, or indeed to swagger about enjoying ourselves, or to relax in idleness. No, for the discerning it is time for action; it is the time to gather in fruits; it is the time for repentance; it is the time for everyone to supplicate Christ with all his heart.

cf Prov 27:1

5. Ask those who lived in days gone by, learn from former generations; consider, during *the days of your empty existence,** where are the wise?³ Where are the philosophers and rhetoricians who gained a reputation for their consummate skills of speech? Where are the kings with their crowns? Or the men with a reputation for strength and might? Ask the earth and it will show you; ask Sheol and it will reveal to you how no realm endures—not even those who grow rich and wealthy.

Qo 7:15, 9:9

6. When you realize this, guard your soul warily so that you do not have regret at the last moment. Strive not to be subservient to the fear of death. Be wary of the pain which is lying in ambush for you, watching your every step, lest it jump out

at you like a snare, and there be no one to rescue you. Pain accompanied by regret when it is too late offers no comfort, for the time for repentance is about to pass by: this is when the exactor who cannot be bribed stands at the door, and earth gives orders to dust. Restraint which has been abused by you will not forget, but will quickly settle upon you.

7. If, then, you chose the monastic life, my brother, be very careful of fame and of negligence [or trifles]. Do not work for a reward, and do not wait expectantly like a hired laborer for the end of the year, or watch out for the evening like a servant. Let nothing ever urge you on except the love of God, for whose sake you should cause yourself to toil. Otherwise what is the use of wearing yourself out, spending your life to no advantage? You would be like the man who laid a plank of wood over a well's mouth and drew up water on one side and poured it out on the other.

8. Do not do or say anything without discernment; do not act out of vainglory. For you are standing in the house of God, and it is God you are serving. Happy are you if God is your paymaster, for he will reward you out of his riches.

9. But be careful, brother, not to let your days be expended in hidden losses; do not wear your life away to no effect, and do not, by your labours and actions, grieve God or the angel who ministers to you, lest you prove to be a useless burden to him. Strive, then, that your life should be God's, and he will rejoice over you as someone

who guards a precious deposit; for it is he who holds the sceptre that should direct your actions.

10. And do not just be zealous over externals, lest you become like someone who wears fine clothes, but who has nothing in his house. Thus you should be zealous over inward matters, like someone who outwardly appears to be poor, but who has gold and treasure in his house. For a wise man to be like this is very easy; but for someone to become wise is not a frequent occurrence.

11. Be a good worker in the house of God, and do not spare your body from weariness, for all your affairs are under God's control. Give yourself to God with your whole heart. In whatever you think, or say, or do, hold in your mind that God is, as it were, watching.

12. Be a servant and at the same time free-born, unconstrained by anything.[4] Give yourself over to contempt, and do not let activities which have a despised character weigh you down, and do not look down on them, supposing yourself to be above them. For if you do not excel in small things, you cannot be confident that you will excel in greater things. Do not hold yourself in honour, or give yourself airs over those who are older than you in the monastery; otherwise you will be the last when the time comes for true honours. Do not act in a superior way to those who come from less noble families than yours, for all men consist of the same dust,

whether they be kings or low-born, rich or poor.

13. Do not speak in the presence of others unless you have been asked a question. Do not look down on those who are less advanced than you in knowledge and labours[5]; do not imagine yourself to be any better than they, for blessed is the man who does not judge himself to be anything special. Otherwise you will lose any benefit you had in order that you may become aware of your low estate, and you will fall into shame and be mocked.

14. If someone considers himself to be something when he has nothing, then he is just a fool. He is like the man who chases after gazelles while riding on a donkey: he fatigues his body, but fails to catch the gazelles. In the same way, a person who is in a state of virtue and has a high opinion of himself, is just bringing toil upon his body without making any progress.

15. Look out, brother, lest he who steals all that is good steal from you too, and you mistakenly think 'that it is sufficient that I should have become a Christian'. Only a senseless man would think like this; for it does not suffice just to receive the mark of holy baptism.[6] No, a person should strive to live his life in accordance with the will of his Creator. If someone has washed after handling a corpse and then goes back to touch it, what is the good of his washing? Grace has acted in you, discerning friend, for when you were toiling in slavery you were invited to freedom, to become a servant of the heavenly King—and not just a

servant, but an associate too, and a minister and a sharer in his Mystery. Now tell me which is better: when you were a tare* all set to go to Gehenna, or now when you are wheat in the granary of joys?

cf Mt
13:37–40

16. Just as the working of grace is so great within you, O penitent, so you should bestow your life on God many times over, much more than anyone else. For God has no need of men.

17. *An attendant admonition.* Be careful, you who travel on this path of humility, lest your heart grow hard, lest you have to repent again and again, pulling down and then having to build up.[7] That a man should pull down and rebuild is an indicator only of his fatigue; he makes his body tired, but no one can see what he has achieved.

18. You should have a heart that is open and patient, a meek attitude which will bear the burden of many. *For the Son of Man did not come to be ministered to, but to serve and give Himself as a ransom for many.* * Let your eyes see while not seeing, let your ears hear while not hearing. Hold in honour those who have grown old in the fear of God; honour them as though they were our Lord, and not men. For no one is greater than he who honours the person who holds the Lord in awe.

Mt 20:28, Mk
10:45

19. Let fools, rather than the wise, be your enemies—not in a metaphorical sense, but rather, just as fraudulent gold is rejected by the goldsmith, so fools should be reproved by your actions, and the proud by your humility. Do not rely on a long life;

do not let your heart deceive you into counting up so and so many years ahead. For it is not days or a quantity of years that can teach you a full quota of wisdom. *Many of those in front shall be last, and those last be first.* * The earth is all one, and so is the Farmer; so is the seed and so is the irrigation. But there is a variety which is prolific in fruit, much richer than the rest. Let it be your care to cultivate the soil of your soul with continual prayer and recitation of the psalms. Do not neglect your soul, but persevere in stilling unclean thoughts in its depths, for they habitually hinder the heart from progressing in purity and holiness by making it impure. For it is these in particular which are bearers of destruction for humanity. They are like rust to iron for people with a pure mind; they are like blindfolds over the eyes of the soul, so that it cannot see clearly what it is doing.

Mt 19:30, 20:16, Lk 13:30

20. If you take care over these things, O penitent, and you truly and wholeheartedly endeavour to investigate them, then you will find something which will benefit your life in no small way. And it will have proved true to you that, unless you become a despised servant in the monastic life entirely of your own free will, you will not be able to attain to the life of penitence, as is fitting. It will have proved all the more true to you that, if you live the monastic life with all your heart in the fear of God, then there will come to you of its own accord, not just what you have been asking for, but also that of which you were not even

aware. And in the end you will understand what I am saying. If, then, the blessed Jacob had not laboured for Rachel with all his strength,* then not even Leah, of whom he was unaware, would have been given him.

Gen 29–31

21. Strive, therefore, with all your strength to ask for that which gives spiritual pleasure to others, rather than to yourself.

22. *On the solitary life.* See, O brother who loves God, whether you love the solitary life, whether you are intent on being a penitent, whether you are happy with the quiet life of the wilderness, and really seek to become a man of God. Strive after the following: wariness over all thoughts, meditation on God, unceasing prayer, purity of heart, a clear conscience, an understanding of what the battle against Satan means, discernment, wariness against shameful passions, recollection and a strict guard against transgressions, the raising up of the soul above the world, and besides all this, continuous fasting, reading of the holy Scriptures, recitation of the psalms, meditation on glorious things.

23. In addition to these things you should endeavour after: spiritual understanding, discernment, patience in all eventualities, stability in one place. For it was by means of spiritual understanding that Joseph dried up the crazed lust that had burst out against him;* it was by discernment that Ananias and his companions overcame the Babylonians and the wise men:* and it was by patience that Job was victorious.

Gen 39:8–9

Dan 3

24. Furthermore, flee from the urge to

write, lest your soul goes out seeking ideas concerning various kinds of knowledge, and your heart is thereby emptied of its reflection on God, through undiscerning utterance; otherwise your affairs will increase, and you will become empty of your proper task.

25. See to it that you do not eat twice a day except in cases of necessity. Be wary of a full stomach, lest you end up with a sick soul as well as a sick body; for illness comes from overeating. He who eats a lot gets ill, whereas someone who is careful about this will prolong his life. It is not the ability of everyone to be pure in matters of eating.

26. Shun conversation with sisters; be careful of a face's looks, lest they affect you unawares, and you are slain without your being aware of it. You would be like the man who rips open his belly and sews up his shirt; or like the man who is wounded by an unskilled doctor with a metal instrument that was intended for his benefit, as a result of which all his blood escapes without his being aware of it. Or it is as though someone was given a honeycomb mixed with poison and all unawares he ate it and ended up dead. So it is that those who associate with sisters and love to meet them: they are spiritually slain without their being aware of it; their soul is blindfolded and befouled inside their bodies, and chastity is unable to reign in their souls. They become like a statue which is decked up with gold, but inside is full of frogs!

27. Take in what I am saying to you, for

my words are to be believed: *Can someone put fire in his lap without his clothes getting burnt? Or can he walk over coals of fire without his feet getting scorched.* *

Prov 6:27-8

28. Do not do anything out of the ordinary or adopt a singular way of life as long as you are with many brethren in the monastery, otherwise when you imagine you are making progress you are in fact retrogressing, and you will be like the man who harvests and then scatters the grain, or the man who plants and then pulls up.

29. Try to ensure as far as possible that it is not men but God who sees your labours and good works. If they are visible to your fellow men, then the moment they are seen, they are befouled. For there is a path which appears to men to be good, but its tracks are those of death. Your religious life will be unacceptable if you show someone your good deeds.

30. It is very easy for someone to hide bread in the grass and then eat it, but to hide grass in bread and live off that is something only the discerning is able to do. It is good to hide one's good deeds: a man whose actions only God sees has reached a high grade.

31. Do not take on many activities lest the day hand you over to the month, and the month then make you subject to the year. * Insofar as you are able, be on the alert not to commit yourself [*lit.* your days] to more than a year at a time, for a penitent who is occupied with village activities belongs to the world, and is like someone who is shown the king, but turns away his

cf Lk 12:58

gaze to look at an elephant. You should
have in your cell more tools for the craft of
looking after the soul than for looking after
the body. It is impossible for you to make
progress if you are occupied with some exterior activity. Let your day be one, and
tomorrow will not be forgotten; otherwise
boredom may give you trouble. When a
certain blind man was on the point of dying
he was asked by someone, 'How old are
you?' The blind man replied, 'one night
old'. So it should be with you, O penitent:
let your day be one with all your heart and
all your strength and all your soul.

32. Make it your care to pray without
ceasing,* for prayer is light to the soul, and   *1 Th 5:17*
it acts as a guard to the body. Pray not just
when you are standing in prayer, but also
when you are moving around or doing
something, and even when you are asleep,
and when you are eating. When your
mouth is occupied with nourishment, let
your heart be occupied with prayer. While
your right hand is looking after your body's
needs at table, let your mind be given to
praise and thanksgiving to him who provides for your needs. In this way your food
will be blessed and hallowed in your body,
without your being concerned about this.

33. Be alert so that you are not overcome by any passions, and error lead you
astray. Instead, while others are having a
good time, giving pleasure to their bodies
at meal time, you should be praying, giving
pleasure to your soul. The greater the variety of delicacies set before you, do you the

more give praises in your soul to Christ the giver of all the good things you have.

34. And whenever you allow yourself some rest of the body, whether in daytime or at night, lie down after the labour of prayer like someone who ceases at evening from harvesting.

35. And if you are going to be assiduous in the activity of prayer, my beloved, do not have many things to attract you; do not omit to say the Office hours on any pretext, lest you find the words *Cast the useless servant into outer darkness** apply to you. Do not get entangled in a large number of activities; they are rust to your soul and disease to your body.

Mt 25:30

36. So do not extend your labour beyond what you have the strength[8] for, otherwise you may be obliged to depart from your place and you will be like the man who gave up carrying cockerel's wings, which was within the bounds of his strength, and was seen carrying a beam, whereupon he fell and was laughed at.

37. Do not abandon the small advantage that is close at hand in the hope of a greater one further off; otherwise when you let go of the small one close at hand, you fail to catch the greater one, and you lose both. You will be like the stupid man who, as he was carrying his son across a river on his shoulders, saw a fish swimming in the water, let go the child to catch the fish; and as a result he lost the child in the river and failed to catch the fish.

38. It is easy for a wise man to exist, but

to become wise is not within everyone's grasp.

39. Beware of the impulses of the body when it is at rest, and do not let evil thoughts take up residence in your heart. Do not let your heart enjoy any physical thought under a false pretext, and do not let yourself accept such a thought with pleasure; otherwise you will be considered an adulterer in the sight of that Eye which sees all. For the Lord is the Lord of knowledge, and if you are neglectful, such a thought will end up as an action. So drive it out from you, and do not let any pleasure at it rest in the depths of your heart. Rather, occupy yourself in the recitation of psalms, in words of prayer, in thinking of God. Whenever you are struggling with sleep, meditate on whichever of these is in your heart as you go to sleep, and if such things pass the night in your soul, then the demon cannot attack your sleep and mislead you with foul dreams.

40. Just as a beggar cannot dare to enter the house where the king is living, so demons do not dare to attack if you go on reciting the psalms or sing continual prayers within yourself.

41. Do not strive to be alone because of being ashamed at some sin or other; but you should strive to be alone in order to be by yourself. For someone to be physically alone is very easy, but to be recollected by himself is not for everyone a simple thing. When you are alone, then struggle not to lose your concentration, or your conscience will rebuke you for neglect.

42. Let the thought of God revolve in
your heart more than breath in your nos-
trils.[9] Take great care, then, not to let error
dominate you, for any recollection,
whether it be advantageous or the opposite, and any thought which is not centred
in God you should drive out: the gaze of
your mind should be on God alone. Now if
the recollection of God dies away from
your heart, then do not consider yourself
as having any part in life; but if your
thought is on God, O penitent, then your
life too will be mingled with the recollection of God and of his grace.

43. God takes thought for you, so do not
rely on yourself if you see yourself doing
well. A person's life should be lived in trepidation as long as he goes to bed in the
evening and gets up early in the morning.

44. Take care not to show your wealth to
cf Is 39:2   your enemy,* otherwise he may take from
you hostages, and so hold you under his
control. For someone to show his wealth to
the enemy is to fight on the side of folly.

45. Be careful not to lose anything in this
world apart from your body. Dissociate
your soul [*or* self] from anything which
does not accompany you out of this world.
Watch your heart with the greatest precaution for all that stirs within it.

46. Do not give yourself all sorts of pre-
texts for going out on journeys, wandering
about different countries and places, living
an evil life, moving from house to house.
The person who does not stay in his own
house distributes winds to his children. Do
not be like the bird that perches on thorns.

47. Receive everyone who comes to you.
Except when you are in real need, do not
get into the habit of leaving your monastery
all of a sudden, for a penitent who loves
wandering about is no different from a man
who takes some thorns and hits himself in
the eyes with them; and just as someone
cannot escape from poverty and need if,
while he is carrying a load, he starts hunt-
ing after a bird, making it fly off, and he
chases after winds and storm, so it is in the
case of the penitent who wanders about: it
is impossible for him to make any progress
in the things of God. And just as someone
caught in a net as he fights in battle cannot
save himself from being killed, so too the
penitent, who settles down one day and
wanders off the next, cannot at all escape
from being wounded by the evil one.

48. Make every effort to love penitence,
and maybe you will be delivered from
things which are harmful to the stable lives
of man.

49. If your soul is held by contrition,
nothing will arouse it to wander about in
the world. Who can persuade a widow
who has lost her only son to give her attention to the sound of music? So it is with the
soul which is commingled in the love of
God and in penitence: it is unable to take
any pleasure in wandering about.

50. For a penitent to exist is very easy,
but to become a penitent belongs only to a
few.

51. Do not get caught up with those who
are rich in this world, and do not take any
delight in talking to well-born women; oth-

erwise your heart will play tricks on you,
and you will find yourself all ruffled. Conversation with them is sweet and delightful
and pleasant for the body, but bad for the
soul; listening to them is a source of error
for the body, but to the soul it is leprosy—a
soul which is caught up in seeking the company of well-born women is unable to escape from leprosy.

52. If a wealthy person approaches you,
keep your distance from him; and avoid
talking with well-born women with all
your strength. The very thought of them is
a deadly snare, a net from which there is no
escape once one is caught.

Ps 144:13

53. *The Lord's words are to be believed*;* and just as a dog which licks a file
not only gets nothing from it, but actually
hurts its tongue [*lit.* body], so too a penitent who likes wealthy people and conversation with well-born women not only gets
no advantage from it, but is actually doing
harm to his soul.

54. Be careful for your soul's salvation:
do not let it be subordinate to your body,
but bring your body into subjection to your
soul, and so your struggle will not be
useless.

55. You should realize that you are walking on the edge of a sharp sword, that you
are standing on the edge of a precipice with
a ravine on either side. Do not let your
thoughts be upset by things here on earth,
but keep your mind's gaze on *Jerusalem
which is above.* *Think of what is above,
and not of what is on earth*;* ensure that
you let go of everything which belongs to

Gal 4:26
Col 3:2

this world. Do not ever let your gaze be captivated by someone's face; and do not speak to no purpose. Excuse yourself from unprofitable and empty conversation, and be wary in your heart of complaining against others, for they are your brothers, and maybe the complaint will rebound on yourself. Do not find fault with anyone in your mind, and do not make your tongue impure by accusing your neighbour. For the words *the deeds of men have not passed my mouth in the utterance of the lips** are *Ps 17:3–4* trustworthy.

56. Do not allow your ears to hear calumny destructive of those dear to you; do not judge those who are close to you, and do not condemn those who are far off. For a penitent who has anything to do with calumny and accusations is not better than someone who 'eats the flesh of his own shoulders.' It is as though a man took stones and battered his own head, without injuring his companion at all; or like a man who tears away his own flesh and eats it. So it is with a penitent who indulges in calumny and accusation: it is not his companion he is injuring, but his own soul that he is destroying.

57. If a man takes the monastic habit, thinks of himself as a penitent, and then gives himself over to wandering about, then his life will prove useless and he will cause the recollection of God to die away from his heart; he will steal away his mind from God who sees all; he will start off in one place and stop in another; he will speak with one person and push away another; he will say

one thing and then another; he will calumni-
ate one person and accuse another, laugh at
his companion and mock his neighbour; he
will act one way and then another, say one
thing to a man's face, and another behind his
back; he will stick out his tongue at his enemy and be a slave to his belly; he will titi-
vate his body with delicacies and indulge in
talk with sisters; he will chatter inanities
endlessly. Such a man deceives his soul, and
all the lamentations of the blessed Jeremiah
will not suffice for his condition. While he
has turned his back on this world and its
joys, he has not given himself over wholly to
the other, and he has voluntarily deprived
himself, as a result of his slackness, of that
delight which has been prepared for those
who are whole-heartedly diligent in their religious practices.

58. What a fate has met him! He has left
the joy of this world, and has failed to
strive fully to attain that joy which has been
prepared for him in the New World. Who
will fail to weep bitterly for this man who
has left his parental home to set out for the
royal city? He began the journey, but then it
seemed to him difficult and hard-going, so
he ended up in indolence and lassitude. He
has left his parent's house, and failed to
reach the royal city; unable to travel on, he
has idly started wandering about villages
and hamlets.

59. *On Self-emptying.*[10] O my beloved,
you have chosen self-emptying for yourself; recall the portion of your joy which
you have left behind in this world, and do
not forget your departure from your par-

ents' house, or the sorrow and sadness in which you left those who are dear to you. Stir up your soul in eagerness to travel uninterruptedly, day and night, in order to reach what your soul is expecting—the portion that has been prepared for you in the *heavenly Jerusalem*,* along with the upright and the confessors, those who have confessed Christ truly and not as a pretence, who have done so with diligence and not superficially.

Heb 12:22

60. Therefore *do not give sleep to your eyes or slumber to your eyelids.** Be eager to acquire Christ in this world of poverty, and do not exchange the love of him for things visible. Be careful not to try to acquire anything else alongside Christ; if you do try to do anything of the sort here, you will not be able to receive that confidence in his presence which is the victor's crown, from the hands of Christ who crowns them on that day of true shame and true glory.

Prov 6:4

61. Be very attentive to your life in Christ. Do not let involvement in this world hold any pleasure for you, do not let it captivate you by its excitements. Do not let your eyes look upon its beauty. For involvement in it will prove many times more bitter to the soul than it is pleasurable to the body, and a man who is caught in its bonds will never extricate himself, for its bonds are the bonds of death, and they bring you down to the chambers of Sheol. So make your escape from them, otherwise little by little, out of negligence, you will get caught up in them, and when you look around there will be no one to deliver you.

It is as though someone was given by his enemy a silk cloth in which a sharp knife was wrapped, and he does not realize there is a knife there until he has cut himself on it. So it is that the snares of this world are hidden, thanks to various devices by the one who is cunning in every evil artifice, with the result that a man does not realize until he has been caught. They are invisible to the physical eye, and so one should flee from them, and they have been devised by the rulers and powers of darkness, and by the evil spirits who reside beneath the heavens. There is no escape from them, except through the mercies of Christ.

62. Do you then, discerning man who have attached yourself to Christ, beseech him with all your heart and all your *cf Mt 22:37*   strength and all your mind,* and do not approach his commandments in a neglectful way, but beseech his mercies so that they may come to your aid.

63. Run away from vain and unprofitable talk, and guard yourself carefully from the company of men who have committed their lives to idleness. Do not associate with those who speak peaceably with their fellow human beings, all the while harbouring evil in their hearts; or with those who occupy themselves with speaking against their brethren, or with people who say one thing to your face, but another behind your back, or with those who hide their hate in a pretence of friendliness, or with those who are bad tempered and hard-hearted, or with those who try to please with their pleasantries and chatter away inanities, or

with those who, abandoning their own
faults, object to the peccadillos of their
companions—people who do not notice
the *beams in their own eyes*,* who show
friendliness outwardly, but who hate in
their heart; or with those who go around
houses and talk with sisters and well-born
women; nor again with those who minister
to such people.

64. Discern all these, then, from a distance, and get your knowledge of them
from what they do. From the mouth of a
cistern can its water be tasted; for the appearance of a man will make manifest his
actions.

65. Flee from such people, Cyriacus, and
with all your strength be wary of them lest
they captivate you with their words, and
they ensnare your life.

66. It is the following to whom you
should attach yourself: to blessed people,
godlike men, who have committed their
whole selves to our Lord. Let people who
have grown old in the religious life be your
neighbours, let them be your source of advice; attach yourself to them and love
them. And if you have your abode among
such people, then emulate their way of life
and become such as they. Do not separate
yourself from them by your actions, lest
you become like lupine seeds strung together amid strings of pearls.

67. And if you are really concerned with
these things, by means of actions with all
your heart, then all that is black in you will
become white in the company of people
who love God. *Seek and find** that day by

*Mt 7:3–5 &
Lk 6:41–2*

cf Mt 7:7

day you are making progress so that in truth you are blessed and there will be good for your soul.

68. But if you love them only with words and outward appearances, then you will be like a piece of ground which is only in outward appearances a garden separate from everything else, grass, seedlings and trees being absent.

69. All this have I indicated to your piety, O lover of God. The rest is left to your powers of discernment to put it all into action. So read discerningly the words of this letter, and do not, because of the mule carrying the holy vessels, let the holy vessels themselves be despised. Whatever is deficient you should store in the place meant for knowledge.

70. May Christ preserve your life of exile in spiritual poverty, may he save your soul from unclean habits, may he protect you *cf Ps 17:8* under the wings of his care* from the sorrows which are going to come upon earth. May peace and tranquillity of Christ be with you, amen. Thus do I remember you in my prayers, I assure you.

71. I have written this to you, my beloved, not just as a matter of course, but that you may recognize your road and gain understanding of the paths in which you are travelling. For human beings know what is behind them, but in front of them is infinity. And for those who seek the Lord, evening and morning is more than enough. Their road goes a long way, but it is close at hand as they travel along it. They rejoice at fatigue, and are upset by comforts; their

soul finds pleasure in what properly belongs to itself, and they are bored with the
things which other people hold in affec-
tion. Their minds are free, and you cannot
carry the weight of their thoughts.

72. Blessed is the person who has caused
his soul to love God, with his foot treading
on truth, hating bad paths, and travelling
blamelessly.

73. Awake, awake, my beloved; awake
and arouse yourself to penitence, for the
world is passing on and weariness will get
its rest; the *Sun of righteousness will shine
out.** In him the courses of night and day   Mal 4:2
find rest, in him the souls that are eager for
his beauty take pleasure, in him the body
which had oppressed itself through opposi-
tion to itself finds rest; in him the righteous
exult, and in him is the crown of glory laid
upon them; in him sinners repent as their
actions are laid bare.

74. Take caution, my beloved, not to frit-
ter your days away in idleness,* for no man   cf Lk 15:13
knows when the day of the Avenger is com-
ing: the time when the thief is coming is
hidden from the owner of the house.* He   cf Mt 24:43
who is wakeful and who watches will es-
cape from fear. *Blessed are these servants
whom the Master shall find awake and
ready when he comes.**   Mt 24:46

75. So remember your soul during your
lifetime, and be eager to give it what is appropriate. The days of our lifetimes are
short,* as the prophet says, and their num-   cf Ps 109:8
ber can be quickly counted. That we should
live our lives in a perfunctory way does not
belong to the discerning.

76. Multiply the guards you keep on your soul, lest it leave you in search of many things, and when you eventually look for it you will fail to find it. Let your search, then, be for one thing. To walk on the earth is something everyone can do, but to walk along a knife edge is something only a mature soul can do.

77. This too you should know: there are three things which are praiseworthy, great, and honoured before God. By these a person can climb up and be exalted to the height of the tower of the religious life; they are inconspicuous, yet upon them the glorious crown of the perfect life of the holy Gospel's commandment is woven, and with them is strung the entire necklace of virtue. They are what the law—that is, the solitary life—ordains.

78. The first has no compare, the second is of great value, the third is magnificent; they are one, not three; they are three, not one. The first gives birth to seven virtues: joy which cannot be dominated by sorrow, wariness over thoughts, toil which weariness cannot prevent, the forgetting of all memories, the uprooting from all worries, the cessation from all worldly affairs, and a heart that does not shift its concern from God.

79. The middle one also gives birth to seven excellent things: love that is far removed from any guile, serene peace which anger cannot perturb, equilibrium which envy cannot upset, purity which resentment does not disturb, a heart which does not despise itself, sleep that is free from

foul dreams, and vigilance which is preserved from miseries.

80. The third one too gives birth to
seven beautiful things: the escape from all
that appears to human beings as important,
the refusal of everything that is attractive,
hope that time cannot impair, pleasure that
does not fall under what tongue can express, confinement and stability in a single
place, a small amount of sustenance, and
confidence in the presence of him who examines all—and that a person should not
keep his eyes fixed on what is close at
hand.

81. Hunt out these things; see that you
run night and day so as to find them: for
they cannot be learnt and they cannot be
taught, but with toil and sweat are they acquired. They can be dissipated in a short
time, but without them the penitent cannot
advance.

82. For he who is not rich in these three
is distant from the first, and not close to the
other two. The soul that is not caught up in
these is still engaged in temporal labour,
and its course is terminated in the same
way as with the course of a sound.

83. So run after those good things to
which you have been invited, O lover of
God, so that we may all be held worthy of
them, our brother, through the grace of
Christ our God and his great mercies,
amen.

THE DISCOURSE OF MAR BABAI IS ENDED:
MAY HIS PRAYER SUCCOUR ALL THE
CHILDREN OF THE HOLY CHURCH.

The Syriac Fathers

BIBLIOGRAPHY AND NOTES

A. The text is translated from my forthcoming edition (whose section numbers are employed here). Extracts from the *Letter to Cyriacus* (containing sections 3–4, 22–37, 39–49, 51–56a, 57b–58, 60–70 and 73) have recently been published in Syriac in a small volume entitled *Martyānūtā d-abāhātā d-ʿīdtā* ('Admonition of the Fathers of the Church'), edited by Metropolitan Mar Yulios Çiçek (Holland: St Ephrem the Syrian Monastery, 1985) 87–98; there the author Babai is specifically identified by the editor as 'Babai, Catholicos of Babylon'.

B. For Babai/Baboway the Catholicos reference may be made to S. Gero, *Barsauma of Nisibis and Persian Christianity in the Fifth Century*, CSCO 426, Subsidia 63; (1981) 97–109.

1. Compare John of Apamea, *Letter to Hesychius*, 32.

2. Legends concerning the Magi were naturally popular among Persian Christians: see U. Monneret de Villar, *Le leggende orientali sui magi evangelici*, Studi e Testi 163 (1952).

3. Such series of rhetorical questions are not uncommon; Babai partly reflects the wording of a homily attributed to Ephrem (ed. T. J. Lamy, *Sancti Ephraem Syri Hymni et Sermones*, II [Malines, 1886] col. 337).

4. Babai here reflects John of Apamea, *Letter to Hesychius*, 25.

164

5. This perhaps reflects John, *Letter to Hesychius*, 14.

6. The 'mark' normally refers to the baptismal anointing in Syriac writers.

7. This perhaps reflects the end of John, *Letter to Hesychius*, 7.

8. This perhaps reflects John, *Letter to Hesychius*, 22.

9. Compare Gregory of Nazianzus, *Oration XXVII.4*, quoted by Martyrius (section 60) 227.

10. For this term see the General Introduction, p. xxxi.

Chapter VIII

Anonymous I

6th Century?

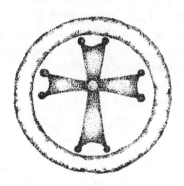

INTRODUCTION

THE TEXT translated below is a 'chapter on prayer' taken from the beginning of an anonymous collection of eighteen hortatory discourses preserved in a single ninth-century manuscript. The work as a whole draws fairly extensively on earlier writers, both Greek and Syriac; in the present excerpt there are explicit quotations from Basil, Gregory of Nyssa, and Jacob of Serugh, while an unacknowledged quotation is also made of Evagrius' *Admonition on Prayer*, translated above in Chapter IV. The work was definitely written in Syriac and may belong to the second half of the sixth century—a *terminus post quem* is provided by the quotations from Jacob of Serugh, who died in 521.

ANONYMOUS I,
On Prayer

W E SHOULD PRAY in faith, without letting our minds be in doubt or be lacking in a firm trust in our God. This is what our Lord himself teaches us when he says *All that you shall ask in prayer* in my name, *having faith, you shall receive.** Potent indeed is prayer that is of- *Mt 21:22* fered in faith from a pure heart. For this reason we should persevere in prayer, my brethren, and not weary of it.

What, then, is prayer? And what is petition? And why do we stand in prayer facing east? And how should we pray? And what advantage do we get from prayer and petition? All this we must set out before you.

We define prayer, then, as a means of escape from misfortunes, a delivery from all that can cause hurt, a key to the gates of heaven, converse and encounter with God.

Petition is a request for the things that are lacking from what is requisite. Supplication is therefore a profound form of the same

169

thing. Thanksgiving is the expression of gratitude for what has been given.

Why is it that we stand in prayer facing east?

The holy Basil tells us in his book on the Holy Spirit:[1] 'So this is the reason why our gaze is directed eastwards when we stand in prayer: it is so that our eyes may gaze in the direction of Paradise, and in this way we may seek for our original abode which we lost when our forefather Adam transgressed the commandment. It is easy to see the point of this, seeing that it is written that *Paradise is in the east*,* and its planter is God.'

Gen 2:8

How should we pray? Our Lord instructs us as follows: *Pray, and do not grow tired of it.** And, wanting to instruct us in what way we should pray, he said, *When you are going to pray, enter your chamber and shut the door* on yourself; *then pray to your Father who is hidden, and your Father who sees you hiddenly will reward you openly.**

Lk 18:1

Mt 6:6

The blessed apostle James says *How great is the potency of the prayer that the just person prays*;* and again *The prayer of many people possesses potency.*

Jas 5:16

The blessed Paul also teaches us as follows: *Pray at all times*;* and again, *exercise yourselves with psalms and songs of praise, and sing in your hearts the odes of the* Holy *Spirit.* He also says, *Be constant in prayer; let your requests be made known before God with all kinds of prayers and petititions.**

Eph 6:18

Phil 4:6

The holy Gregory, the brother of Basil

the Great, teaches us as follows in his exposition of the Lord's Prayer:[2] 'If prayer takes
place prior to worry over particular things,
then sin is unable to find any entrance into
the soul. The same is the case if someone is
going on a journey, or is facing some crisis,
or is going to get married: if he does everything accompanied by prayer, then his
course will go well.'

From the fact of our praying it so happens that we are with God; and whoever is
with God is well away from the Enemy:
prayer thus preserves chastity, it beats
down anger, it drowns pride, it gets rid of
resentment, it destroys envy, it causes evil
to vanish, it reforms wicked ways. Prayer,
then, is the seal of virginity, the firm basis
of marriage, the armour of those who
travel, the protection of those who are
asleep, the source of confidence for those
who are awake. In brief, prayer is talking
to, and encountering, God.

The blessed teacher Mar Jacob says:[3]

Prayer reveals the profundities of the
   Divine,
by it one enters to behold the
   mystery of hidden things.
It is the key able to open all doors.
From it one can clearly espy what is
   hidden,
by it the soul can approach to speak
   with God,
it raises up the mind so that it
   reaches the Majesty.
It is easy for prayer to learn the
   mysteries of the divinity,

for it can go in and out unhindered
  by the angelic powers:
no angel is as swift-winged as prayer,
nor do the seraphim fly up with it as
  it ascends;
it whispers its words in the ears of
  the Lord, without any
  intermediary,
it murmurs in the heart, and God
  hears it in his exalted place.
Where it ascends not even the
  Watchers have ever reached,
for it is capable of approaching the
  very Divinity.
The seraph hides its face from the

cf Is 6:2   divine Being with its wings,*

but prayer stands there unveiled
  before the Majesty:
nothing at all stands in the way
  between it and the Lord,
for it converses with him and he
  hears it gladly.
The Watchers tremble and the
  heavenly hosts in their modesty are
  held back,
whereas prayer goes in and relates its
  affairs before God.
The cherubim are harnessed and
  cannot see him whom they bear,
but prayer goes up and speaks with
  him lovingly.
In its love[4] prayer speedily attains the
  exalted place,
in its love prayer advances to be
  raised up above the heavenly
  orders.

The cherub is afraid to raise its eyes
    to the Majesty,
being harnessed in its modesty with
    the pure yoke of flame;
the ranks of fire do not approach the
    Hidden One,
whereas prayer has authority to speak
    with him.
Prayer enters closer in than they and
    speaks unashamed;
above the myriads of heavenly hosts
does it pass in flight, unhindered by
    their ranks.
As though to a close relation prayer
    reveals its secret to the Lord of the
    Watchers,
asking of him what is appropriate in
    all sorts of activities.
Prayer does not bend down to the
    angels to speak with them,
for it asks God himself, and he bids
    the angels attend to its affairs.

For this reason, seeing that such advantage comes to us from prayer, these being the kinds of fruits we can gather from it, we urge you, beloved brethren, let us be eager to perform it with constancy and without any slackening, as we meditate and occupy ourselves with it continually, day and night. When we arise from our beds let our mouths not utter anything else before we have given praise and thanks to God. Just as buildings which are constructed with dressed beams do not collapse all of a sudden, even if fierce gales buffet against them, so it is with us: provided we gird our actions and our way of life with prayers all the days of our lives, we will not suddenly fall.

We can observe how soldiers have their swords, shields, and cuirasses hung up at the ready in their own homes, thus indicating their profession. In our case God has provided us with an armour not forged from gold, silver, iron, or bronze, but deriving from a good disposition and a firm faith. So hang up this armour on the walls of your house, and on going to bed, at table, and when you are leaving home, make the sign of the cross on your forehead and give mental thanks to God; then, clothed in this armour, you can walk out in the street with firm trust in God and with thankfulness of heart. And when you get back home, draw close to the presence of your Lord many times over in prayer. When you are about to eat and to drink, do not break bread or drink a cup of anything without first signing it with the cross and hallowing it with prayer. And when you have had sufficient give praise and thanks to him whose good things you have enjoyed.

At the times when you stand before your Lord in prayer, do not start off in a languid fashion, otherwise you will perform your entire prayer in a lax and lazy way. Rather, when you stand in prayer sign yourself with the cross, collect your thoughts together and prepare yourself properly; concentrate on him to whom you are praying, and take care that your thought does not depart from him until your prayer has reached its conclusion. At the very begin-

ning of your prayer, compel yourself so
that your tears flow and your mind is filled
with suffering: in this way your whole
prayer will gain advantage. For any prayer
in which reflection on God and mental contemplation is not mingled is a mere weariness of the flesh. Take care that your mind
does not wander off during the time of
prayer as it thinks about empty matters: in
that case, instead of arousing the Judge to
reconciliation, you will stir him to anger,
having been insulted by you. You are full of
fear before the world's judges, but in God's
presence you show contempt: if someone
is not aware of where he is standing and
what he is saying, how can he suppose that
he is offering up prayer? No, arouse yourself and concentrate your mind at the times
when you stand in prayer; your Lord is
speaking with you, so do not wander off;
his chosen angels surround you, so do not
be perturbed; ranks of demons are standing
in front of you, so do not slacken. Rather,
take refuge in trust in your Lord and start
off on the road of prayer confidently, turning aside neither to the right nor to the left;
then all of a sudden you will arrive at the
place of tranquillity which is exempt from
any element of fear, and the offering of
your prayer will be accepted, as was
Abel's,* your mind being attentive and *Gen 4:4*
aware: whereas the Adversary who opposes
you is put to shame, for he becomes fearful
of you during your time of prayer, seeing
that the words of your mouth correspond
to the will of God.⁵

From prayer you will gain the benefit of

protection, so that you can travel along the road of God's righteousness without danger, until you can recline in the haven of rest.

Being aware of all this, my beloved, we urge and advise that we should not pray as if it was some ordinary thing, but when we pray we should do so with divine love, for without love prayer and suplication are not acceptable to God.

BIBLIOGRAPHY AND NOTES

A. The translation is made from British Library, Add. 14535, fol. 22a–24a, of the ninth century; this manuscript is remarkable since it is one of the few extant Syriac manuscripts of monothelete provenance. An edition, translation, and commentary are forthcoming in *Parole de l'Orient*.

1. Basil, *On the Holy Spirit*, Ch. XXVII (PG 32; 189C–192A), expanded.

2. Gregory of Nyssa, *Hom. 1 on the Lord's Prayer* (PG 44: 1121D–1124A).

3. Jacob of Serugh, *Homily* 123, on Nebuchadnezzar's Dream (ed. Bedjan, IV, pp. 493–4). The beginning of this quotation usefully fills a lacuna in the printed text.

4. Jacob has 'in its impudence', using the word *ḥutzpā*, familiar from Yiddish slang, 'brazen cheek'; he is reflecting the wording of Ephrem, *Hymns on Faith*, V.5 (see my *The Luminous Eye*, p. 52).

5. This paragraph combines together elements taken from Evagrius' *Admonition on Prayer* (Chapter IV, pp. 70–73).

Chapter IX

Anonymous II

6th/7th Century?

INTRODUCTION

THIS ANONYMOUS TEXT, entitled 'On Prayer, from the Teaching of the Solitaries', is to be found in a single manuscript of the tenth or eleventh century. Presumably we are dealing with a short anthology, but no sources for the texts are indicated. The piece ends with a prayer, whose style suggests that it may be derived from the works of John of Apamea.

ANONYMOUS II,
On Prayer, from the teaching of the Solitaries

PRAYER IS A LADDER leading up to God; for there is nothing more powerful than prayer. There is no sin which cannot be forgiven by means of prayer, and there is no sentence of punishment which it cannot undo. There is no revelation which does not have prayer as its cause, and there are no types or symbols which prayer cannot interpret.

In the hands of prayer are laid the keys to the Kingdom into which you are desirous of entering; without it you cannot be an heir there, becoming one of the firstborn *whose names are inscribed in the Book of Life.** Prayer is the narrow and confined gate through which the saints enter the Jerusalem which is in heaven. *Dan 12:1*

Continual prayer is the light of the soul: by it the soul rejoices at that glorious place of light which is true love for God and for one's neighbour. Prayer embraces all the commandments. This is why our Lord also

181

Lk 18:1
Mt 26:41

gave instructions concerning it, saying, *Pray at all times and do not be wearied,** and *Be wakeful and praying continually.** This is how our Lord instructed those who wish to travel on the road to excellence that leads to the city situated in the height of heaven, which is love.

I am not talking about prayer for special times or appointed moments, but about continual prayer which has no stopping point at all. For there is no time which anyone spends in prayer with God when his thought is not entirely focussed on God. Constancy in prayer is the fulfilment of all the commandments—and this is the figurative cross about which our Lord spoke: Everyone who takes it up and follows me will
cf Mt 16:24
inherit eternal life.*

There are three modes by which prayer may be prayed, apart from prayer which is with the body. The first consists in the movement of the stirring of the natural impulses. Another mode arises out of the propinquity of the angels of protection. Yet another belongs to the good intention which is desirous of what is beautiful.

Attendant upon the first movement of prayer is compunction, together with an ardent love on the part of the thoughts which burn in the heart like fire. The second is accompanied by the activating of insights, along with tears of joy, while to the third belongs a love of bodily labours, together with tears which stir up the thoughts to some extent. Apart from these three kinds of movement which I have mentioned there is no other movement which can be called prayer, but only that wonder which is called 'light without form' by the sages. Outside these three kinds, any movement that is set into motion is destructive of pure prayer. Now if the mind is standing at the time of prayer in a place which belongs to the demons, then they cause disturbance and distraction of thoughts to dominate over the soul.

Listen to what, in brief, is the reward of God's commandments. The first reward is the crown of impassibility, which consists in freedom from the passions; the vision of the light that is in yourself; insight into the true natures of created things; wisdom full of spiritual insight hidden therein.

The second reward is the contemplative vision of judgement and of providence and of the end, along with tears full of utter delight.

The third reward is the immaterial contemplative vision, together with that discernment of spirit which gathers together all kinds of joys, a holy fragrance, bursting into spiritual utterance, a taste that gives sweetness to the mind's palate by its delight. And after all these things comes the contemplative vision of the Holy Trinity, though this does not come as a reward, but rather it is only granted by grace.

Compassion is the gate by which the saints enter into knowledge of God. You should realize, brother, that whenever movements of compassion are stirred in you, they are insights into the spiritual understanding of judgement and providence.

PRAYER

Grant me, Lord, by your grace that my
mind may have converse with the greatness
of that grace—not by means of that converse which is constructed from the body's
voice or which is carried on by the tongue
of flesh, but grant rather that converse
which praises you in silence, you the Silent
One who are praised in ineffable silence.

Grant me, Lord, at this time a mind filled
with love of you, and one that bears a
knowledge of you, an intellect filled with
insight into you, and a pure heart in which
the light of the vision of you shines out.

Make me worthy, Lord, that my mind
may become a fountain of wisdom to
which the mysteries of the New World are
revealed. And I beg you, Child of the Father
and Radiance of his Essence, do not deprive
me at this time of that ardent love with
which the souls of your saints are so inflamed as to be united with you in that
inexpressible joy. Yes, Lord, in your grace
make me worthy at this time to hear with
the ears of my soul that awesome cry of the
supernal hosts who escort your Majesty:
grant that I may hear at this time the psalmody and halleluiahs that are heard at this
time by the minds of the saints. Grant me,
Lord, in your grace that I may be made
worthy of the vision of those fiery insights
which are revealed at the time of prayer,
and may I enjoy that delightful fragrance
which wafts from them.

BIBLIOGRAPHY

A. The translation is made from British Library, Add. 14615, fol. 74b–76b, of tenth/eleventh century. An edition of this, as well as of several other texts included in the present volume, is to be published by the monastery of St Ephrem (Holland) under the title, *Malpānūtā d-abāhātā suryāye 'al ṣlōtā.*

Chapter X

Abraham of Nathpar

fl. c. 600

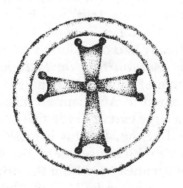

INTRODUCTION

A CONSIDERABLE NUMBER OF texts on the monastic life are transmitted under the name of Abraham of Nathpar, a monk of the Church of the East who flourished around the turn of the sixth to seventh century, at the height of the monastic revival in this Church. Only a few of his works have so far been published. Practically nothing for certain is known about his life and it is not even clear whether Nathpar (modern Guwair on the Great Zab, south east of Mosul, Iraq) was his birthplace or the location of his monastery.

As we have already had occasion to see from the attribution of Evagrius' *Admonition on Prayer* in some manuscripts to Abraham of Nathpar (Chapter IV, above), not all the works attributed to Abraham are necessarily by him. This applies to a large extent to the fine text on prayer and silence translated below, for this is little more than a recycling of a work which elsewhere circulated under the name of John of Apamea (to whom the original form in all probability belongs) or under that of Philoxenus of Mabbug: all that Abraham has done is to preface the work with some sentences taken from Aphrahat's *Demonstration on Prayer* (translated above, Chapter I), and to expand a little here and there. In the translation below the section numbers of the original text by John are given.

The work is primarily concerned with 'the prayer of silence'. It starts out by distinguishing two kinds of prayer, that of 'the just' who employ vocal prayer, and the silent

188

'spiritual prayer' of those who 'worship God in Spirit and in truth' (John 4:23). Spiritual prayer can only be achieved after considerable experience in vocal prayer, and requires an attitude of profound and utter humility. No less than five different kinds of silence are described: of the tongue, of the entire body, of the soul, of the mind, and of the spirit. The short piece ends, however, by urging the reader to be content with vocal prayer if he has not managed to attain to truly silent prayer. But, the author adds in conclusion, such vocal prayer has no advantage unless the words used actually 'become embodied in you in the form of actions'.

ABRAHAM OF NATHPAR,
On prayer: how it is necessary for someone who prays to be eager and vigilant in himself.

B E EAGER IN PRAYER, and vigilant, without wearying; and remove from yourself drowsiness and sleep. You should be watchful both by night and by day; do not be disheartened.[1]

I will show you the different occasions for prayer. At the time when you are in trouble, offer up petition; and when you are well supplied with the good things of God, give thanks to the Giver; and when your mind rejoices, offer up praise. Let all these prayers be made with discernment.[2]

I am convinced, my beloved, that everything that people ask in diligence and faith, God will grant them. But when someone offers up prayer in mockery or contempt or doubt, he does not receive his request,[3] seeing that he is not firm in heart or believing that he will receive an answer. One needs to offer up prayer, being purified of all doubt and blemish, and he offers up his offering

190

in purity, so that it may be received. He will also take care lest there be found in it anything which will result in it being rejected.

Out of all offerings, pure prayer is the most excellent. Therefore be eager in prayer, my son, and labour in it. At the beginning of all your prayers use the prayer which our Lord taught.[4]

ON PRAYER AND SILENCE

1. Do not imagine, my beloved, that prayer consists solely of words, or that it can be learnt by means of words. No, listen to the truth of the matter from our Lord: spiritual prayer is not learnt and does not reach fullness as a result of either learning or the repetition of words; for it is not to a man that you are praying, before whom you can repeat a well-composed speech: it is to him who is Spirit that you are directing the movements of prayer. You should pray, therefore, in spirit, seeing that he is spirit.

2. To show that no special place or vocal utterance is required for someone who prays in fulness to God, our Lord said, *The hour is coming when you will not be worshipping the Father in this mountain or in Jerusalem*;* and again, to show that a special place was not required, he also taught that *Those who worship God should worship him in spirit and in truth.** And in the course of His instructing us why we should pray thus, He said '*For God is spirit*,'* and he should be praised spiritually, in the spirit. Paul too tells us about this spiritual prayer and psalmody which we should employ: 'What then shall I do?', he

Jn 4:21

Jn 4:23

Jn 4:24

says, '*I will pray in spirit and in my
mind*'.* It is in spirit and in mind, then,
that he says that one should pray and sing
to God; he does not say anything at all
about the tongue. The reason is that this
spiritual prayer is not offered up by the
tongue or prayed by the tongue, for it is
more interior than the lips and the tongue,
more interiorized than any composite
sounds, lying beyond psalmody and wisdom. When someone prays this kind of
prayer his worship is more perfect than that
of the company of Gabriel and Michael;[5]
like them, he utters 'holy' without any
words.* But if he cease from this kind of
prayer and recommence the prayer of vocal
song, then he is distanced from the region
of the angels, and he becomes an ordinary
man again.

3. Whoever sings, using his tongue and
body, and perseveres in this worship both
night and day, such a person is one of the
'just'. But the person who has been held
worthy to enter deeper than this, singing in
mind and in spirit, such a person is a 'spiritual being'. A 'spiritual being' is more exalted than the 'just', but one becomes a
'spiritual being' after being 'just'. For until
someone has worshipped for a considerable time in this exterior manner—employing continual fasting, using the voice for
psalmody, with repeated periods on his
knees, with petitions, constant vigils, recitation of the psalms, arduous labour, supplication, abstinence, paucity of food, and
other such things appropriate for his way of
life, along with a careful watch over the

1 Cor 14:15

cf Is 6:3

senses, being filled with the remembrance
of God, full of due fear and trembling at his
name, seeing that he has a firm belief that
the rustling movements of his thoughts are
not hidden from God's knowledge, hum-
bling himself before everyone, considering
everyone better than himself—even when
he sees a debauched person, or an adulterer,
or a drunkard, or a murderer, or someone
full of effrontery or abuse, or a blasphemer,
or indeed a person with even worse sins
than these: on seeing such a man he still
acts humbly before them and thinks 'He is
better than me, and closer to God'; for the
vision of the thought of his heart is fixed
with all the concentration of his thought on
his own transgressions, and he does not approach such a man hypocritically, but with
his whole self he acts humbly before him
and asks him with groaning to pray for him
and to supplicate God on his behalf, 'For I
have done great wrong before God'. Only
when someone achieves all this—and
greater things than these things which, if
they truly seem to him to be so, he should
suffer, seeing that he is far removed from
what is proper—when someone can do all
this, and achieve it in himself, he will arrive
at singing to God in the psalmody that spiritual beings use to praise him.

4. For God is silence, and in silence is he
sung and glorified by means of that psalmody and praise of which he is worthy. I am
not speaking of the silence of the tongue,
for if someone merely keeps his tongue silent, without knowing how to sing and give
praise in mind and spirit, then he is simply

idle in his silence and evil wandering
thoughts, since hateful ideas surge up and
corrupt him. He is just keeping an exterior
silence, and he does not know how to sing
or give praise in an interior way, seeing that
the tongue of his 'hidden person' has not
yet learnt to stretch itself out even to bab-
ble. You should look on the spiritual infant
that is within you in the same way as you
do on an ordinary child or infant: just as
the tongue placed in an infant's mouth is
still because it does not yet know speech or
possess the correct movements for speaking, so it is with that interior tongue of the
mind; it will be still from all speech and
from all thought, it will simply be placed
there, ready to learn the first babblings of
spiritual utterance.

5. Thus there is a silence of the tongue,
there is a silence of the whole body, there is
the silence of the soul, there is the silence
of the mind, and there is the silence of the
spirit. The silence of the tongue is merely
when it is not incited to evil and cruel
speech, or to utter something full of anger,
or liable to stir up trouble, or some calumny or accusation. The silence of the entire body is when all its senses are not
occupied by a propensity to evil deeds or
improper actions; or when the body is in a
sort of death, unoccupied by anything. The
silence of the soul is when there are no ugly
thoughts bursting forth within it, hindering
anything good. The silence of the mind is
when it is purified from any harmful
knowledge or wisdom—otherwise called
cunning and inventive craftiness, such as

operates in those inclined to wicked actions upon which they continuously ponder, to the harm of their fellow human beings. The silence of the spirit is when the mind ceases even from stirrings caused by spiritual beings, and when all its movements are stirred solely by Being; in this state it is truly silent, aware that the silence which is upon it is itself silent.

6. These are the degrees and measures to be found in silence and utterance. But if you have not reached these higher states and you find yourself still far away from them, remain where you are lower down, for this is the psalmody and praise of the tongue. Use these to sing and praise God; do this with the application and reverence that befits God, singing and praising him with the voice and the tongue. Toil in your service until you arrive at love. Stand in awe of God, as is only right, and thus you will be held worthy to love, with that natural love, him who was given to us at our renewal.

7. And when you recite the words of the prayer which you know to be appropriate for requests before God, be careful not to repeat them merely out of obligation, but let your very self become these words, as they manifest themselves in you as actual deeds. For there is no advantage in the reciting unless the words you are reciting become embodied in you in the form of action, and you become as though they were mingled into your very being, so that even in this world you will be seen to be a

man of God, and many will imitate you and benefit from their imitation of you.

BIBLIOGRAPHY AND NOTES

A. The translation is made from British Library, Or. 6714, fol. 81b–83a, of the ninth/tenth century. For the edition and English translation of the original form of the work, by John of Apamea, see bibliography to Chapter V, above. B. Information on Abraham of Nathpar and his works can be found in A. Penna, 'Abramo di Nathpar', *Rivista degli Studi Orientali* 32 (1957) 415–31, and R. Tonneau, 'Abraham de Nathpar', *L'Orient Syrien* 4 (1975) 337–50.

1. Based on Aphrahat, *Demonstration* IV.16 (end).
2. Based on Aphrahat, *Dem.* IV.17.
3. Based on Aphrahat, *Dem.* IV.18 (beginning).
4. Based on Aphrahat, *Dem.* IV.19 (end).
5. For the phrase see Chapter VI, note 4.

Chapter XI

Martyrius
Sahdona

First half of 7th Century

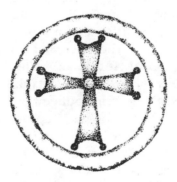

INTRODUCTION

MARTYRIUS, or Sahdona (to use his Syriac name), was born in the vicinity of Kirkuk in modern Iraq, towards the end of the sixth century; at an early age he became a monk at one of the most famous monasteries of the time in north Iraq, known as Bēth Ābē. He seems to have owed his monastic vocation to the influence of his mother and a remarkable holy woman named Shirin, to whom his mother had often taken him in his youth. Some time in the late 630s he was appointed bishop of Beth Garmai (the region around Kirkuk). There he became involved in the doctrinal controversies (concerning christological formulae) which troubled the Church of the East in the 640s. Martyrius was accused of innovation and seeking to introduce the formulation used by the Byzantine Church; he was deposed by a synod, but after a short exile in 'the west' (perhaps Edessa) he was recalled, thanks to the influence of his supporters, only to be driven out once again by a new Patriarch of Seleucia—Ktesiphon, Ishoyahb III. This time Martyrius did not return, but spent the rest of his life, probably as a solitary attached to a monastery, in the vicinity of Edessa.

Of Martyrius' writings there survive the *Book of Perfection* (not quite complete), five letters to fellow monks, and a set of spiritual maxims; undoubtedly the most important of these is the long *Book of Perfection* which certainly ranks as one of the masterpieces of Syriac monastic literature. Deeply rooted in the Bible, it is remarkable for the sense of fervour which it conveys. The *Book of Perfection* is a work of edification rather than a theoretical exposition, and in the course of it much information about monastic life in the Syriac Church at the time of the Arab invasions can be gleaned. The cenobitic life is seen by Martyrius as the essential preparatory training for the solitary life with its ideal of 'perfection', or spiritual maturity. In fact, the solitary was never totally cut off from the cenobitic community to which he belonged, for he would normally return to participate in the Sunday Office and Divine Liturgy. Such a semi-anchoretic life seems to have become a normal feature in many Syriac monasteries by Martyrius' time.

The *Book of Perfection* is divided into two parts. The mainly lost opening treatises of Part I evidently dealt with the dogmatic foundations of the Christian life and contained an exhortation to the life of virtue. There follow two treatises on the solitary life and the preparation for this in the cenobitic life. Part II, preserved complete, consists of fourteen chapters, with Chapters 2–13 devoted, a chapter apiece, to the following topics: faith, hope, love, self-emptying (*msarrqūtā*), chastity, fasting, prayer, repentance, humility, obedience, endurance, and watchfulness. It is the eighth chapter from Part II, on prayer, which is translated in its entirety below (as the full title indicates, the chapter also deals with the monastic Office and reading the Bible). In this chapter Martyrius develops the theme, already found notably in Aphrahat and the *Book of Steps*, of prayer as an interior offering of the heart. Section 20, in particular, is remarkable for its description of the descent of 'the fire of the Spirit' upon this offering of prayer when it proves to be acceptable: the fire of the Spirit 'will consume our sacrifices and raise up our mind along with them to heaven; then we shall see the Lord, to our delight and not to our destruction, as the stillness of his revelation falls upon us and the hidden things of the knowledge of him will be portrayed in us'. Implicit in all this is the parallelism with the decent of the Spirit at the epiclesis in the eucharistic Liturgy.

Martyrius's spirituality is centered on the heart, following the biblical anthropology. Throughout his work there is great emphasis on the need for purity of heart and for love: 'the person who possesses love becomes the abode of the Trinity', says Martyrius in the chapter on this topic (Part II, Chapter 4), and later in this chapter we find him exclaiming:

> Happy is that person of love who has caused God,
>   who is love, to dwell in his heart.
> Happy are you, O heart, so small and confined, yet
>   you have caused him whom heaven and earth
>   cannot contain to dwell spiritually in your
>   womb, as in a restful abode.
> Happy that luminous eye of the heart which, in its
>   purity, clearly beholds him before whose sight
>   the seraphs veil their face. . .
> *Blessed indeed are the pure in heart, for they shall*
>   *see God. . .* [a]
> Blessed are you, O heart that is luminous, the
>   abode of the Divinity;
> Blessed are you, heart that is pure, which beholds
>   the hidden Being.
> Happy are you, O flesh and blood, the dwelling
>   place of the Consuming Fire;
> Happy are you, mortal body made out of dust,
>   wherein resides the Fire that sets the worlds
>   alight.
> It is truly a matter for wonder and astonishment
>   that he, before whom the heavens are not pure,
>   who puts awe into his angels, should take delight
>   and pleasure in a heart of flesh that is filled with
>   love for him, that is open to him, that is purified
>   so as to act as his holy dwelling place, joyfully
>   serving and ministering to him in whose presence

thousand upon thousand, ten thousand upon ten thousand[β] fiery angels stand in awe, as they minister to his glory.

MARTYRIUS,
From the *Book of Perfection*

On the Office, and on prayer, vigils and reading the Bible.

2. At every moment we need to have wakefulness, recollected thoughts, and a careful watch on the intellect. This applies above all when we stand before God* in spiritual ministry, speaking in a hidden way, in prayer, with God's majesty: at such a time it is appropriate that we stand with a wakeful and attentive mind, combining a sense of awe and trembling* with the spiritual fervour of joy and deep love.*

3. When we collect together our outward senses, gathering in the thoughts of our minds from all over the place, then, as we are being raised up from earth and from the body by the interior movements of our soul, and we become like those who dwell in heaven, let us speak with God, stretching out towards him the gaze of the eyes of our heart; in a hidden way let us look upon his

cf Dan 7:10

cf Ps 2:11

cf Rom 12: 11–12

202

majesty in awe, and behold *as though in a mirror** as it were *the likeness of Him who cannot be seen.** Let us realize, even just a little and insofar as we are capable, the extent of the greatness of the God whom we have been held worthy to serve.* We should consider how wretched we are, where we are actually standing, and in whose presence. Right at the beginning of our converse with God, as we stand before him, we should use those humble words of the blessed patriarch Abraham: *See, I have begun to speak in the Lord's presence, I who am but dust and ashes!**

1 Cor 13:12

Col 1:15

cf Is 6:5

Gen 18:27

4. Let us also ponder this: how we, who are mortal beings continually bespattered with the mud of sins, have been held worthy to stand before *the King of kings and Lord of lords* who *dwells in* the resplendent *light that none can approach,** to whose honour *thousands upon thousands* and *myriads of myriads* of angels and archangels *minister** as they stand before Him in fear and trembling; how he, *before whom even the heavens are not pure,** even though he strikes wonder in his angels, yet he condescends to speak with weak and wretched human beings who have rendered themselves unclean by sins.* For he said through the prophet to the sinful people of Israel who were befouled by ugly deeds: *Wash, and be cleansed; remove the foulness of your actions from my sight. Come, let us speak with one another, says the Lord.**

1 Tim 6:15–16

Dan 7:10

Job 15:15

cf Is 6:5

Is 1:16,18

5. How immense is the grace of the divine compassion and condescension that

knows no limit! God comes down to the level of sinful men and women; the good Lord speaks with his rebellious servants; the Holy One calls those who are impure to forgiveness. Humanity created out of mud addresses its Fashioner with familiarity, *cf Is 29:16* dust converses with its Maker.* Let us, therefore, show awe when we sinners stand in the presence of this Majesty and speak. Even though we are so impure in our deeds he draws us close to the sight of himself in the spirit; let us therefore repeat with trembling the words of the blessed prophet Isaiah: *Woe is me, for I am dazed: I am a man of unclean lips, yet my eyes have be-* *Is 6:5* *held the King, the Lord Almighty.**

6. He can be seen by us in the spirit even now, if we wish—not that he is contained on the throne in any form external to his nature, just *filling the Temple with the ex-* *Is 6:1* *tremity of his train,** as the prophet beheld. No, he is hidden in the loftiness of his hiddenness in the inaccessible light of his nature where he lives and reigns over all the extremities of the universe in the majesty of his dominion, *almighty in the power of his* *Heb 1:3* *word,** grasping *the round sphere of the* *Is 40:22* *earth with all its inhabitants like locusts.** In the boundlessness of his Being he is everything, *for he is not far away from each one of us, for in him we live and move* *Acts 17:27–8* *and have our being*;* and while he is in us and in everything, he exists in the majestic glory of his divinity and in his utter exaltedness.

7. His creation is full of the splendour of *Is 6:2* his glory: *the seraphs** of fire *stand* there

to honour him, the ranks of the many-eyed
*cherubim** escort His majesty Being, the   *Ez 10:12*
bands of spiritual powers dash around ministering to him, the throngs of angels fly
hither and thither with their wings, and all
the orders of spiritual beings serve his Being in awe, crying 'Holy' in trembling and
love, *as they cover their faces** with their   *Is 6:2*
wings at the splendour of his great and fear-
ful radiance, ceaselessly crying out to one
another the threefold sanctification of his
exalted glory, *saying 'Holy, holy, holy,*
Lord Almighty, with whose glories both
heaven and *earth are full.'**   *Is 6:3*

8. Let us therefore tremble at the magnitude of the sight of the Ineffable One, and
at the sound which ceaselessly utters the
praise of the Hidden Being. And let us be
filled with awe and trembling, falling on
our faces in fear before him. Let us recognize our earth-born nature, let us be aware
of the base character of the dust we are
made from, let us join the prophet in saying, with feeling and with a penitent heart,
'Woe is our state of confusion';* let us lay   *cf Is 6:5*
bare the foulness of our sins quite openly,
accusing ourselves forcefully—just as it is
said: *The just man condemns himself at*
*the very beginning of his words.**   *Prov 18:17*

9. This is what we too should do at the
commencement of our prayer, stating
before God that we are not worthy to stand
in his presence in our wretched state; and
that, because our blind hearts have lost
their sight through concentrating on what
is below, dwelling in the darkness of the
earth, we are unable to gaze on the great

sight of him whose glory blinds the vision of the angels of light. Again, how are we able to speak with unclean lips with his

cf Is 6:5   great holiness?*

Ps 46:6   10. For at his *voice the earth quakes*,* and who can endure the sight of his face? Nothing that has breath is left able to speak in his presence. Our entire inner being is

cf Dan 10:8   *overwhelmed** at the sight of him, out of awe our mouths are stopped in silence. And even if we regain just a little strength to speak before him, our consciences rebuke us, seeing that *we have sinned* and *done*

Ps 106:6   *wrong** in his presence. If we should imagine that we have been put in a state of righteousness, then all our righteousness is

Is 64:6   *like a menstrual rag*,* for the victory belongs to him, whereas *ours is the shamefac-*

Bar 1:15   *edness** and reproach.

11. These are the things we should have in mind at the beginning of our time of prayer. So let us pray *Our Father who are*

Mt 6:9   *in heaven*,* we have *sinned against heaven and before you, and* are *not worthy*

Lk 15:18–19   *to be called your sons** or to praise your holy name. Let us keep our eyes down in humility of heart and cry out with feeling and tears from our hearts' depths to *the Lord who is enthroned on high*, yet listens

Ps 113:5–6   and *sees what is in the depths*,* as we say 'O God, have mercy on us sinners who are

cf Lk 18:13   not worthy to look in your direction,* towards your highest heavens; grant us the ability to sanctify your name on earth as it is in heaven, for you, O Lord our God, are

cf Mt 6:9–10   holy, and your mercy is for ever.'*

12. These are the things we should val-

iantly lay bare in his presence, coming from the heart and accompanied by the soul's bitter weeping. For thus, when we declare our own guilt and set ourselves among those who deserve punishment, we will draw God, the Judge of all, to compassion and mercy, with the result that he will send for our cleansing, not just *one of the seraphs** who sanctify him, but he himself will draw close to us to sanctify us—that is to say, he will bring us close to himself in burning love. And with the fire of his Spirit he will burn up our wickedness and remove our impurity, forgiving our sins and wiping out our filthy stains as he illuminates our darkness with the light of his revelation,* making us worthy of the gift of his grace. He will then grant that we be singled out spiritually, chosen for his work, so that we may stand in undistracted service and prayer before the divine Majesty, full of both awe and love. In this way we will acquire righteousness for ourselves,* even though we are extremely sinful.

13. This is exactly what the sinful tax-collector did:* being someone guilty of a great wrong, he asked for mercy and compassion, and by so doing he amply acquired righteousness for himself; not only did he succeed in removing from himself his sins, but in his self-abasement he was exalted as someone righteous even more than the Pharisee,* who destroyed his righteousness thanks to his pride, for instead of accusing himself, he was detracting others in his prayer:* while he proudly recounted his own good deeds, he was thereby rebuking

Is 6:6

cf Lk 2:32

cf Lk 18:14

Lk 18:13

cf Mt 23:12 & Lk 18:14

cf Lk 18:11–14

others—and especially that *tax-collector* who *stood at a distance* from him, humble of heart and with downcast eyes, yet whose prayer was far better answered for he drew close to God in justification because he had condemned himself in God's presence.

14. If the tax-collector was so benefitted by accusing himself—not that it was out of humility, for he was indicating the very truth of the matter—how much more benefit will accrue to the person who accuses himself of sins he has not committed: He does indeed have sins, but they may not be many, and he does continually transgress, though not in the matter of mortal sins.*

cf 1 Jn 5:17

15. Thus self-accusation before God is something that is very necessary for us; and humility of heart is extremely advantageous in our lives, above all at the time of prayer. For prayer requires great attention and needs a proper awareness, otherwise it will turn out to be unacceptable and rejected, and *it will be turned back empty** to our bosom.

Is 55:11

16. Prayer is rejected if it contains a blemish from one of the emotions that are alien to it: resentment, or hatred, or pride, or deceitfulness, or ingratitude, or hypocrisy. For God was speaking with reference to us when he said 'Your prayer is rejected by me; *my soul abhors* the service of your psalms: *it is a weight upon me that I have grown weary of carrying. When you lift up your hands I will avert my eyes from you; and if you pray at great length, I will not listen,** for your hearts are full of evil

Is 1:14–18

passions, and your minds are befouled with hateful thoughts. Your countenances have been made hideous by corrupt dealing. Therefore *wash and be made clean. Remove* your foul passions *from my sight*; then you may come to see me, and *speak with me** in prayer.'

Is 1:16, 18

17. We should accordingly be in fear of the word of our God, cleansing our hearts of these passions, so that we may become worthy to see him in prayer, and so that our sacrifice may be accepted.

It is not just from the passions that are of evil origin that we should distance ourselves in prayer, but also from any kind of contempt that stems from lassitude or negligence. For even if our prayer should be pure of the other bitter passions and of self-love, nevertheless if it is offered accompanied by signs of contempt or scorn it will be rejected, in that the pristine beauty of divine and reverential love is not raised up with it, to convey it eagerly and with joy to God.

18. Such was the offering of the murderous Cain which was rejected. He had been told by God *If you act well, I will receive it.** Such again were all the offerings of the Israelites which were rejected, whereby they received the curse of the prophet who says *Cursed is the man who has a ram in his flock, and he vows and sacrifices to the Lord one that is sickly.** He rebukes and reproaches them saying, *Try offering it to your ruler, to see if he will be pleased with it or show you favour; this is what the Lord says.** So how will any address made

Gen 4:7

Mal 1:14

Mal 1:8

to God during the ministry of prayer that shows any contempt prove acceptable to God—an address that is full of all sorts of distractions, that is 'sickly' and broken up by interruptions? This sort of thing would not be acceptable even to the most insignificant of human beings, if he were thus addressed. The offering of turbulent prayer and the ministration of a heart that shows contempt is exactly like the sacrifice of a blemished ram.

19. Accordingly we should not offer up offerings like those blemished ones of the People who were rejected. We should not offer to God in a contemptible way any sacrifices of thanks and praise—the whole burnt offerings of prayer which he loves. Otherwise he will return the offering. Just as this kind of offering, with its use of words, is superior to one consisting of dumb animals, so we should accordingly look at it more carefully to see whether there is concealed in it any kind of blemish; and if there is, we should cleanse it, washing it with tears and removing whatever blemish there is; only then should we offer it, with love and reverential eagerness, in purity before the Lord, *lifting our hands* upwards towards God in prayer, raising at the same time our minds, *without any hint of anger or any such thoughts*,* as we ask, amidst tears and sighs from the heart, that our offering be accepted, along with the prophet's, as an evening offering.*

1 Tim 2:8

Ps 140:2

20. So, if the commencement of our prayer is wakeful and attentive, and we wet our cheeks with tears stemming from the

emotion of our hearts, then our prayer will be made perfect, in accordance with God's wish; being without blemish, it will be accepted in his presence, and the Lord will be pleased with us and have delight in our offering. As *he perceives the pleasing scent** of our heart's pure fragrance, He will send the fire of his Spirit to consume our sacrifices* and raise up our mind along with them in the flames to heaven. Then we shall behold the Lord, to our delight and not to our destruction, as *the stillness** of his revelation falls upon us and the hidden things of the knowledge of him will be portrayed in us; our hearts will be given spiritual joy, along with hidden mysteries which I am unable to disclose in words to the simple.* In this way we make our *bodies a living holy and acceptable sacrifice*, one that pleases God in our *rational service.**

Gen 8:21

cf 1Kgs 18:38 & 2 Chr 7:1

Gen 15:12

cf 2 Cor 12:4

Rom 12:1

21. If, on the contrary, we stand at the outset showing contempt, with our slovenlines and dullness of heart,* with our darkened thoughts distracted hither and thither, then our entire ministration proves useless. We hear but we do not understand, and we see but we have no awareness, as a result of the dullness of our heart and the heaviness of hearing of our mind's ear that fails to understand the Spirit's words.

cf Is 6:10

22. As one of the saints says: 'Any service of prayer that is not addressed to the Lord of all with wakefulness of soul and reverent awe is without any benefit'.* Rather, our entire service and prayer, if it is offered with contempt, will prove to our soul's condemnation: like servants who

Source unknown

cf Mt 24:
48–51

make bold to treat in contempt the service of their master,* we will be handed over to grave punishment. Not that our case is like that of servants who serve their fellow human beings who are mortals like ourselves, for whereas they stand in wakefulness and reverential fear before someone who is like themselves, we, by contrast, stand before God our Maker, *the King of*

1 Tim 6:15

kings and Lord of lords. * So how do we not manifestly prove to be dishonouring him, seeing that when we imagine we are standing serving him, we are immersed in the thought of all sorts of other far away things, and we are really speaking with other people in our thoughts.

23. Do you suppose that this will be tolerated with indulgence and be imputed to the weakness of our dust-born nature,* and

cf Gen 3:19

that, whereas we ourselves do not wish it, we are led hither and thither in flighty distraction under compulsion from the agitation of the thoughts confined in the body?—even though in fact we could easily drive them away, if we just forced ourselves by stirring our mind and rebuking our thoughts.

24. Not only is this not the case, but we actually utter aloud empty words with our tongues when we are gathered for prayer and in our folly we provoke floods of laughter. How will God put up with us, seeing that in his presence the *thousands*

Dan 7:10

*and myriads** of angels quake with fear? Will he not straightway impose upon us the stern wrath of punishment when we are lax in serving him and speaking with him, turning instead to each other to chatter and laugh?

25. Suppose we are talking with someone like ourselves: if that person does not listen carefully to us, but instead abandons us, turning away to other people, thus showing contempt for us, we will instantly be filled with a great anger against him, thinking him to be openly despising and insulting us. How much greater—and more worthy of punishment—does the insult seem when we act in precisely the same way towards God, interjecting into our service of him all sorts of alien talk.

26. Look at those who offered alien fire in God's presence* in that Tabernacle which was but a shadow* that would come to an end: he burnt up their bodies with fire from himself that needs no kindling. How do you suppose he will put up with those who, in the course of their rational and holy ministry* that takes place in his bodily and indissoluble temple, make an offering in his presence of alien conversation that belongs to the world? If he does not finish us off it is only because he is kind and patient, inviting us in his great patience to repentance.*

Lev 10:2

cf Heb 8:5

cf Rom 12:1

cf 2 Pet 3:9

27. Why do I say this? We stand laxly in his presence as though it were just a game, and we do not show any patience in our service even for a short period of time; instead, like people who have been set on fire, we dash in and out. How can we expect to recollect our minds when our eyes are fixed on the doors that lead outside? We

are distracted by each other, as we scrutinize everyone who comes in or goes out.

28. Finally, when it was appropriate that we pay just a little attention to our souls, asking for mercy at the conclusion of our Office, supplicating with feeling in our prayer that grace will compassionately treat us with mercy despite the fact that we have been remiss in the entire Office and thus have shown contempt; and when we should be praying that we be accepted in a small way, even just to a thousandth degree, and that God have mercy on us and in his grace hold us worthy of a wage in reward,

29. instead, we have omitted to do this, acting like runaway fugitives, or like slack hired workmen and lazy servants* who look only for rest in the shade: we are like people who stand nonchalantly against their will,* held bound by the custom and outward rules of the monastic *schema*.[1] And even if we have managed to complete the entire Office with our minds applied but did not wait till it was completely ended, I do not think that even so our offering will be accepted—so how much less will it be accepted when quite the opposite is manifestly happening?

30. That someone should turn up at the last moment and receive a wage along with those who came at the beginning—this is something just and acceptable: it happened in the case of those who came at the eleventh hour to work in the vineyard.* But look at the case of the man who worked from the beginning who, when the time came at the end for payment of wages,

cf Mt 25:26

cf Mt 20:6

cf Mt 20:7–9

went off and showed contempt for his em-
ployer: this man's labours proved in vain,
and instead he was handed over to judgement for showing contempt. The same is
the case with the person who gives in right
at the end of the contest, feebly rushing off
from his position.

31. How is such a man not worthy of
sentence, who, when his fellow monks are
kneeling in prayer and supplicating with
fervour of heart, is himself lazily sleeping,
like a mummy; or failing that, he is sitting
and talking idly.

32. I shudder to mention something else
that is the most dreadful thing of all done
by people who show contempt: at that
dread moment which makes even the rebel
demons shake, I mean at that awesome
point when the Divine Mysteries are con-
summated, when angels and archangels
hover around the altar in fear and trembling, as Christ is sacrificed and the Spirit
hovers,[2] many of these people will, on one
occasion wander about outside, on another
will come in according to their whim and
stand there, showing their contempt by
yawning as though at their excessive burden, being tired of standing up.

33. At the moment when the priest is
making this great supplication on their behalf, deep sleep gets the better of them, so
slack are they; at this moment which causes
even the dead to awaken, here are these
people, fully alive and supposedly running
after perfection, nevertheless sunk in sleep,
or wandering about, waiting expectantly
for when they can quickly leave their place

of confinement; for the Jerusalem of light
and life is like a prison to these people—the
place where Father, Son, and Spirit dwell,
where spiritual beings and the bands of
saints together give praise and glory before
God in holy fashion.*

cf Heb 12: 22–23

34. And once they have received the Living Sacrament they push their way out in
haste, before the communal thanksgiving is
made. They never quit the table which belongs to the belly that perishes before everyone else has had his fill and departed, yet
they quit and leave the Table of the Bread of
Spiritual Life in a matter of fact way, without rendering thanks to God, not even with
words merely on their lips.

35. Do you realize what you are doing,
O man? I hesitate to say who it is that you
resemble, for it would be something hard to
listen to. Nevertheless it must be said, by
way of a warning. That person who leaves
the spiritual Table of the Mysteries and goes
out before the priest's final thanksgiving is
showing a resemblance to Judas:* Judas did
exactly the same thing, for once he had
received the bread, he went outside, showing contempt for his Master and his fellow
apostles by going off. It was for this reason
that *Satan entered him* * and he became the
traitor of his Master. The other apostles,
however, remained with their Master, giving praise and going out to the Mount of
Olives.* The last act of praise after the Mysteries is a type of that episode, and so let no
one show contempt for it, as did Judas.

36. Indeed, anyone who has enjoyed the
good things of an ordinary meal ought to

cf Jn 13:30

Jn 13:27

Mt 26:30

render thanks* for this enjoyment, other-   *cf 1 Tim 4:3*
wise he will be reckoned as animal-like and
lacking is discernment. As one of the saints
said, 'A table from which the praise of God
does not ascend is no different from an
animal sty', and it is not that the table is
reckoned to be like a sty, but rather the
person eating from it resembles an animal
owing to his lack of thanksgiving. For anyone who receives the nourishment of food
ought to be discerning and take notice of
the good things before him, and so give
praise to him who gave them. How much
more, then, ought we to thank and praise
without cease him who at the Table of Life
nourishes us with the incorruptible Body
and Blood of Christ?

37. Is it something too onerous for you,
O man, to repay with words him who gave
you his Body as food and his Blood as
drink,* who was slain and laid upon the   *cf Jn 6:56*
altar in your presence for your joy and for
the salvation of your life? But you have
been straying about, neglectful of him—
and even more so of your own soul—when
you should have been standing before him
pressing your requests as you would to
someone who is close at hand. More so
than at any other time is he receptive of
your request at that moment of his being
sacrificed on your behalf; for it was then
that he even asked of his Father forgiveness
for the men who had crucified him.* This   *Lk 23:34*
is the reason why he was sacrificed—in order to forgive our sins. It was on behalf of
our salvation and that of the entire world

that *He broke* His holy Body *and shed* His
venerable Blood, *for the remission of sins.**

Mt 26:26, 28

38. We should be discerning and aware
of the grace that has been effected in us,
giving thanks for it to the Maker, praising
God for this great and *ineffable gift** to us.

2 Cor 9:15

We should put aside from ourselves any
hateful habits of slackness and neglect
which only destroy our lives; instead, we
should persevere from the beginning to the
end of the times of our Offices. And we
should behave with all the greater awe and
love during the great and perfect Mysteries
of our salvation, standing firmly before
God continually with wakefulness of heart
in spiritual service, resembling servants
who are eagerly at the ready to serve their
master.

39. We should not confine our ministry
to the specific fixed times of the Hours;
rather, it should be continuous all the time,
in accordance with the Apostle's bidding to
*pray at all times** in the spirit, keeping
vigil in prayer at every moment, praying
continuously without cease. And again he
says *Let your requests be made known
before God with all sorts of supplication,**
and *Be constant in prayer;** *be filled with
the Spirit; speak with yourselves with
psalms and praise; sing spiritual songs in
your hearts to the Lord.** Everywhere in his
letters he urges strongly that we be constant
in prayer; for he knows that prayer is a
mighty weapon for Christians, an impreg-
nable rampart, made strong by God.

Eph 6:18

Phil 4:6
Rom 12:12

Eph 5:18–19

40. Prayer may do what it likes—just as
God can. It gives orders on earth, it holds

back in heaven. Prayer is a god amongst human beings: it forgives sins and decrees healing. For *the prayer of faith heals the person who is sick, and if he has committed sins, they are forgiven. Great is the power of the prayer which the righteous person prays. Elijah was a human being subject to suffering just like us, yet he prayed** on earth and held back the heavens; he prayed over a dead person and brought him back to life.*

Jas 5:15–17

cf 1 Kgs 17:22

41. Prayer sometimes brings the dead back to life, but sometimes it may slay the living, as happened with the godly Peter: he brought Tabitha* back to life by prayer, but he effected the death of Ananias and Sapphira.* Elisha, that spiritual man, brought to life the young son of the Shunamite woman,* but he brought to their end the wicked children, through the bears which he brought out against them with the curse.* The case of Hezekiah was also astonishing: through prayer he added to the days of his life as king,* but he routed the mighty army of the Assyrian through the agency of a spiritual being.*

Acts 9:40

Acts 5:3–10

2 Kgs 4:32–36

2 Kgs 2:23–24

Is 38:1–5

2 Kgs 19:35

42. How potent and mighty is the power of prayer! Prayer is able to put pressure on Satan who puts pressure on the human race; it can rescue from his hands and bring deliverance from all the temptations in the world. For this reason our Lord does well to bid us *Be wakeful and pray, so that you do not enter into temptation,** and again *Be watchful at all times and pray, so that you may be held worthy to escape from the*

Mt 26:41

Lk 21:36 *things to come and to take your stand before the Son of Man.**

43. Those who stand in Christ's presence, whose whole concern is with things divine, who are liberated from all the cares of the world, should accordingly persevere at all times in the hidden prayer of the heart and in spiritual thoughts of the mind, rejecting and pushing aside every worldly thought which darkens the soul, preventing it from engaging in thoughts of God.

44. The cares and desires of this world are a great obstacle to the soul's engaging in pure prayer addressed to God, just as that holy teacher, beloved by God, John Chrysostom said[3]: 'Nothing so much perturbs and troubles the eye of the soul as the importunity of this world's cares and yearnings.' For as long as we are strung about with all this earthly weight we cannot fly up to heaven. It is far preferable and more desirable that we should be able to travel along this road completely denuded of everything. Even so, this ascent cannot take place without the wings of the Spirit. What is required in order for us to ascend to this height is a combination of an unburdened mind and the grace of the Spirit; but if one of these is not present at all, but instead we are strung about with things that are actually hindrances, how will we be enabled to fly upwards, seeing that we are held back by all these heavy burdens?

45. Accordingly, my beloved, let us shake off from us the burden of worldly concern, and let us spend all our time in thoughts of God, for this will purify our soul and make

it soar heavenward towards God. For divine
words polish away rust from the mind and
lighten it of the weight of earthly things;
they raise the mind to a vision of the divinity. It is imperative, then, that we meditate
continually on the divine Scriptures, for it
is in them that God speaks. Meditation of
this sort gives birth in the soul to love towards him, and to purity.

46. To illustrate this, let us take the example of Mary, the sister of Lazarus, *who
sat at the feet of our Lord listening to his
words*;* by her love she caused her soul to
fly up to heaven at His words. This is the
reason why our Lord gave good testimony
concerning her, saying *Mary has chosen the
good portion; it shall not be taken away
from her.**

*cf Jn 11:1 &
Lk 10:39*

Lk 10:42

47. Let us too imitate this blessed woman in 'the good part' which she chose.
For our Lord is close at hand for us even
now: as he sits in heaven with his Father,*
he is speaking in his Gospel with us on
earth, calling out *Blessed are those who are
pure in heart, for they shall see God.** Let
us incline our ear towards him, and purify
our hearts with his words, so that we may
hear his living voice with the ears of our
minds, and behold with the eyes of our
hearts his great beauty. In this way we shall
receive from Him a second blessing, for he
said *Blessed are your eyes which see and
your ears which hear.**

cf Col 3:1

Mt 5:8

Mt 13:16

48. So let us open up our hearts so as to
understand the Scriptures which are filled
with spiritual life and wisdom. In them
there speaks the Spirit of God who gives

life and knowledge. The blessed Apostle, who was well aware of the great power to be found in the reading of them, exhorts his disciple concerning them in no small way, emphatically bidding him *Until I* *1 Tim 4:13* *come, be eager in reading them,** and again *Exercise yourself* in religious teach- *1 Tim 4:7–8* ing, for it is *beneficial in every way*;* and, praising him for his study, he says *From your youth up you have been instructed in the holy books: they are able to endow you with wisdom for life. Every Scripture which has been written in the Spirit is beneficial for instruction, for admonishing, for correction and for education in righteousness, so that the man of God may be* *2 Tim 3:* *come perfect, performing everything well* *15–17* *and fully.**

49. For all the wisdom of Life is hidden in the Scriptures. In them we are able to gain knowledge of God and of his creative activity, of his wonderful governance and providence; likewise of his goodness and, at the same time, of his righteousness, and, in sum, of his great and mighty power.* *cf Eph 1:19* Anyone who is deprived of a knowledge of the Scriptures cannot withstand the power of God; just as our Lord said to the Jews: *You do not know the Scriptures or the* *Mt 22:29* *power of God.** And when He sent them off to examine them, he said *Examine the Scriptures, for in them you imagine that you have eternal life; they will testify to* *Jn 5:39* *me.**

50. Again, it is from the Scriptures that we learn how to travel on the road of virtuous conduct, for in them all the fine deeds

of the just life are delineated. Just as one cannot see anything without light, for it is light that enables us to see, as it is written *By your light we see light*,* similarly, without the light of the Scriptures we are unable to see God, who is Light,* or his justice, which is filled with light.*

Ps 36:9

cf 1 Jn 1:5
cf Ps 37:6

51. The effort involved in reading the Scriptures is thus greatly beneficial to us, all the more so since it causes us to become illumined in prayer. For anyone whose soul, after having laboured in reading and been purified by spiritual meditation, is fervent with love for God, will pray in a luminous manner when he turns to prayer and the Office, and he will recite the psalms without distraction. This is because his mind has laboured in meditating on divine providence and so is filled with joy. In his soul he carries the model for virtue that he has received from training through the agency of the Spirit; he has depicted before his eyes, as though in a picture, the lovely beauty of the saints' way of life: wrapped up in reading about these things, he will exult over them and become fervent in spirit, so that the words of his Office and the incense of his prayer become illumined and pure, seeing that they flow out from the pure spring of his heart.

52. It is entirely right that the person who neglects his way of life should also be wrapped up in the labour of reading the Scriptures, for as a result of continually meditating upon them he will come to his senses and feel ashamed of himself. Then, little by little, his soul will begin to become

illumined and be purified of the passions;
he will habituate himself to good habits,
providing training for a virtuous life.

53. Truly great and mighty is the power
of God's word. For the word of God has

Mt 3:7

changed *the offspring of vipers** into children of God. So let us constantly sow it

cf Mt 13:5

within the hard soil of our heart,* waiting
for it to soften it so that the wheat-ear of
life may sprout up in it. For the word of
God is at the same time the seed and the
water; and even though we have *a heart*

*cf Ez 11:19,
36:26*

*like stone,** it will be softened and split up
by the water of the Spirit, so that it can
bring forth holy fruit that is pleasing to
God.

54. Therefore let no one neglect meditation of the divine words or the labour of
reading the appointed measure. As our
honoured teacher said, from such meditation the soul acquires great benefit and
finds salvation. Futhermore, we please God
by this occupation, and our mouths are
cleansed of both abuse and of shameful and
frivolous talk, seeing that we are constantly
meditating on the holy words. We also become objects of fear for the demons as we
arm our tongues with these words. Above
all, we bring close to ourselves the grace of
the Spirit, and the eye of our soul is made
to shine by the understanding we receive
from him. This is why God gave us eyes,
mouth and hearing, so that all our limbs
might be filled with service of him, as we
recount his words, carry our his wishes,
continuously sing his praises and cease-

lessly offer up to him thanksgiving. By these means we shall purify our minds.

55. Just as the body that benefits from clean air will acquire good health and will be kept pure, so too the soul that enjoys the divine words—as it were, God's wind—will be restored to health and rejuvenated in purity, and made holy. Its eye will be illumined so that it can gaze all the time on God. Just as is the case with the body's eye, provided it is open and clear, it never ceases from seeing things and does not know how to have its fill; so too it is with the illumined *eye** of the mind: provided it is *straightforward* and pure, it is occupied with spiritual vision; and when it is opened so as to peer into the mysteries of divine knowledge and into the world above, it will become even more illumined and purified, thus enabled to approach the essential light of the divinity that exists above the world.

Mt 6:22

56. When the vision of the body's eye is clear and its light is mingled with the luminous rays of the sun, it is able to see with the sun's light. Analogously, when the heart is purified and the eye of its awareness is illumined, the light of its vision being commingled with the essential radiance of the Spirit of God, then, by means of the radiance of the grace from the spiritual brightness provided from above, the heart begins to behold, in a spiritual way, the great *Sun of Righteousness** and to enjoy his beauty.

Mal 4:2

57. If we take great trouble over this, then maybe the air we feel around us will not be as close to our exterior senses as is the Spirit of God who is continuously in

our hearts. Through him the memory of
him is clear at every moment, and in this
way he dwells all the more in us and is seen
by us. He also nourishes our souls just as
the air nourishes our bodies, for the soul at
every moment depicts in itself the thought
of God and the praise of his name: it becomes a hidden church[4] where the Godhead is ministered to in an excellent way.

58. Blessed is the soul which has been
accounted worthy of this, for it enjoys spiritual life with God. Alas for the soul that is
deprived of this, for it is shrouded in darkness and its very name is covered in darkness: while it lives to the world it is dead to
God. For the soul in which no thought of
God is to be found, and whose intellect is
deprived of the recollection of him, is in
very truth dead as far as the life of the Spirit
is concerned. For just as the body dies and
its life departs when it is prevented from
breathing, so too when the soul's mental
faculty is held back from the recollection of
God, the soul dies as far as the life of righteousness is concerned, and the Holy Spirit,
whose grace it had breathed in at baptism,
departs from it.

59. Accordingly we ought to open our
mouths at all times to God, and breathe in
the breath of his grace that nourishes our
souls with the recollection of him.[5] We
should be even more assiduous in this than
we are with external breathing. As one of
the saints said: 'Let the recollection of God
be even more continuous than your breathing', and again, 'Let psalmody be continuous, for when God is named, he causes

demons to flee';[6] or again, 'You should remember God at every moment; then your mind will become heaven'.

60. The holy Gregory the Theologian teaches the same thing when he says[7] 'We should remember God even more than our breathing'; and if one may say so, we should not do anything apart from this. I am one of those who applaud this law which bids us *to meditate day and night*,* reciting the Lord's name and blessing Him at all times, *evening, morning and noon.** And if necessary, let us say with Moses, 'When I lie down and when I get up, and when I set off, and whatever else I do'.* Let us be conformed to purity by the recollection of him; and let us gaze at ourselves, and sculpt the theologian into an object of beauty. And again, 'Meditate on these divine matters, and speak the things of the Spirit; and as far as possible do not speak or breathe in anything else. For it is excellent, and something divine, that we should be continually grafted into God by recollection of the things of God'.[8]

Ps 1:2

Ps 55:17

cf Deut 6:7

61. Let us too do this, meditating continuously on the things of God, and by means of the Lord's law, let our wills be grafted on to him. For the person who *meditates on the law of the Lord night and day*,* as David said, and who sings *his praises at all times** and blesses him, is *like the tree planted by a stream of water** in fair and excellent soil, *providing fruit** all the time, *without its leaves ever falling.** The pride of such a person's soul is continually in the Lord, and the Lord delivers him from all

Ps 1:2

Ps 34:1
Ps 1:3
cf Mt 13:23
Ps 1:3

afflictions,* seeing that his gaze is continuously upon God.

62. Let us therefore also gaze upon God,* raising up and exalting his holy name in praise. Let us take refuge with his purity by continual recollection of his name; let us sculpt out the beauty of our souls by gazing on the likeness of his glory,* so that we may be seen to be glorious statues of his divinity within creation.

63. For this is how we were established by him in the world: we were smelted down from dust,* just like other natural beings, but when we were poured out he clothed us in the beauty of his own image* and caused us to acquire the radiance of his likeness, adorning us with the glory of his divinity—or rather, making us as secondary gods on earth,[9] giving us an authority like his own within creation.

64. We should accordingly worship and glorify him who raised our dust to such state, recounting ceaselessly the holiness of him who mingled our spirit with his Spirit, and mixed into our bodies the gift of his grace, causing the fire of his Holy Spirit to burst into flames in us. For *he has shone out in our hearts** which had been submerged in darkness.

65. Let no one of us henceforth *walk in darkness*,* or *quench* the light of *the Spirit** by neglecting his praise. Let not the deep sleep of night cause us labour, let not its darkness hold sway over us, making the limbs of our bodies go slack, and obscuring the light of our souls by means of its dreams, making us like dead corpses that lie

cf Ps 34:3

cf Ps 34:5

cf 2 Cor 3:18

cf Gen 2:7

cf Gen 1:27

2 Cor 4:6

Jn 8:12
1 Th 5:19

in the dark. Rather, let our light grow strong in him by means of the brightness of his radiance; for it is by means of spiritual prayer and utterances of thanksgiving that we are raised up from earth to the heights.

66. When servants are waiting for their master to return from a banquet they need to stay awake all night, awaiting his arrival: their *loins should be girded* and their *lamps lighted*;* they cannot allow themselves to drop off into deep sleep, seeing that they do not know whether their master will be returning that evening, or in the middle of the night, or at cock-crow,* or the next morning; they are afraid he may suddenly come and find them asleep. We too, then, should be wakeful and prepared, just as our Lord bade us: *You too should be prepared, for the Son of Man will come at a moment when you are not expecting him.* *

Lk 12:35

cf Lk 12:38

Mt 24:44

67. This applies particularly to the holy day of Sunday, the great day of the Resurrection on which we expect our King to return from on high to take us off to the wedding feast he has prepared for us. We should especially display our eager readiness by our wakefulness in singing psalms and in praying during the long vigil that lasts the entire night, after the example that our Lord taught us when he went up alone to the mountain, watching without sleep the whole night in prayer to God.*

cf Lk 6:12

68. This is also what the apostles used to do when they gathered together, spending the entire night in praise, prayer, and addresses to the faithful. Thus Paul went on

talking to the disciples *until the middle of*
the night;* even after he had restored to life
Eutyches* who had dozed off and fallen
from the third floor to his death, they
found delight in songs of praise and in the
Mysteries, and Paul went on talking with
them until dawn. This custom is preserved
to this very day in the churches of the By-
zantines: their faithful do not sleep during
the Saturday night, but keep vigil with
prayer, the Office, and readings.

69. Likewise we Christians who are
Christ's servants should truly stand valiantly in wakefulness like *good and faithful*
*servants** who are eager to do honour to
their master. Let us gird ourselves in asceticism, inwardly strengthened by austerity,
having the lamps of our hearts filled with
the oil of grace* from the Spirit and illumined by prayer; in this way we shall valiantly do battle with the powerful
incitement provided by the sweetness of
sleep. In this way *the dark will be light for*
us, just as the prophet said, *and night will*
be illumined by our faces:* the darkness
will not make our minds dark, so let us
spend the dark night awake as if it were
bright daylight.

70. If the Son of Darkness wants to make
us children of the dark* night like himself,
causing us to sink into sleep, he will press
us particularly hard when, at the time of
night when darkness reigns and *he is on the*
*prowl**—as Scripture says of the wild animals*—he being himself darkness and a
lover of darkness, he sees us in the light of
prayer keeping vigil with our Lord, resem-

Ac 20:7
Ac 20:9–12

Mt 25:23

cf Lk 12:35 &
Mt 25:4

Ps 139:11

cf 1 Th 5:5

1 Pet 5:8
cf Ps 104:20

bling the angels of light, *with our spiritual songs and praises** as we give glory to God our Maker. Burning with a furious jealousy, full of envy at the sight of human beings exhibiting the wakefulness of the angels, he will try to submerge us in the heaviness of sleep, making us share in his own darkness.

Eph 5:19

71. But we, being *children of light** and of the day share in the likeness of Christ, should *ease away from ourselves the works of darkness**—empty vigils, unprofitable talk, deep sleep. *Let us put on the armour of light,** taking our stand in the Office for the utterance of praise that sends our minds towards God, for the supplications made in his presence made on our knees, for the prayers of petition accompanied by spiritual groaning of the heart, for the outpouring of tears, for fervour of spirit** when we are set on fire by love, for eagerness of mind as we gaze undistractedly on God.

1 Th 5:5

Rom 8:29

Rom 13:12

cf Rom 12:11

72. Girded with such things to serve as invincible armour, let us take our stand against the Evil One, being wakeful and well prepared, as though it was day. Let us transfix him with the mighty arrows of the Spirit's words, and cut off all his hopes, joining David, the son of Jesse, in adjuring him by the covenant that does not fail: 'Depart from us and go to your ill fate, you mad *dog** that audaciously barks against its master, for we have sworn to the Lord and made our vow to the God of Jacob that we shall *not allow sleep to touch* our *eyes, or drowsiness* our *eyelids, until* we have *found a place for the Lord* to rest in our souls, *a tent for the God of Jacob** to dwell

cf 1 Sam 17:43

Ps 132:4–5

in inside our hearts. We will certainly not cease from vigil, prayer, toil and labour until the Lord is pleased at our soul and chooses it as a place in which to live, saying, *This is my resting place for eternal ages; here shall I reside, for I have desired it'.*

Ps 132:14

73. If Satan is still unwilling to depart, but instead insolently grows stronger against us, at one moment enticing us with blandishments in order to bite us the better, at the next growling* and barking out in his bitterness in order to frighten our hearts, even so we should not prove weak and timidly collapse before him; rather, we should strengthen ourselves all the more against him, using whatever means we can find to withstand him and drive him from us, gasping out to God, begging him to save us from him.* Yes, from the very depths of our heart we should *offer up earnest supplication and tears** as we call upon him to hear our cry and deliver us from Satan's hands; for he has the power to save us and enable us to drive Satan away from our presence full of shame and with his head pounded by the spiritual stones that are hurled against him from our mouths.*

cf 1 Pet 5:8

cf Ps 55:16

Heb 5:7

cf 1 Sam 17:49

74. If we go on crying out and do not receive any answer, this is for our advantage: instead of losing heart and growing weary, we should go on brazenly asking God, for it is certain that *at an acceptable time** and at the appropriate hour he will answer us and deliver us. When we go on brazenly asking him, even though we have no legitimate claim of *friendship* on him on

2 Cor 6:2

the basis of which we might be answered,
yet *because of the insistency** of our re-   *Lk 11:8*
quest *he will arise and grant* what we are
asking for, on seeing us standing in great
fatigue at his door in the middle of the
night. We stand there, cruelly aflicted and
maltreated by the Evil One, isolated and
alone, like the widow* who had no one to   *cf Lk 18:3*
help her, so how will the merciful God hold
himself back when he sees our wretched
state of oppression at Satan's hands, and
not quickly avenge us and deliver us from
him?

75. For, as our Saviour pointed out, even
the cruel and wicked judge eventually saw
to the poor widow's case because she had
wearied him with her importunity.* But it   *Lk 18:2–5*
is quite clear that God does not neglect us.
Even if he makes us wait, he will nonetheless answer us and *see to our case all of a
sudden.** When we pray all the time, we   *Lk 18:8*
should not weary, but eagerly cry out to
him day and night, supplicating him with a
broken heart and a humble spirit: *for a
humble spirit is a sacrifice to God, and
God will not reject a broken heart.**   *Ps 51:17*

76. If you offer to God the sacrifice of
prayer in humility, he will answer you and
deliver you, granting you all sorts of good
things. Our Lord said: *If then you who are
evil know how to give good things to your
children, how much more will your good
Father give good things from heaven to
those who ask him.** For he will not go on   *Mt 7:11*
holding back from us *his kingdom and his
righteousness** which have been prepared   *Mt 6:33*
for us, provided we persevere valiantly in

knowledge and humility of spirit, making our request to him with the broken heart and afflicted spirit which he desires.

77. If, on the contrary, we pray and recite the psalms before him in a proud and critical way, giving ourselves airs, or if we complete the Office in a distracted way, not only will he not listen to us or deliver us from the Evil One, but we will be making ourselves and our requests abominable before him, so that he will turn out to be

Is 63:10 our *opponent* who *strives* against *us*;* in other words, he will drive us out from his presence, and *hand* us *over to Satan to be punished, to stop us acting*

1 Tim 1:20 *blasphemously.**

78. Thus whoever offers to God sacrifices of praise—the rational *fruits of the*

Heb 13:15 *lips that confess his name**—should be very wary of the ambushes of the Evil One. For Satan lies in ambush ready to catch you by surprise at the very time of thanksgiving: he will get up and accuse you before God, just as he did with your fellow

cf Lk 18:11–14 Pharisee in the temple;* this time he will not be puffing you up with pride over good works, as he did with the Pharisee, but he will be making you drunk with a different kind of pride—pride in the lovely and sweet sound of your own voice, the beauty of your chants that are *sweeter than honey*

Ps 19:10 *and the honeycomb,**—with the result that you do not realize that these belong to God, and not to yourself.

79. You should understand this from the case of the harp or lyre or *cymbals when*

1 Cor 13:1 *they make a sound*:* does the sweetness of

the melody and song come from the harp or the lyre, or does it belong to the person plucking the instrument and singing? You, who are endowed with reason, should receive instruction from what is not endowed with senses, and you should realize that the Spirit of God is playing on your tongue, and singing his melodies in your mouth.

80. Therefore do not be proud of the sweetness of the words that does not belong to you: you may be too deaf to understand them, perhaps even more so than the sounding brass cymbals.* For you are much *cf 1 Cor 13:1* more inferior to the Spirit who sings in you than is the ten-stringed harp to the musician. Therefore do not be proud over the Spirit who speaks in you, even though you may know his intention well—whereas the Apostle was gazing upon it in wonder, saying *Who has known the mind of the Lord, or who has been his counsellor?** Accord- *Rom 11:34* ingly, reader, if you suppose that you have some understanding or knowledge, you should learn from Paul that *you have not yet understood anything in the way you should properly understand it.** *1 Cor 8:2*

81. There is another way in which the Evil One may surreptitiously ensnare you in pride, this time not through the voice's chanting or the comprehension of the words of the readings, but through the still silence of prayer. This applies to the person who attracts people to look at his sad countenance and to observe his state*—which *cf Mt 6:16* gives the appearance of someone whose mind has been snatched up towards God and raised far above mankind in what it is

experiencing. What an inflated supposition, and one that destroys prayer—when that prayer should have been sincere! Such a man is an associate of the Pharisee in his wish to be praised; as our Lord said, *They loved to stand in synagogues and on street corners to pray, so that they might be* applauded *by men—thus getting their*

Mt 6:5

*reward.**

82. My beloved, let us keep far away from anything like all this. Rather, let us pray in a hidden way with humility of heart, without having any desire to be puffed up with pride at the demonstration of our prayer, thus losing our reward. Our Lord bids us, *When you pray, enter your*

Mt 6:6

*chamber and close your door.** What, then, is this chamber, if not the inner house of the heart, whose door is kept closed by humility, which abhors praise from men.

83. This is how we should pray to God, asking what is fitting and appropriate. Do not let us *stammer out* empty words before

Mt 6:7

him *like the pagans,** for these things are inappropriate for Christians to ask; rather we should ask for whatever is worthy of his holiness and is to the glory of his name—in other words, *His Kingdom and its right-*

Mt 6:33

*eousness.** The Kingdom is for our delight and adornment, and the righteousness is for his exaltation and the glory of his majesty. These two things, then, are for our elevation and for the adorning of our place of honour with him.

84. You should pray as follows: *Our Father in heaven, may your name be sanctified, may your kingdom come. . . .** These

Mt 6:9–10

are words appropriate for the children of God to pray, having their minds raised up from earth, as they dwell in heaven in the Kingdom with their Father, assembled as though in the chamber of the heart's hiddenness, away from the sight of anyone outside. This is the model we should imitate in our prayer, when our mouths give thanks before God our Father.

85. In this way, being occupied in prayer night and day in purity of conscience, as we delight in the hidden light of spiritual vision within our minds, singing God's praises with our mouths and in our hearts without cease, hidden away as though in some secret hiding place by means of humility of a modest soul, to prevent our losing the reward of our prayer by allowing it to be destroyed by the empty praise of men, let us prove worthy of that sure reward that is given by God who sees inside the heart, as our Saviour said, *Your Father who sees your hidden prayer in a hidden place will reward you openly.** Mt 6:6

86. Praise be to God, and may he give us the joy of converse with him for ever, amen.

BIBLIOGRAPHY AND NOTES

A. The translation is made from A. de Halleux's edition, *Martyrius (Sahdona): Oeuvres spirituelles*, III, CSCO 252, Scriptores Syri 110 (1965) 1–27.
B. A good orientation is given by L. Leloir in *DSpir* 10 (1980) cols. 737–42; see also his 'La pensée monastique d'Ephrem et Martyrius', in *OCA* 197 (1974) 105–34. A. de Halleux's edition of Martyrius' works also includes a complete French translation (CSCO 201, 215, 253 and 255; 1960–1965). Some further fragments of lost portions of the *Book of Perfection* have subsequently been found: see *Le Muséon* 81 (1968) 139–54, and 88 (1975) 253–95.

1. I.e. the monastic habit. Martyrius uses the Greek term.
2. See Chapter III, note 2.
3. Compare perhaps John Chrysostom, *On Psalm 6* (PG 55: 77), and *Homily 20 on Matthew 5* (PG 57: 291).
4. The idea of the 'hidden church' is based on the *Book of Steps, Discourse XII* (Chapter III, above).
5. Compare John of Apamea, *Letter to Hesychius*, 42, and the passage from Gregory of Nazianzus quoted in section 60.
6. Compare perhaps Nilus, *Letters* I, 239 (PG 79; 169D), and E. A. W. Budge, *The Wit and Wisdom of the Christian Fathers of Egypt* (London, 1934) p. 31 (nos 106–7).

7. Gregory of Nazianzus, *Oration* XXVII.4 (PG 36: 16B–C and 20B = *Sources chrétiennes* 250: pp. 78–81, 86–7).

8. Unidentified (not from *Oration* XXVII).

9. Compare Ephrem, *Hymns on Faith* XXIX.1, 'God in his mercy has called mortals gods through grace' (cf. note 21 to the General Introduction).

Chapter XII

Isaac of Nineveh

Second half of 7th Century

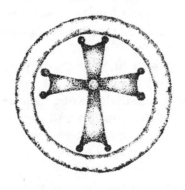

INTRODUCTION

S T ISAAC OF NINEVEH, or St Isaac the Syrian as he is
often known, is indubitably one of the most
profound writers on spirituality produced by the
Syriac Churches; he has also proved to be one of the most
influential, thanks to early translations of many of his
works into Greek and Arabic, whence they have reached
many other languages.

Isaac was born in the region of Qatar, in the Persian
Gulf. In the seventh century Qatar was still an important
centre of Christianity and it produced a number of writers
of note in the Church of the East. Isaac first became a
monk and a teacher in his home country, but may have
moved north to the mountains of Khuzistan (Syriac Bēth
Hūzāyē) during a schism which occurred between the Patriarchate of Seleucia-Ktesiphon and the bishops in Qatar.
But Isaac was evidently back in the Qatar region when the
Catholicos-Patriarch Giwargis (George) I visited the area in
676, when the schism was healed, for the Catholicos took
him back with him and ordained him bishop of Nineveh
(Mosul) in the great monastery of Bēth Ābē (in north Iraq).
After five months, however, Isaac abdicated his episco-
pacy 'for a reason which God knows' (as one biographical
source puts it), and retired to the mountains of Khuzistan
to lead a solitary life in the vicinity of other anchorites. In
old age he moved to the nearby monastery of Rabban
Shabur. The date of his death is unknown, and one source
says that he became blind in the later years of his life.

Isaac's extensive writings all seem to be the product of his old age; they thus date approximately to the last decade or so of the seventh century. One biographical account states that he wrote 'five volumes of instruction for monks'; if this is correct, then much will have been lost, for the works which have come down to us and which are definitely genuine are divided into two 'parts'. These two parts were clearly put together after Isaac's death. The First Part appears to have had much the widest circulation, and texts from it were soon copied by Syrian Orthodox monks as well as those belonging to the Church of the East; similarly the Greek translation, made by the Greek Orthodox monks Abraamios and Patrikios at the monastery of St Saba in the eighth or ninth century, was entirely composed of texts taken from the First Part. The complete Syriac text of the First Part was published in 1909 by the Lazarist Father Paul Bedjan, an indefatigable editor of Syriac texts, and it was from this edition that A. J. Wensinck made his English translation in 1923. In Syriac the First Part comprises eighty-two separate texts or chapters.

Bedjan had temporary access to a single manuscript of the much rarer Second Part, and he printed a few excerpts which he had been able to copy; these were not included by Wensinck in his English translation. This manuscript has unfortunately subsequently disappeared, and only recently has another old and complete manuscript of this Second Part been discovered in the Bodleian Library, Oxford. The Second Part turns out to contain some forty new texts, of which by far the longest is a set of four Centuries of 'Headings [*Kephalaia*] on Knowledge', described by the person who first collected together these works of Isaac as 'containing exalted spiritual meanings and perfect knowledge, abundant and wondrous meanings and great mysteries; appropriate for the joy and delight of the soul and for its growth in things spiritual'.

Besides these collected works there is also ascribed to Isaac the *Book of Grace*, consisting of a collection of seven Centuries on various topics concerning the spiritual life. This has not yet been published and its attribution to Isaac is not certain.

In the excerpts translated below, 1–2 are taken from the First Part and are given in a new English translation. Excerpts 3–5, on the other hand, are all drawn from the as yet unpublished Second Part; 3 gives some extracts from the *Kephalaia* on Knowledge, while 4 and 5 provide two complete discourses, both on aspects of prayer. In 1(a) Isaac underlines the importance of praying for the right things, and goes on to give advice about situations where God appears to be slow in answering prayer. In 1(b) the benefits of humility in prayer are described while the brief excerpt 1(c) emphasizes the importance of the body in prayer, a topic developed in 4. In 1(d) Isaac states that the whole purpose of prayer is to love God, and in 1(e) he gives some definitions of repentance, purity, perfection and prayer. The long discourse given in 2 contains some of Isaac's most characteristic teaching on 'pure prayer' and 'spiritual prayer' which lies beyond it: in 'spiritual prayer' the movement of prayer is 'cut off' and prayer actually ceases as a sense of utter wonder takes over. The excerpts in 3 from the *Kephalaia* on Knowledge are mainly concerned with different states of prayer. In 4 Isaac stresses the great importance of posture in prayer and then goes on to discuss the relationship between prayer and the monastic Office. Finally, in 5 he returns to the subject of 'pure prayer' and offers some advice on wandering in prayer.

Isaac is not a systematic writer and his spirituality draws on many different sources, notable Evagrius, John of Apamea (whose threefold pattern of the spiritual life he sometimes employs), the *Macarian Homilies*, the *Apophthegmata* and related literature of the Egyptian Fathers (this had been made readily accessible by Ananisho in the mid-seventh century to monks of the Church of the East in a massive compilation known as the *Paradise of the Fathers*), Theodore of Mopsuestia (to whom Isaac normally refers as 'the Exegete', *par excellence*), Abba Isaiah and Mark the Hermit. Although 'Dionysius the Areopagite' (whose works had been translated into Syriac in the early sixth century) is also mentioned by Isaac on a few occasions, he does not appear to have had a formative influence on his thought.

1. ISAAC OF NINEVEH,
Excerpts from Part I

(a) From *Discourse III*

DO NOT BE FOOLISH in the requests you make to God, otherwise you will insult God through your ignorance. Act wisely in prayer, so that you may become worthy of glorious things. Ask for things that are honourable from him who will not hold back, so that you may receive honour from him as a result of the wise choice your free will has made. Solomon asked for wisdom*—and along with it he also received the earthly kingdom, for he knew how to ask wisely of the heavenly King, that is, for things that are important.

Elisha asked for twice the gift of the Spirit* that his master had had, and his request was not withheld from him.

On the other hand, a king's honour is diminished by the person who requests

1 Kgs 3:9–14

2 Kgs 2:9

contemptible things from him. Israel asked
for despicable things—and received in return God's anger. For, failing to wonder at
God's actions and the awesome character of
his works, they asked for things that the
belly desires. Then, *while the food was still
in their mouths, God's anger rose up
against them.* *   Ps 78:30–31

Make your request to God in accordance
with his glorious nature, then he will hold
you in greater honour and will rejoice at
you.

When someone asks a human king for a
load of manure, not only will he be despised as a result of his despicable request—seeing that he has accused himself
by means of his own ignorance—but he has
also offered an insult to the king by means
of his stupid request. Exactly the same applies when someone asks God for the
things of the body in prayer.[1]

If God is slow in answering your request,
and you ask but do not promptly receive
anything, do not be upset, for you are not
wiser than God.[2] When you remain as you
were before, without anything happening,
it is either because your behaviour is not
worthy of your request, or because the
paths in which your heart was travelling
were far removed from the aim of your
prayer, or because your interior condition
is far too childish, when compared with the
magnitude of the thing for which you have
asked.

It is not appropriate that things of great
magnitude should fall easily into our hands;
otherwise God's gift will be held in con-

tempt as a result of the ease with which it is
to be found. Anything that is easily found is
also easily lost, whereas what is found after
much labour will be guarded with
vigilance.

Thirst for Jesus, so that he may inebriate
you with his love. Blind your eyes to all
that is held in honour in the world, so that
you may be held worthy to have the peace
which comes from God reign in your heart.

Fast from the allurements that make the
eyes glitter, in order that you may become
worthy of spiritual joy. If your way of life is
unworthy of God, then do not ask him for
glorious things, otherwise you will appear
as someone who tempts God. Prayer accords strictly with behaviour.

(b) From *Discourse VIII*

Humility restrains the heart. Then, once
someone has become humble, immediately
God's mercy surrounds him and embraces
him. Once this mercy has drawn close, the
heart straightaway becomes aware of its
benefit, for a certain confidence and power
surge up within it. Having become aware of
the advent of divine succour to support and
help it, then the heart is immediately filled
with faith, and now realizes and understands that prayer is the haven of help, the
fountain of salvation, the treasury of confidence, the anchor that brings rescue amid
storms, the illumination of those in the
dark, the staff of the weak, a shelter in time
of temptation, giver of health in time of

sickness, beneficial shield in battle, and sharp arrow against adversaries.

Because a person has found an entrance to all these good things by way of prayer, henceforward he will take delight in prayer of faith, his heart exulting out of confidence, and no longer blindly and as a result of hearsay, as had hitherto been the case.

Once a person knows this, he will have acquired prayer as a treasure within himself, and as a result of his joy he will change the direction of his prayer to songs of thanksgiving. This accords with the words of Evagrius[3] wise among the saints, who had a purpose for everything: 'Prayer is joy which expresses itself in thanksgiving'. Concerning this prayer which follows the receiving of the awareness of God he says, 'In this prayer which expresses itself in thanksgiving a person does not pray or labour', as happens with other kinds of prayer involving sufferings that are prior to the perception which comes by grace; rather the heart, being filled with joy and wonder, bursts forth abundantly with impulses of thanksgiving and gratitude amid the silence of kneeling. Then, as a result of the inner impulse which is greatly stirred by wonder at insights into God's graces, all of a sudden he will raise his voice and utter praise insatiably, as the inner impulse gives expression to thanksgiving on the tongue as well. He will go on repeating this for a long period and in a marvellous way. Anyone who has experienced these things, not in a dim way, but clearly, and has been distinctly aware of them, will understand

when I say that this happens without varia-
tion, for it has been experienced many
times. From then on this person will cease
from empty occupations, and will be with
God constantly, without any break, in continual prayer, fearful of being deprived of
the flow of benefits that this brings.

(c) From *Discourse XVIII*

Every prayer in which the body does not
toil, and the heart does not feel suffering,
you should reckon as an abortion without a
soul.

(d) From *Discourse LXIII*

The purpose of prayer is for us to acquire
love of God, for in prayer can be discovered
all sorts of reasons for loving God.[4]
Love of God proceeds from conversing
with him; this conversation of prayer
comes about through stillness, and stillness
comes with the stripping away of the self.

(e) From *Discourse LXXIV*

The sum of the entire ascetic course consists in these three things—repentance, purity, and perfection.
What is repentance? Desisting from former sins, and feeling pain at them.
What is purity, in a nutshell? A heart
which has compassion on every natural
thing in creation.

What is perfection? Profound humility, which consists in the abandoning of everything visible and invisible: visible meaning everything involved with the senses; invisible meaning all thinking about them. The same elder was asked on another occasion, 'What is repentance?', and he said, 'A broken heart'. And what is humility? He replied, 'Embracing[5] a voluntary mortification with regard to everything'. And what is a merciful heart? He replied, 'The heart's burning for all creation, for human beings, for birds and animals, and for demons, and everything there is. At the recollection of them and at the sight of them his eyes gush forth with tears owing to the force of the compassion which constrains his heart, so that, as a result of its abundant sense of mercy, the heart shrinks and cannot bear to hear or examine any harm or small suffering of anything in creation. For this reason he offers up prayer with tears at all times, even for irrational animals, and for the enemies of truth, and for those who harm him, for their preservation and being forgiven.[6] As a result of the immense compassion infused in his heart without measure—like God's—he even does this for reptiles.[7]

What is prayer? The emptying of the mind of all that belongs here, and a heart which has completely turned its gaze to a longing for that future hope. Whosoever departs from this ideal is like someone who sows mixed seed in his furrow, or like someone who ploughs with an ox and an ass at the same time.

2. ISAAC OF NINEVEH,
Discourse XXII

ON VARIOUS EXPERIENCES DURING PRAYER,
AND ON THE LIMITS OF THE MIND'S
POWER;
HOW FAR IT IS CAPABLE OF MOVING ITS
ARBITRARY IMPULSES BY VARIOUS HABITS
OF PRAYER. AND ON THE LIMIT PRESCRIBED
TO NATURE DURING PRAYER, THE LIMIT
BEYOND WHICH PRAYER IS NOT ABLE TO
PASS;
AND ON HOW, WHEN IT HAS PROCEEDED
FURTHER, IT IS NO LONGER PRAYER, EVEN
THOUGH IT HAPPENS TO BE CALLED
PRAYER.

GLORY TO HIM whose gift is poured
out over humanity. Even though
the human race is of flesh, yet He
has effected that it should perform on earth
the role of beings who are by nature incorporeal, holding those whose nature comes
from dust worthy to speak of such mysteries—including sinners such as we, who are
quite unworthy even to hear any utterance
on such matters. But in his grace he has
opened the eyes of our blind hearts so that
we can gain understanding from the spiritual meaning* the Scriptures and from the
teaching of the great Fathers—even though
I have not been worthy as a result of my
own application to have had experience of
a thousandth part of all that my hand has
written, especially in the present chapter,

theoria

which we only ventured to embark upon for the purpose of illumining and goading our own soul and that of anyone who might come across it; maybe our soul will be awakened—even by its own desire—to draw close to action.

What then? Delight during prayer is different from vision during prayer. The latter is superior to the former, just as a fully grown man is superior to a small child. Sometimes biblical verses themselves will grow sweet in the mouth,* and a simple phrase of prayer is repeated innumerable times, without one having had enough of it and wanting to pass on to another. And sometimes out of prayer contemplation* is born: this cuts prayer off from the lips, and the person who beholds this is like a corpse without soul in wonder. We call this the faculty of 'vision in prayer'; it does not consist in any image or portrayable form, as foolish people say. This contemplation in prayer also has its degrees and different gifts, but up to this point it is still prayer, for thought has not yet passed into the state when there is non-prayer—for there is something even more excellent than prayer. For the movements of the tongue and of the heart during prayer act as the keys;[8] what comes after these is the actual entry into the treasury: from this point onward mouth and tongue become still, as do the heart—the treasurer to the thoughts—, the mind—the governor of the senses—, and the bold spirit—that swift bird—, along with all the means and uses they possess.

cf Ps 119:103

theoria

Requests too cease here, for the master of
the house has come.

Just as the whole force of the law and the
commandments laid down by God for humanity has its boundary extending up to
purity of heart, as the Fathers have said, so
all the types and varieties of prayer which
human beings address to God have their
boundaries extending up to purity of heart.
Groans, prostrations, heartfelt requests and
supplications, sweet tears and all the other
varieties of prayer, as I have said, have their
authorized boundary only as far as pure
prayer. Moving inwards from purity of
prayer, once one has passed this boundary,
the mind has no prayer, no movement, no
tears, no authority, no freedom, no requests, no desire, no longing for anything
that is hoped for in this world or the world
to come. For this reason, after pure prayer
there is no longer any prayer: all the various stirrings of prayer convey the mind up
to that point through their free authority;
that is why struggle is involved in prayer.
But beyond the boundary, there exists wonder, not prayer. From that point onwards
the mind ceases from prayer; there is the
capacity to see, but the mind is not praying
at all.

Every kind of prayer that exists is set in
motion through stirrings of the soul. But
once the intellect has entered the stirrings
of spiritual existence, it cannot pray there.
Prayer is one thing, but contemplation during it is quite another—even though they
have their cause in each other, the former
being the seed and the latter the load of

sheaves—*where the harvester is full of wonder at the sight he sees which cannot be described: out of the miserable bare seeds that he has sown, what glorious ears of corn have all of a sudden sprouted forth in front of him! As he gazes, he ceases from all motion.

cf Ps 126:6

Every kind of prayer that there is consists in asking, or petition, or praise, or thanks. Examine whether any of these—or any kind of asking—exists once the intellect has passed this boundary and entered that sphere. I am asking this of those who know the truth; these distinctions are not for everyone to investigate, but only for those who in their own persons have become spectators and ministers of this matter, or who have grown up in the presence of Fathers such as these, having received the truth from their mouth, and having passed their days in this sort of converse, with questioning and with answering concerning what is true.

Just as there is scarcely one person to be found out of ten thousand who has more or less fulfilled the commandments and laws, and so been held worthy of limpidity of soul,[9] so only one out of many has been held worthy, as a result of much vigilance, of pure prayer, and has breached this boundary and been considered worthy of that mystery as well. Not many are considered worthy even of pure prayer—only a few; but in the case of the other mystery beyond it, scarcely is anyone in each generation to be found who has approached this knowledge through God's grace.

Prayer is supplication, or concern and yearning for something; or the wish to escape from present or future evils, or a desire for the promises, or some request by which a person is aided in drawing closer to God. Within these stirrings all the various kinds of prayer are included.

Prayer's purity or lack of purity consists in the following. If, at the times when the mind invites one of these stirrings we have specified to offer a sacrifice, it mingles in this sacrifice some alien thought or distraction, then it is called impure, seeing that it has placed on the Lord's altar—that is, the

cf Gen 28:18

heart, the spiritual pillar*—one of the animals that is not permitted.

But when the mind is longingly involved with one of these stirrings—this depends on the urgency of the matter at the time of supplication, and is the result of its great eagerness—the gaze of its stirring is drawn by the eye of faith inside the veil of the heart, and the entries of the soul are thereby fenced off, keeping out those alien thoughts which are called 'strangers' who are not permitted by the Law to enter inside

cf Ez 44:9

the Tent of Witness.* This is what they designate as 'an acceptable sacrifice of the heart' and 'pure prayer'. Prayer's boundaries reach this point: afterwards it is not to be named prayer.

If anyone should introduce mention of what is called 'spiritual prayer' by the Fathers, without understanding the meaning of the Fathers' words, claiming 'This too belongs inside the boundaries of prayer', I think that if that person were to come to an accurate understanding he would realize that it is blasphemous for any created person to say that spiritual prayer can be prayed at all. For every kind of prayer that can be prayed lies this side of the spiritual realm, whereas all that is spiritual enjoys a state that is quite apart from any stirring or prayer. Now if a human being can scarcely pray in a pure manner, what can one say of it being done in a spiritual manner? The Fathers have the habit of designating by the term 'prayer' every excellent impulse, and every spiritual activity. And not just these, but the blessed Interpreter[10] also includes good actions under the heading of prayer, even though it is obvious that prayer is one thing and actions which are carried out are another thing. But sometimes they designate as 'contemplation'* what they elsewhere call 'spiritual prayer'; or sometimes they term it as 'knowledge' or 'revelations of spiritual things'.

    theoria

You see how varied are the terms used by the Fathers of spiritual matters. Precise terms can be established only for earthy matters; for matters concerning the New World this is not possible: all there is is a single straightforward awareness which goes beyond all names, signs, depictions, colours, forms, and invented terms. For this reason, once the soul's awareness has been raised up above this *circle** of the visible world, the Fathers employ whatever designation they like concerning this awareness, since no one knows what the exact names should be. But in order that the soul's thoughts may have something to

    Is 40:22

hold on to, we employ various metaphorical terms—in accordance with the words of the holy Dionysios,[11] who said 'we employ letters, syllables, ordinary names and words with reference to the senses. But when our soul is stirred by the Spirit's activity to divine matters, then the senses and their workings are superfluous to us; just as the spiritual powers of the soul are superfluous when our soul becomes the likeness of the divinity through unattainable union, and it shines out with rays of light which belong to the sublime, by means of visionless stirrings.'

So, my brother, you may be assured of this: the intellect has the authority to initiate discernment between different stirrings up to that point where it has purity in prayer. But once it has reached that place, then it either turns back or it ceases from being prayer. Thus prayer serves as the mediary between the state of existence and spiritual existence. As long as prayer is stirred, it belongs to the sphere of the soul's existence, but when it has entered that other sphere, then prayer stops.

Just as the saints do not actually pray in the New World, once the intellect has been swallowed up in the spirit, but dwell in wonder in that delightful glory, so too, when the intellect has been held worthy of perceiving that blessed state of bliss which is to come, it forgets itself and everything else here; and it is no longer stirred by the thought of anything.

One can confidently go so far as to say that every virtue that exists, all the various

kinds of prayers—whether bodily or
mental—are initiated and governed by the
will's free choice; this also includes the intellect which has authority over the senses.
But once the Spirit's activity starts to reign
over the intellect—the orderer of senses
and thoughts—, then the inborn, natural
free choice is removed, and the intellect is
then itself guided, and no longer guides. So
how can there be prayer at that time, when
what is endowed by nature no longer has
authority over itself, being guided in a direction which it does not know? It does not
direct the stirrings in the mind in the way it
wants, but a captive state reigns over what
is endowed by nature at that time, guiding
it in a direction of which it is not aware.
For a person no longer has a will at that
time, and does not even know whether he
is in a body or without a body—as Scrip-
ture testifies.* Can a person who is taken   *cf 2 Cor 12:2*
captive in this way have prayer, when he
does not even know himself? Accordingly
no one should blasphemously claim that
there is someone who can make bold to say
that it is possible to pray spiritual prayer.
This audacity is something which the Mes-
salians claim for themselves—haughty
ignorants who let it be known of themselves that whenever they wish for prayer
of the Spirit they are able to pray it. But the
humble, who have insight and submit
themselves to learn from the Fathers, and
who know what are the bounds of the natural person, give no thought to such
audacity.

Why, then, is this ineffable gift given the

name of 'prayer' when it is not prayer? The
reason, we say, is this: as the gift is granted
to those who are worthy at the time of
prayer, so it has prayer as its starting point.
For there is no other occasion for so glorious a gift to be granted apart from this time
of prayer, as the Fathers testify. Furthermore we observe from the lives of saints
that in the case of many of them, their intellect was seized while they were standing
in prayer.

Someone may ask, 'Why do these great
and ineffable gifts only occur at this time of
prayer?' Our reply is, 'It is because at this
time, more than at any other, a person is
recollected and in a state of preparedness to
gaze towards God, yearning and hoping for
mercy from him.' In brief, it is the time
when a person is standing at the King's
door, making his request, and it is appropriate that the request of someone who supplicates with real desire should be accorded
to him then. For when is a person so attentive, and in such a state of readiness and
preparedness, as he is at the time when he
prays? Or would it be befitting that a person be held worthy of it while he is asleep,
or doing something, or is distracted in his
mind? The saints, however, have not ever
had any moment of idleness, for all their
time is spent occupied with things spiritual: when they are not standing in readiness for prayer, they will usually be
meditating on certain stories in the Scriptures, or their intellect is meditating in contemplation of creation, or other such things
as are profitable for meditation. But it is

particularly at the time of prayer that the gaze is fixed upon God, and the entire momentum of its movement is stretched out toward him, as it offers to him supplications from the heart with an impelling and fervent intensity. For this reason it is appropriate that divine grace should spring up just at the moment when a single thought occupies the soul.

For we can see the same thing with the gift of the Spirit upon the visible Offering we make. When everyone is standing in prayer in readiness, making earnest supplication, with the intellect concentrated on God, it is then that the Spirit descends upon the Bread and Wine that are laid upon the altar.

It was also at the time of prayer that the angel appeared to Zechariah, announcing to him the conception of John;* and in Peter's case, it was when he was praying on the roof, at the prayer of the sixth hour,* that the revelation was seen by him, indicating the accession of the Peoples by means of the sheet let down from heaven with wild animals on it. And what is written about Cornelius' vision happened when he was praying.* And in the case of Joshua son of Nun, God spoke with him when he was prostrate on his face in prayer.* The same applied to the plate† placed on top of the Ark,* from which the priest learnt from God whatever was necessary by revelation once a year, when the High Priest entered,† at the solemn moment of prayer, while all the tribes of Israel were gathered and standing in awe and

Lk 1:13

Ac 10:9–16

Ac 10:1–8

Josh 7:6–15
†*[NEB 'cover'; RSV 'mercy seat']*
Ex 25:21–2
†*Lev 16 & Heb 9:7*

Num 20:6 trembling in the outer tent* in prayer: the
High Priest entered the inner sanctuary, and
while he lay prostrate on his face, the utterances of God were audible from within that
plate which was over the Ark, by means of
an awesome and ineffable revelation. How
fearful was that mystery which was carried
out on that occasion. It is the same with all
the revelations and visions which have
come to the saints: they have all occurred at
the time of prayer.

What time is more holy and more appropriate for sanctification and for the receiving of divine gifts than the time of prayer,
when a person is speaking with God? It is
then, when someone is engaged in supplicating and beseeching God, with every
stirring and every thought forcibly concentrated, as he thinks on God alone, with his
entire mind swallowed up in discourse with
him, his heart filled with him. It is from this
point onwards that the Holy Spirit, in accordance with a person's capacity and
complementing what he is praying, sets in
motion in him certain inaccessible insights,
with the result that prayer is cut off from
any movement by these very insights, and
the intellect is swallowed up in wonder,
forgetting the desired object of its supplication: instead its stirrings are submerged (*or*
baptized) in a profound inebriation, and the
person is no longer in this world. There is
no longer any discernment of either body
or soul there, or any recollection of anything. As Evagrius says,[12] 'Prayer is the state
of the mind which is only cut off from the
light of the Holy Trinity by wonder'. You

have seen how prayer is cut off by wonder at the insights which are born in the mind as a result of prayer as I said at the beginning of this treatise, and in many other places hitherto.

Evagrius also says,[13] 'The state of the intellect is the summit of intelligible reality; it resembles the colour of the heaven, for in it at the time of prayer there arises the light of the Holy Trinity'. And when someone is held worthy of this grace being raised to this majestic state at the time of prayer, he says:[14] 'When the intellect strips off the old person and through graces puts on the new,* then it sees its state at the time of prayer to resemble sapphire,† the colour of the heaven, which was named the "place of God"* by the Elders of Israel by whom it was seen on the mountain'.

cf Eph 4:22–4, Col 3:9–10
†Ex 24:9–10
*Ex 24:11 (LXX)

Accordingly, as I have said, this gift should not be called 'spiritual prayer'. What should it be called? The offspring of pure prayer that is swallowed up by the Spirit. From that point on, the mind is beyond prayer, and prayer has ceased from it now that it has found something even more excellent. No longer does the mind actually pray, but there is a gaze of wonder at the inaccessible things which do not belong to the world of mortal beings, and the mind is stilled, not having knowledge of anything here. This is the 'unknowing' of which it is said, 'Blessed is the person who has reached the unknowing during prayer which cannot be surpassed', as Evagrius said.[15]

3. ISAAC OF NINEVEH,
Selections from *Centuries on Knowledge*

I.42. Prayer deprived of contemplation is full of interruption, and such prayer can hardly be prayed. This occurs as a result of thick darkness of mind, which in turn is caused by the senses being greatly fragmented: fragmentation of the senses leads to fragmentation of the intellect; out of this a thick darkness springs up in the mind.

Whosoever prays in a state of contemplation resides in delights: he prays with pleasure and remains in prayer without any effort.

IV.32. Purity of prayer is silence from the converse of bodily thoughts, and the uniterrupted movement of the things which give delight to the soul.

IV.34. You should not wait until you are cleansed of wandering thoughts before you desire to pray: such distraction is not banished from the mind except by assiduous prayer entailing much labour. If you only begin on prayer when you see that your mind has become perfect and exalted above all recollection of the world, then you will never pray.

IV.63. We should realize this too: the consolation given to someone in prayer and in the Office is better than the consolation that comes in reading or in contemplating the created world—even though these are important activities. Belonging to a separate category of their own amongst the consolations which give joy to those at an intermediary stage are those consolations which people of an advanced stage also receive from Scripture and the verses which cause them wonder. But you should understand that the consolation which a solitary receives from external sources—through the movement of the tongue, or by sight or hearing—is inferior to the consolation which stems solely from the heart, without any mediator. This may occur either by means of prayer which is more interiorized than any prayer on the lips[16] or it may suddenly occur in the mind, manifesting itself without any material vehicle. Such a revelation belongs to the Spirit, and is a kind of prophecy, for the heart is in fact prophesying, in that the Spirit is revealing to it hidden matters, over which not even the Holy Scriptures have authority. What Scripture was not permitted to reveal, the pure mind is authorized to know—something that goes beyond what was entrusted to Scripture! Nevertheless the fountainhead for all these things is the reading of Scripture: from it comes the mind's beauty.

Comment:[17] All these things are born out of the reading of Scripture: even pure prayer itself is born from such reading. Likewise recollection of the mind comes from this reading. Out of it all these things are fashioned, and have reached the mind's perception. Any prayer which is not born out of much assiduousness in reading Scripture is like a body which has no legs but wishes to run. I am speaking of the kind of reading which is appropriate for such minds, urging them on to their goal by means of its insights.

64. Since we are going to speak on the topic of prayer and since many people are desirous of knowing the stage they have reached by means of those stages which are recognizable in prayer, we propose briefly to distinguish these stages in prayer. So sharpen your senses and purify and recollect your understanding from distraction, then let us pay especial attention to the intellect as we cross over, with its help, to the wondrous staging post which consists in rest for all one's way of life, for within it is situated divine rest. Indeed the entire upright course and fair human endeavour of those who have despised the spectacle of things visible and subject to corruption has its gaze fixed on this goal, seeking to be held worthy of pure prayer and the enjoyment of this.

65. First of all, bear this in mind: we are not prepared to speak about things which go beyond nature, only about things that belong to nature and come under the category of pure prayer, for many are hesitant about such things. I do this because the majority of diligent and illumined brethren experience these things, having reached this staging post, each travelling according to his different stage of advancement.

From these things it is also possible for human nature to pass on to those other stages.

Anyone who is watchful, has a rule of prayer, and is a disciple of stillness will find this appropriate reading. But for someone

with a different way of life, who is at a
different stage, the labour involved in such
things, as well as any investigation into
them, will seem like a waste of time, as will
the guarding of the mind's boundaries in
prayer and the learning about its different
kinds of impulses.

Therefore examine carefully the mind's
path during times of prayer to see what the
aim of its course is; see whether its prayer
flows forth smoothly and abundantly, or
whether it is cut short and comes spasmod-
ically: and if the latter, observe whether it
is the result of the mind's stammering or
whether it is held back from advancing as a
result of the immense light of some insight.
Prayer may flow for one person, whereas
for another this other situation may apply.
Again, one person's prayer may be tranquil,
and another's agitated and fervent; one person will pray from the depths of the mind,
while another from the flow of his
thoughts. Sometimes prayer issues from a
person's groaning, at other times unbear-
able stirrings from within cause prayer to
burst forth. A person's particular stage is
made clear by these different things which
happen, and which stage is superior is
made clear from the occurence of the stirrings that belong to each of these stages.
For from the perseverance of particular stirrings a man will recognize that he is standing in the ranks of the penitent; the same
applies to someone who has begun to see
the splendour of his own soul, or who is
travelling half-way along the road of repentance, or who has completed it and begun

to receive the pledge of delights—I refer to
the gifts that follow after repentance. But
all these things belong only to the diligent:
none of what has been mentioned applies
to the lax—only to those who take care in
the matter of prayer, who have an obliga-
tory rule of prayer to ensure that it is
cherished.

But let us come on to real prayer and
briefly illumine the lower stages by means
of those which are more exalted.

66. Intensity of stirrings in prayer is not
an exalted part of pure prayer, even though
it is good; this belongs to fervour. When it
occurs having repentance as its aim, being
intermingled with suffering, or attendant
on joy, then it is very good. Nevertheless it
belongs only to the second or third rank. I
do not mean to say that you are not travelling on the right path when these things
apply to you; rather I just mean that these
things belong not to the highest, but only
to the intermediate stages. What is the most
precious and the principle characteristic in
pure prayer is the brevity and smallness of
any stirrings, and the fact that the mind
simply gazes as though in wonder during
this diminution of active prayer. From this,
one of two things occurs to the mind in
connection with that brief stirring which
wells up in it: either it withdraws into silence, as a result of the overpowering might
of the knowledge which the intellect has
received in a particular verse; or it is held
in delight at that point at which it was aiming at during the prayer when it was stirred,

and the heart cultivates it with an insatiable yearning of love.

These are the principal characteristics of pure prayer. Let these serve as indications for you during the time of prayer. Observe in which of these different states the mind is to be fixed during these various parts of prayer: whether in the former states, or in those that follow on.

67. If the heart flows forth smoothly and abundantly with long drawn out prayer, combined with intensity of diverse stirrings, then this is a sign of fervour; it is an indication that the mind has not yet become aware of the light contained in the words, nor yet received experience of the knowledge which illumines the inner eye during the time of prayer; but the mind nonetheless receives strength from the things that the heart—or the lips—cause to flow forth.

If the mind becomes aware of the power inherent in what it is praying and becomes illumined by the truth inherent in the words, this is a sign that this awareness is not allowing him to travel on and add to the wealth of utterance, but is straightway about to bind him by means of one of two ways which we explained a little earlier.

68. This too we should realize: the length and duration of prayer does not come from a superabundance of words or from the use of long and varied phrases; rather it is the result of the fountain of knowledge and the power of the utterances that is revealed to the mind at that moment. From this we should learn that when the

mind is illumined in prayer, insight does
not shine out for it in all the words of one's
supplication or in all the verses used in the
Office; no, the mind only receives the
power of one small verse when it is illumined; and as a result of that verse by
which it was illumined it turns to perception. Up to this point its course was bub-
bling forth, but as long as the illumination
from that particular verse lasts in the mind,
the natural faculties are powerless to leave
that verse and pass on to another. But once
the illumination is removed, then they can
pass on to other verses, though wherever
the mind is illumined by one of them, it
pauses there, being brought to a stop.
Where then is the need for an intense flow
of stirrings when all is well with the mind?
Or for long strings of words and sequence
of varied verses, if there is no longer any
reason to turn to multiplicity, once a person has prayed attentively, resulting in the
opening up of the understanding?

69. In all this it is not a limping mind
that I am extolling; all I am saying is that
the mind may be held back from its course
as a result of much illumination. Nor do I
reject intensity of prayer or object to
lengthy Offices; rather, it is the more excellent ordering to be found in them that I am
trying to illumine, illustrating the gifts that
occur during them, thus providing an indication of the stature that someone's mind
has reached during prayer and the Office.
For this reason we should not test the illumination of our mind during the time of
supplications by means of the abundance

and wealth of words of our prayer. Rather, we should rely on the fact that even if our prayer is only limited, it will be easily obvious when the mind receives the power to be found there: the mind will clothe itself in the delight that exists in these words which have been made the vehicle of prayer, through whose mediation the intellect receives an outpouring of words which are beyond articulation, and within which is located the silence of insight: this is precisely the prayer which exists naturally within us in unembodied form; it is the enlightened mind.

4. ISAAC OF NINEVEH,
Texts On Prayer And Outward Posture During Prayer

IN SUMMARY the topic of this discourse concerns the following:

That it is not right for us to be idle, with empty minds, from the bodily labours and reverent postures that are appropriate for prayer, even if we should be raised to the heights in our way of life. What I have in mind here is the appointed period of standing during the Office and the visible prostration of the body, etc.

From what great evils the Office of the Psalms delivers us.

On how we should consider, on those occasions when we are held worthy of this gift, that purity of prayer and the mind's vision that belongs to it, consisting in spiritual insights, constitute the fulfilment of the Office and of its entire ordering.

On the misfortunes that will overtake, as a result of abandonment by God, those who despise the reverent outward forms, along with the awe and reverence that should properly be shown during prayer.

And some other topics.

1. There are four kinds of change of activity applicable to all persons, at whatever stage they are. One can change one's activity as a result of a wise and laudable discernment and a godly disposition. Or change can occur as a result of a corrupted mind and a lax and foolish disposition. Or it can happen under the constraint of pressing reasons and unavoidable circumstances. It can also happen as a result of the activity of divine compassion.

This also applies to the case of the wonderful mode of life of solitaries: any change in this way of life that occurs to anyone can be recognized by that person as belonging to one of these four varieties of which I have spoken: either it comes about through the wisdom of the love of God, when someone sets his mind on some excellent goal; or it may be the result of a corrupted disposition and a laxity which has got the better of someone, when he exchanges the ministry of his former customary and laud-

able way of life for one that is inferior; or
there is the case where, under the constraint of the spiritual delight in God which
he glimpses, thanks to divine working, the
customary labouring after virtue is altered
by grace and rejuvenated, so as to become a
more exalted kind of toil: then, as a result
of the wonderful taste and discovery of a
more exalted knowledge, his former course
of labour is rebuked when he glimpses
something sweeter in taste and more glorious than the labour at which he was previously toiling. And sometimes the mind is
enriched by the stirring of the things with
which it is occupied, and it becomes interiorized from the outward labour involving
the senses, according to the recognized
norm of all ascetics. This occurs in accordance with the measure, time and strength
of one's way of life. There is also the case
where change results from the constraint of
demonic attack, or the inroads of sickness
and weakness.

Accordingly, my brethren, whenever
some change is to be seen in our way of
life. We should immediately rush off to see
its cause, and find out from what quarter
the altered custom is peering out, and
whence comes that novelty that does not
resemble the normal course of solitaries or
their common monastic rule. Then either
our joy will increase, or we will fittingly be
put to confusion when we do not act well.
In this we can always be in a state of awareness concerning our way of life, being
above that understanding which looks in a
corporeal fashion at both the outward as-

pects of the thoughts, and at words and actions; rather we can gain wisdom at once, right at the start, for the thoughts, words and actions are the product of these various causes.

2. The following is a bad sign when it appears: that someone should neglect the duty of the Offices without any pressing reason. But if it is prayer which has drawn someone to neglect these times, and if it is the compulsion and weighty experience of long drawn out prayer which has led him to desist from them, or if the delay brought about by prayer's overpowering pleasure causes him to neglect the time of Office, then this person has chanced upon a splendid piece of merchandise, as a result of the change brought about by the enviable object which has fallen into his hands. As it is written, *The lines have fallen for me in excellent places.** All is well, provided he does not neglect the time of the Office as a result of empty ideas or a contemptuous attitude, but rather the sweet delight found in prayer has held him fast, as a result of the constraint of divine love—for this, after all, is the fulfilment of our religious worship, and is not constrained by, or subject to, any rule. And if such things occur to someone continually—and they are a sign of divine gifts and a mighty opening to purity of prayer—, and especially if he manifests a reverential outward posture and profound reverence during his prayer, then that person is quickly raised to the rank of the perfected.

But if someone decides to abandon what

Ps 16:6

belongs first of all, without yet having found what comes afterwards, then it is clear that he is being mocked by the demons, and through their agency he is going to fall away completely from his life; from this point onwards the beginning of his downward path gets the better of him.

We should be aware of this too: the search for these discoveries is superfluous for beginners, even though such people may be well trained in doctrine. This also applies to those who wish to become aware of these things in themselves without possessing strict vigilance and the awareness that comes from stillness.

3. There cannot be recollection of mind and purity in prayer without much vigilance over speech and action, as well as a guard over the senses; nor can the awareness that is given by grace come about unless a person has acquired much discernment by means of stillness.

4. It is in proportion to the honour which someone shows in his person to God during the time of prayer, both with his body and with the mind, that the door to assistance will be opened for him, leading to the purifying of the impulses and to illumination in prayer.

5. Someone who shows a reverential posture during prayer, by stretching out his hands to heaven as he stands in modesty, or by falling on his face to the ground, will be accounted worthy of much grace from on high as a result of these lowly actions.

Anyone who continuously adorns his prayer with such outward postures will swiftly and quickly be accounted worthy of the activity of the Holy Spirit, for the Lord is accounted great in his eyes, thanks to the honour he shows in the sacrifices which he presents before the Lord at those times which have been set apart for him, [*or* by him] by the law of free will.

6. You should realize, my brethren, that in all our service God very much wants outward postures, specific kinds of honour, and visible forms of prayer—not for his own sake, but for our benefit. He himself is not profited by such things, nor does he lose anything when they are neglected; rather, they are for the sake of our feeble nature. Had such things not been requisite, he would not have adopted such postures for himself during his incarnation—thus speaking with us in the Holy Scriptures.

He cannot be dishonoured by anything, seeing that honour belongs to him by his very nature. But we, as a result of slovenly habits and various outward actions which lack reverence, acquire an attitude of mind that dishonours him. Consequently we fall from grace of our own will, seeing that we are subject to backsliding: then we are assailed by incessant attacks and continual deception from the demons, as we acquire a nature that loves ease and is easily swayed to evil actions.

7. Many people despise these outward forms in their thoughts and suppose that prayer of the heart suffices by itself for God, claiming, as they lie on their backs or are sitting in a disrespectful manner, that there should only be an interior recollec-

tion of God; they are not concerned at all
with adorning the visible side of their worship with prolonged standing, corresponding to their body's strength, or with making
the venerable sign of the cross over their
organs of senses. Nor are they concerned,
as they kneel on the ground, to act like
those about to draw close to a flame and to
take upon themselves, both inwardly and
outwardly, a reverential attitude, or to accord special honour to the Lord, honouring
him with all their limbs and with reverence
on their faces. This is because they have not
perceived the might of the Adversary they
have, and as a result they are handed over
to the workings of falsehood, not having
understood that they are still mortal and
liable to be stirred by their soul, which is
subject to backsliding; they do not realize
that they have not yet reached the state of
spiritual beings, or that the resurrection has
not yet taken place and they have not yet
achieved a state of immutability. During the
body's life, when human nature is in need
of labour and training in new things all the
time, they have wanted to lead their lives in
a purely spiritual state, without being involved in those things which necessarily
daily constrain the world which is subject
to the passions. Imagining in themselves
that they are wise, they have acted with
disrespect, in that the sign of pride and disrespect for God has appeared in them. As a
result they have doubled their perdition by
means of prayer—which is properly the
fountainhead of all life; this is because they
supposed they could offer disrespect to that

Honour which is not to be disrespected,
and who is to be honoured by all created
beings.

8. We do not force the sick or the infirm
to abide by a rule, nor do we say that someone should subject himself to impossibili-
ties. Everything that takes place with
reverence and trembling and as a result of
the exigency of the occasion is seen by God
as a choice offering, even if it lies outside
the custom of the rule. Not only does he
attach no blame to the person who so acts,
but he accepts with a good will the paltry
and insignificant things done for his sake
along with mighty and perfect actions. And
even if they are blameworthy, they are
borne with mercy, and are forgiven their
author, without any blame, by the omni-
scient God to whom all things are revealed
before they happen, and who was aware of
the constraints of our human nature before
he created us. For God, who is good and
compassionate, is not in the habit of judg-
ing the infirmities of human nature or actions brought about by necessity—even
though they may be reprehensible; but he
does judge actions that are possible, but
which are nonetheless scorned. He does
not judge human nature's inclination towards anything—even if it were to result in
some great and voluntary sin on taking effect: rather, it is the eventual action that he
judges, making exaction with justice, wherever he knows that it will be followed by
compunction and mental suffering. This is
all the more the case when someone has
not given himself wholly over to perdition:

suffering affects him as he gazes at the
plight of his enslavement that leads no-
where; he despises himself and is eager to
make amends, as he grieves over his short-
comings or over his lapses. Not only is such
a person not rejected by the Will which
performs all things, but without any doubt
he is actually close to mercy.

Though we have said all this, we nevertheless reprove those who upset the order
of prayer out of their own wilfulness,
whose foolish mind feigns perfection, and
with a false knowledge they contrive to create one thing or another by themselves.

9. The heart acquires greater freedom of
speech with God during prayer than it does
during the Office. But complete neglect of
the Office causes pride, and it is out of
pride that one falls away from God. You
see, the very fact that someone forces himself to be subjected to a rule—when he is
quite free in his way of life—keeps the soul
humble, and offers no opportunity for the
demon of pride to dangle before him some
evil thought. By continually considering
himself as insignificant and not capable of
freedom, he humbles and brings low any
haughtiness of thought. There is no more
effective bridle than this to place in the
mouth of the mind that exalts itself.

This is why the holy Fathers—even
though they possessed continual prayer, being filled with the Spirit and never ceasing
for a moment from prayer—used to observe, not only in the matter of the Office,
but also in that of prayer as well, all that
was ordained in the matter of times set

apart, and the specifically fixed numbers of
prayers, involving the visible participation
of the body and performed with kneelings;
all this they did following the aim of
the rule which they had decreed for
themselves.

10. It was not to no purpose that these
Fathers imposed upon themselves, in some
cases one hundred, in others fifty or sixty,
etc., prayers—even though they had already entirely become altars of prayer. Why
were fixed numbers so necessary, when
they never ceased from prayer? It is said
that Evagrius had one hundred, the blessed
Macarius sixty, and Moses the Black, the
Ethiopian, had fifty, whereas a certain great
solitary, Paul, had three hundred; and so
on.[18] The reason why these blessed Fathers
compelled themselves actively to keep such
rules was fear of pride. They carried out
these fixed numbers of prayers accompanied by labour of the body, involving specific acts of worship, with prostrations in
front of the cross. It was not the case, as
detractors say, that these fixed numbers of
prayers related concerning them were
prayers which just took place in the heart;
this is what people with Messalian opinions
proclaim concerning them, those who say
that outward forms of worship are unneces-
sary. Far be it that such a thing should be
said of the holy Fathers! We are not concerned here to rebuke or censure the faults
of others—nor do we despise those who do
this; but seeing that we are about to speak
of and to transmit the truth, unless falsehood is first openly rebuked, one cannot

have assurance of the truth, or cultivate it with a clearly defined attitude of love, or be wary of its opposite. And even those who travel on a straight path walk all the more confidently upon it once the road that leads astray has been openly pointed out.

These Fathers' acts of worship were very real, and in particular by their means the soul was kept humble. They carried them all out, taking care to stand up from their places as they did so—provided they were not prevented by physical weakness—with great reverence and deep humility of mind, lying prostrate on their faces before the cross. These acts of worship were quite separate from those which took place in the heart. Nevertheless, each time they stood up, they performed many acts of worship, their body assisting them as the occasion might allow, kissing the cross five or maybe ten times, reckoning each act of worship and kiss as a single prayer. During such acts all of a sudden someone might sometimes discover a pearl which in a single prayer would encompass the number of all the others. Sometimes a man would be standing on his feet, or kneeling, his mind seized by the wonder of prayer—a state not under the control of the will of flesh and blood and the soul's impulses. Or he might be in one of those states of purity of prayer which we will later elucidate.

In this manner the Fathers used to carry out their large numbers of prayers, just as I have described. It was not, as many people suppose, and as others also claim, that they distinguished a separate time of standing for each prayer individually—for the wretched body is not capable of such numbers, standing up separately for each separate prayer. On this reckoning all the prayers would never be achieved, if someone were to arise from his place a hundred times in a day, or fifty, or sixty times—not to mention three hundred or more, as was the custom of some of the saints; otherwise there would not have been any room for reading or any of the other requirements. Nor would there have been any opportunity for prolonging prayer, should it happen that the gift of tears were granted by grace during someone's prayer, or the limpid stirrings to draw out one's prayer, as is the case with those who have been counted worthy of one of these kinds of grace at such times. Instead, such a person's Office would be turbulent, and he would be filled with turmoil in all he did.

If someone does not believe this, let him experiment on himself and see whether he can get up tranquilly from his place fifty times during a day—let alone a hundred or two hundred times—, being undisturbed in himself and his prayer remaining peaceful, fulfilling his Office, and his appointed scriptural reading—which contributes a large part of prayer—still unperturbed; will he manage to do this for seven days—let alone all the days of his life?

11. Sometimes gifts that are partial occur during prayer, such as a profusion of tears, or a delight welling up in the heart resembling honey from a honeycomb, or a burst-

ing up of thanksgiving, which silence the
tongue with the humbleness of the joy; or
it may be a sudden stirring of hope during
prayer, or some insight into divine providence, such as is wont to burst forth from
prayer itself or from the recollection of
what one has read just before it; this sort of
insight lingers on many hours, as a person
lies prostrate on his face, overcome by one
of those altered states which belong to the
gift of purity of prayer with its concomitant
delights. Or sometimes this occurs when a
person is standing, or when he is kneeling.
Such things are reckoned by the Fathers as
purity of prayer, and not as rapture of the
intellect. This latter is a gift which is all
inclusive, the sum of divine workings,
which is accorded to the perfect. Now
these partial gifts are granted to those at an
intermediate stage as well as to the advanced during the remainder of their time
of prayer. They belong to the natural world
and are given in accordance with diligence
and vigilance, whereas the other gift is
supernatural.

Gifts, such as illumination of insights and
a precise understanding of the verses of
Scripture, act for the intellect of the saints
during prayer and the Office as a rope by
which the naked intellect is held back from
distraction and brought close to God. Without them there is no other laudable way
for the intellect to cease from external
thoughts and recollect itself during the Office and in prayer—unless of course one
follows those who teach that we should
abandon divine reflection and the exact en-

quiry into the senses of the verses, while
they cause their mind to wander with
imaginings, as though they possessed a capability for this which excelled that of
secular people. But what occasions illumination of the thoughts during prayer, as a
result of some stirring during the divine
Mysteries, is a thing which most people
lack, and which is to be found only with a
few, being something which requires tranquillity and great wariness and purity of
mind. Imaginings of the mind, and the voluntary binding of the thought to some image or phantasy, is something within the
grasp of a secular person as well: it does
not require purity or tranquillity, or living
in the desert. If these people were right,
what would be the purpose of all the
trouble of the solitary life and of purity
from the 'world' or the illumination of
thoughts resulting from the time of prayer?
We would be enduring all this to no purpose, and our labours would be in vain, if
the object of our hope only extended to
that which a secular person, despite being
involved in the world, and tied to a wife
and children, is capable of achieving.

12. The true vision of Jesus Christ our
Lord consists in our realizing the meaning
of his Incarnation for our sakes, and becoming inebriated with love of him as a
result of the insights into the many wondrous elements contained in that vision.

13. The Office of psalmody is a rule
which subjects the soul to the humility that
belongs to servitude.

14. In this rule there is liberty, and in

liberty there is a rule. Some people are tested and excel as a result of the rule, others as a result of the liberty which comes from it.

15. In freedom someone makes more progress than when subject to a rule. Nevertheless often enough out of freedom there spring up many paths leading to error; in freedom there lurk many varieties of downfall. Whereas with a rule no one ever goes astray; those who persevere under the yoke of some rule will only be driven to some downfall once they have abandoned that rule and disregarded it. For this reason the saints of old who completed their course without going astray, governed themselves by means of some rule. Many people, however, having left behind the requirements of their rule, and by labouring far beyond what was laid down, have added to their diligence; nevertheless their extra labours have not prevented them from falling into the hands of demons once they had left their rule. No one is able to gainsay this, for the narratives concerning these men shine forth like the rays of the sun for our enlightenment.

16. There is a rule involving liberty and there is a rule for slaves: a rule that enslaves says 'I will recite such and such psalms during the Office, and every time I pray I will say the same fixed number'. Such a person is inalterably bound by obligation, without the possibility of change, to these same psalms all his days—all because he is tied to the obligation to follow the details of the number, length, and fixed character of the

psalms which he has decreed and fixed for himself. All this is utterly alien to the path of true knowledge, for such a person does not bear in mind either divine activity or the feebleness of nature, or the hazard of frequent battles: in the first case grace may be given so that he tarries beyond what his will has decreed; in the second case human nature may prove too weak to fulfill the rule, under the constraint of the demons by whom it is attacked—demons who are specifically provided for the subduing of pride.

17. The rule of liberty consists in one's unfailing observance of the seven Offices, ordained for our chaste mode of life by the holy Church at the hands of the Fathers who were assembled by the Holy Spirit for the ecumenical synod [at Nicaea]. Far be it from us solitaries that we should not be subject to the Church or her hierarchs or rulers. This is precisely the reason why we observe the ordinance of the seven times of the Office, in conformity with what the Church has laid down for us, as her children. This does not mean, however, that for each Office I should perform the same particular fixed number of psalms; nor does one fix a particular number of prayers to be said between these Offices, during both night and day. And one does not set a time limit for each of these prayers, nor does one decide upon specific words to use. Rather, one spends as long on each prayer as grace provides the strength, asking whatever the pressing need of the moment may require, using whatever prayer one is stirred to use. And while such a person

prays he is all the more recollected and undistracted in view of the delight of this
kind of prayer. During such prayers a person measures his request in conformity
with the strength of human nature and the
wisdom that the Lord accords to him.

18. If someone says that we should recite
the prayer uttered by our Saviour in all our
prayers using the same wording and keeping the exact order of the words, rather
than their sense, such a person is very deficient in his understanding of our Saviour's
purpose in uttering this prayer, nor has he
ever drawn close to the thinking of the
blessed Interpreter.[19] Our Lord did not
teach us a particular sequence of words
here; rather the teaching he provided in
this prayer consists in showing us what we
should be focussing our minds on during
the entire course of this life. It was the
sense that he gave us, and not the precise
sequence of words to be recited by our lips.
Thus, whenever we set this prayer before
our minds as something to aim at, we will
pray following its sense, and we will direct
the movements of our own prayer in accordance with it, as we ask for the Kingdom
and righteousness,* or, as may sometimes   *cf Mt 6:33*
be the case, for escape from temptations;
and at times we may be asking for the needs
of our human nature, that is, for sustenance
for the day; likewise with all the other
things, in accordance with the aims with
which he provided us, telling us what we
should pray for. So our prayer should be
inspired by its sense, and we should conduct ourselves in strict accordance with it

as we pray this prayer that our Lord taught us.

This is the way those who are illumined and endowed in insight understand this tradition handed down by our Lord in the form of a prayer; they are not concerned with the sequence and order of words. Nor indeed was our Lord concerned here with the precise order of words when he provided teaching suited to the wording of a prayer, instilling insight into the disciples. Rather, he was instructing us not to intermingle into prayer, as do the pagans, all sorts of other things which are contrary to his commandments.

It is a childish mentality which investigates and is concerned with the exact sequence of words, rather than setting its sights on their sense, out of which spring forth prayers, requests and reflections excellently suited to conduct in the New World. Altering the outward form of the words of the prayer which our Lord handed down makes no difference provided our prayer stems from its sense, and that the mind follows that sense.

19. I am anxious that whoever loves instruction should be preserved from all harm—that is to say, that anyone who is concerned with discovering the true meaning of the Scriptures should not stumble in anything and reckon advantageous things to be harmful, or understand anything solely on the basis of its simple outer form.

When you hear stories about certain of the solitaries, how so-and-so was harmed by continuous prayer, or how some of them

were led astray by demons because they despised the psalms or did nothing else except pray continuously, and afterwards
many of them came to harm or were
mocked by delusions, etc., do not be perturbed or upset here as a result of superficial external report; and do not fall into
doubt over things that are beneficial in the
process of setting right all our corrupt
state. It is not continuous prayer which is
the cause of going astray, nor the omission
of some psalms, provided there is an appropriate reason for this, nor do we go on to
account prayer, the source of life, and the
labour involved in it as something which
leads to error. Rather, error came when certain people abandoned the prayers' venerable outward forms, turning instead to
their own rules and special customs which
they had laid down for themselves according to their own whim, and when they
completely deprived themselves of the
Holy Mysteries, instead despising and
scorning them; when they deprived themselves furthermore of the light of the divine
Scriptures, and failed to study the teaching
of the words of the Fathers which give instructions about stratagems against the demons; when they gave up the various acts
of humility, prostrations, continual falling
upon the ground, a suffering heart, and the
submissive postures appropriate to prayer,
modest standing, hands clasped in submissive fashion, or stretched out to heaven, the
senses respectful during prayer. Instead
they seized upon various forms of pride, as
a result mingling with their prayer insult

towards God; they accompanied their
prayer with haughty outward postures, forgetting how exalted is the Divine Nature
and how their own nature is but dust. Yet in
all this the words of their prayer were no
different from those of the psalms.

Most prayers, in fact, consist of words
chosen from psalms containing ideas and
sentiments of grief and supplication, or of
thanksgiving and praise, etc. Thus sometimes when someone is kneeling with his
face bowed, or has his fingers and gaze
raised to heaven, he will add feeling to the
words and repeat them slowly. On occasion the feeling and pain of his heart will
cause all sorts of deeply-felt words of
prayer; or joy may burst forth in response
to something, stirring that person to alter
his prayer to praises owing to the delight
his mind feels. The same applies to the
other stirrings comprised in prayer which
the Holy Spirit sets in motion in the saints,
in whose utterances are ineffable mysteries
and insights. And when the outward form
of prayer provides some sign of the insights
they contain, this is an indication of the
mysteries and the perfect knowledge which
saints receive during their prayers, through
the wisdom of the Spirit.

A person either draws near to God or he
falls away from truth; this depends on the
direction towards which his mind is aimed
and not on the external features of what is
performed or neglected. Many of the early
Fathers—I refer to some of the great solitaries—did not even know the psalms, yet
their prayer ascended to God like fire, as a

result of their excellent ways and the
humility of mind which they had acquired.
Their words chased away demons like flies
which buzzed off as they approached. Many
people, however, have used prayer as an
excuse for slackness and pride: failing to
grasp the *better part,** they also lost the
part they had. Though they held nothing in
their hands, they imagined that they stood
in perfection. Others, merely on the basis
of the educational training they have had,
have supposed that this would be sufficient
to enable them to discover true knowledge:
relying on secular culture and ordinary
reading, they fell away from truth, and
failed to humble themselves so as to stand
up again.

Lk 10:42

20. If prayer is fulfilled together with its
outward forms, then this is the fulfilment,
not only of psalmody, but also of all the
virtues. To prevent us just listening to this
statement as something ordinary, let us examine and learn the truth by means of precise enquiry. Tell me, my brother, suppose
there is someone who, for three nights and
days, more or less, will lie prostrate before
the cross, as did some of the Fathers; or he
may receive the gift of tears during the Office—something which the majority of
rightminded brethren experience—tears
which so compel that brother with their
quantity that he is unable to complete the
Office, even though he struggles greatly to
do so: instead he has to abandon the Office
because of abundant weeping, and he is like
someone aroused from the depths, his
whole body becoming, so to say, a fountain

of weeping, stemming from the groaning of
heart produced by the grace that has been
stirred within him; he is drenched in tears;
or his tongue being silenced because of
some particular joy, in his stillness tears
burst forth and soak his face, owing to the
wondrous insights he has, while his soul
exults and is filled with hope that cannot be
cut off. Do you, my brother, consider as
idleness this abandonment of the Office,
this excellent altered state, along with the
various other things that happened to the
solitaries as they were in prayer during the
Office, not all of which is it permitted to
relate? What I have said applies to psalmody when it is swallowed up by purity of
prayer; it does *not* apply when this happens as a result of a corrupted Messalian
mentality, or out of lassitude and sloth.
Such an Office should be considered by us
as a completed work, for in it we have been
brought close to the succour that comes
from grace.

May God make us worthy of a taste of his
grace at all times, for by it we approach the
wonder that surrounds him, thanks to an
awareness, during our Offices and prayers,
of his great majesty. May he grant us the
wisdom of his mysteries, for by this we
shall be separated from the world and mingled in his love; through the prayer of our
Fathers who travelled along this road and
pleased him, ministering well before him,
amen.

5. ISAAC OF NINEVEH,
On Pure Prayer

A SECTION WHICH NICELY INDICATES AND
CLEARLY EXPLAINS WHAT IS PURE AND
UNDISTRACTED PRAYER

A WISE MAN, if he sets his face upon running off to find something that is both requisite and needful, for whose acquisition he lovingly yearns, should not proceed relying just on a superficial report, or rush off to find it without any further investigation, or without having first learnt how and what it is. Otherwise, when the acquisition of it is actually within his grasp, he may easily let it slip away through having failed to recognize it. Rather, he needs carefully to get a knowledge and understanding of the matter in hand—the sort of knowledge that is not mistaken; then, once he knows what it is like, he will know how to take care over its acquisition: exactly what he is running after and what to expect. Otherwise, his expectations may be set upon things that are impossible, rather than upon the reality of the matter in hand, which is quite possible to attain.

Purity of heart, O disciple of the truth, and the recollection of mind that exists in it, consist in the exact reflection on virtue in which we carefully engage at the time of prayer. Just as purity of heart, concerning which the Fathers diligently exhort, is not a

matter of someone being totally without
thought or reflection or movement, but
rather it consists in the heart being purified
of all evil, and in gazing favourably on everything, and considering it from God's point
of view. It is the same with pure and undistracted prayer: this does not mean that the
mind is entirely devoid of any thought or
wandering of any kind, but that it does not
wander about on empty subjects during the
time of prayer. It is not the case that the
mind is outside purity of prayer unless it
wanders about on something specifically
good, but it may also ponder on things that
are appropriate and think thoughts pleasing
to God during the time of prayer. Nor is it
required of someone that empty recollections should not come at all when he prays,
but he should not occupy himself with them
and be distracted by them. For there is a
good kind of wandering and a bad kind of
wandering. When you are in prayer, do not
seek to be entirely free of mental wandering,
which is impossible, but seek to wander following something that is good. For even
pure prayer consists in a wandering which
follows something—but this wandering is
excellent, seeing that the search for something good is excellent. Wandering is bad
when someone is distracted by empty
thoughts or by pondering on something
bad, and so he thinks evil thoughts when he
is praying before God.

Wandering is good when the mind
wanders on God during the entire extent of
his prayer, on his glory and majesty, stemming from a recollection of the Scriptures,

from an understanding of the divine utterances and holy words of the Spirit. In the
case of someone who struggles to tie down
his thought from wandering on such
things, or his mind from wandering of its
own accord on them during prayer, he is of
unparalleled stupidity if he thinks that this
kind of wandering is alien to, and outside
the limits of, pure prayer. For we do not
consider as alien to purity of prayer and
detrimental to recollection of thoughts in
prayer any profitable recollections that may
spring up from the Writings of the Spirit,
resulting in insights and spiritual understanding of the divine world during the
time of prayer. For someone to examine and
think in a recollected manner about the object of his supplication and the request of
his prayer, is an excellent kind of prayer,
provided it is consonant with the intention
of our Lord's commandments. This kind of
recollection of mind is very good.

If the mind is released from this prayer
and becomes diffused in things divine, or if
some excellent thought occurs to it, arising
out of Scripture's insights on God, insights
that are either individual to the person or
belong to the whole Christian community,
insights into God's dispensations and acts
of providence, whether they be those belonging to each successive day or universal
ones—all things by which the depth of the
heart is stirred towards the praise of God,
or to thanksgiving and joy at the immensity
of his compassion and love towards us; if
this happens this kind of wandering is even
better than prayer: however exalted and

pure someone's supplication may be, this is
the culmination of every kind of collected-
ness of mind and of excellence of prayer.
When the mind is entirely without any kind
of thought, this is silence of the mind and
not purity of prayer. It is one thing to pray
purely, and quite another for the mind to be
silent from any wandering at all or insight
into the words of prayer, and to remain
without any movement. No one is so stupid
as to want to find this by means of struggle
and the strength of his own will; for this is
the gift of the revelation of the intellect,
and it is not within the reach of pure
prayer, or a matter of the will.

Apart from this, the mind is able to
wander in prayer in the two ways we spoke
of, either in reflection on its requests, or in
contemplation on the Scriptures and a sage
reflection on God, the Lord of all, carried
out in a sensible way.[20]

If anyone thinks otherwise with respect
to purity of thoughts and recollection of
mind, supposing that there is some other
means of finding them, then he is infirm in
his ignorance and he is held back by a boor-
ish mind.

You are wise enough not to require of the
mind motionlessness—as do the fools; for
this cannot be asked of human nature.
Rather, strive to discover stirrings that are
good during the time of prayer, as the wise
do. These consist in: reflection on the
Spirit's insights, and sagacious thought
which considers during the time of prayer
how to please the will of the Maker of all:

this is the final end of all virtue and of all prayer.

When in these matters you receive the power that stems from grace to be bound firmly to their continual stirrings, you will become a *man of God** and will be close to spiritual things; close, too, to finding that for which you yearn without your being aware of it, namely, the apperception of God, the wonderment of mind that is free of all images, and the spiritual silence of which the Fathers speak. Blessed will you be, and held worthy of the great joy and gladness which exists in our Lord—to whom be praise and honour. And may he perfect us with knowledge of his mysteries, forever and ever, Amen.

1 Tim 6:11 2 Tim 3:7

BIBLIOGRAPHY AND NOTES

A. Discourse XXII and the other extracts from Part I of Isaac's collected works are translated from the edition by P. Bedjan, *Mar Isaacus Ninivita de Perfectione Religiosa* (Paris-Leipzig, 1909) as follows: 1(a) = pp. 32, 34; 1(b) = pp. 105–7; 1(c) = p. 144; 1(d) = pp. 439, 440; 1(e) = pp. 507–8; 2 = pp. 163–75. The remaining texts are all from the newly recovered Part II, and are translated from Oxford Bodleian MS syr.e.7, of the tenth/ eleventh century, as follows: text 3 = fol. 26b–27a, 88a–b, 96b–99b (roman numerals refer to the Century, arabic ones to the number of the text within the Century); text 4 = fol. 138a–146b; text 5 = fol. 146b–148b.

B. The article on Isaac by E. Khalifé-Hachem in *DSpir* 7 (1971) cols. 2041–54, gives a good overview. Brief introductions in English can be found in my 'St Isaac of Nineveh and Syriac spirituality', *Sobornost* 7:2 (1975) 79–89, and 'St Isaac of Nineveh', *The Way*, (Jan. 1981) 68–74. There is a complete English translation of the original Syriac text of Part I by A. J. Wensinck, *Mystic Treatises by Isaac of Nineveh* (Amsterdam, 1923; reprinted Wiesbaden, 1969). The French translation by J. Touraille, *Isaac le Syrien: oeuvres spirituelles* (Paris, 1981), and the more recent English translation, *The Ascetical Homilies of Saint Isaac the Syrian*, translated by the Holy Transfiguration Monastery (Boston, 1984), are both made from the Greek translation; this English translation (made by D. Miller) also has an excellent introduction and provides a table giving a concordance to differing numeration of the homilies in the Syriac and Greek traditions and includes translations of the Syriac homilies 49, 56, 71, 75, and 76 (pp. 387–396). There is also a recent Italian translation, from the Syriac original, of the first six chapters of Bedjan's edition by M. Gallo and P. Bettiolo, *Isacco di Ninive: Discorsi ascetici,* I (Rome, 1984). P. Bettiolo has also translated the four Centuries on Knowledge (which constitute nearly half of Part II of Isaac's works), *Isacco di Ninive: Discorsi spirituali* (Magnano; Communità di Bose, 1985). Some preliminary information on Part II of Isaac's works can be found in my 'Isaac of Nineveh: some newly discovered works', *Sobornost/Eastern Churches Review* 8:1 (1986) 28–33, and 'Lost—and refound: Part II of the Works of St Isaac of Nineveh', *Studia Patristica* XVIII (forthcoming). For the Book of Grace see G. Bunge, 'Mar Isaak von Nineveh und sein 'Buch der Gnade'', *Ostkirchliche Studien* 34 (1985) 3–22; some excerpts in English are given by D. Miller in *The Ascetical Homilies of St Isaac the Syrian* 397–426 (he doubts that they are by Isaac).

1. There follow some paragraphs which are not included in the extracts translated here.

2. Compare Evagrius, *Chapters on Prayer* 32 (CS4:60 = *Philokalia*, p. 60).

3. Evagrius, *Chapters on Prayer*, 15 (CS 4:58 = *Philokalia*, p. 58).

4. There follow some paragraphs which are not included in the extract translated here.

5. Reading *ᶜpyqwt* for *ᶜpypwt* ('redoubling'); so too (evidently) Wensinck in his translation.

6. Reading *wlmtḥsyw* for *wlmtḥsnw* ('being strengthened'), with the Greek and some Syriac manuscripts. For tears in Isaac, see D. A. Lichter in *Diakonia* 11 (1976) 239–58, and P. T. Mascia in *Diakonia* 14 (1979) 255–65.

7. Isaac singles out reptiles since, according to Zoroastrian belief they are part of the evil creation of Ahriman.

8. Isaac may reflect John of Apamea, *Letter to Hesychius*, 1.

9. For 'limpidity' (*shafyūtā*), see General Introduction, pp. xxviii–xxx, with notes 40–43.

10. Compare A. Mingana, *Commentary of Theodore of Mopsuestia on the Lord's Prayer and on the Sacraments of Baptism and the Eucharist,* Woodbrooke Studies 6 (1933) p.3 (translation), p. 126 (text). Similarly Aphrahat in *Demonstration* IV (see Chapter I).

11. Dionysius the Areopagite, *Divine Names* IV.11.

12. Evagrius, *Capita Cognoscitiva* 30 (ed. Frankenberg, p. 454). The Greek text, for which see *Le Muséon* 44 (1931) p. 377 (no 27) and p. 383 (no 4), reads *proseuchē esti katastasis nou hupo phōtos monou ginomenē tēs hagias triados*, but the Syriac translator evidently read *temnomenē* 'cut off' for *ginomenē* 'occurring': see I. Hausherr, 'Par delà l'oraison pure, grace à une coquille. A propos d'un texte d'Evagre', *RAM 13* (1932) 184–8, reprinted in his *Hesychasme et prière*, OCA 176 (1966) 8–12. As E. Khalifé-Hachem has pointed out, while it is true that Isaac uses a mistranslation to support his understanding of 'prayer beyond prayer', he is nevertheless also building on the teaching of John of Apamea: see his 'La prière pure et la prière spirituelle selon Isaac de Ninive', *Mémorial Mgr G. Khouri-Sarkis* (Louvain, 1969) 157–73.

13. Evagrius, *Capita Cognoscitiva* 4 (ed. Frankenberg, p. 426; Greek in *Le Muséon* 44 (1931) p. 374 (no 4) = p. 382 (no 2).

14. Evagrius, *Capita Cognoscitiva* 25 (ed. Frankenberg, p. 450).

15. Evagrius, *Kephalaia Gnostica* III. 88 (ed. Guillaumont, PO 29: pp. 134–5). Cf. Hausherr, *Hesychasme et prière*, pp. 38–49, 238–46.

16. Isaac here reflects the wording of John of Apamea, *On Prayer*, 2.

17. The comments seem to be the work of the person who collected together Isaac's works into the two parts.

18. Cf. Budge, *The Wit and Wisdom*, p. 295 (no 355).

19. Isaac will be referring to Theodore of Mopsuestia's *Commentary on the Lord's Prayer* (see note 10, above).

20. The editor who collected Isaac's works together at this point adds a comment which is not translated here.

Chapter XIII

Dadisho

Second half of 7th Century

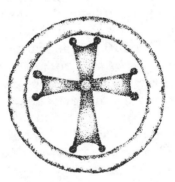

INTRODUCTION

D ADISHO APPEARS to have been a contemporary of St Isaac, living in the second half of the seventh century; like Isaac, he originated from Qatar, but seems to have spent most of his life as a monk in north Iraq. He is known to have been the author of a number of works of monastic concern, but the only two which have come down complete are his *Discourse on Solitude* (or Stillness) and an interesting *Commentary* on the *Asceticon* of Abba Isaiah, a work which had wide circulation in Syriac translation; the *Commentary* shows Dadisho to have been a man of considerable learning.

The *Discourse on Solitude* concerns the aspirations and way of life of solitary monks. Besides giving much practical advice, the work also happens to contain a considerable amount of information about different types of monastic life current in the Church of the East. At the outset Dadisho distinguished between monks who live in monasteries situated on public highways, where the monks till the monastery fields and receive guests, and solitaries who live in, or are connected with, more remote and inaccessible monasteries; in western terms this division would correspond approximately to that between active and contemplative orders. Amongst the solitary monks Dadisho lists six different categories, ranging from the novices, who remain in the community all the time, to the anchorites, who live completely on their own. In between come those who live in their cells all week, emerging only on Saturday evenings to join the rest of the community; those who retire to solitude for various periods of fasting during the ecclesiastical year; the hermits who live separately; and the itinerant solitaries.

Like Isaac, Dadisho draws on Evagrius, the *Apophthegmata* and related literature, the *Macarian Homilies*, Abba Isaiah, and Mark the Hermit, as well as on earlier Syriac writers. In the present extract he describes the four virtues by which 'pure prayer' may be achieved, and the four passions which obstruct it.

DADISHO,
On Pure Prayer

PURE PRAYER that is without any distraction and without any disturbance is accomplished, brought to perfection, established and preserved by means of four virtues; and by four passions it is diminished, tarnished, rendered ineffective and obstructed. The four virtues are these: fasting, vigil, peaceableness, and humility. Two of these concern the soul and two the body. The passions which render it ineffective are: greediness for food, and too much sleep, anger, and vainglory, as I indicated above [in a previous section]. Those illuminated [gnostic] instructors of solitaries, the blessed Mark [the Hermit] and the blessed Evagrius give us clear teaching on the subject of these four virtues which constitute the pure prayer whereby the solitary can vanquish all the passions and demons. The blessed Mark teaches us concerning them in one of his Kephalaia,[1] as follows: 'He who wishes to cross with discernment the

306

spiritual sea of the passions and demons, just as Moses and the Israelites discerningly crossed the Red Sea, should show patience, humble himself, keep vigil, persevere in asceticism. Without these four virtues, even if someone forces himself to enter [this sea], he will be forcing his heart to do so, but he will not be able to proceed with discernment'.[2]

He goes on:[3] 'Stillness is advantageous, provided it has ceased from anything evil. But if he receives assistance in prayer with these four virtues, no one will more speedily reach perfect well-being'. Again he says: 'The intellect cannot be stilled apart from the body. Nor can it dismantle the barrier to these four virtues without stillness and prayer'.[4] He calls peaceableness 'patience', for in another passage he shows that these two are the same, saying: 'A patient man is exceedingly wise',[5] and again 'He who is gentle in our Lord is wiser than the wise'.[6] He attributes wisdom to both patience and peaceableness, as having the same meaning.

These two virtues of the soul by which pure prayer is constituted—I mean peaceableness and humility—are the ones taught by our Lord: *Learn from me, for I am peaceable and humble in my heart, and you shall find peace for your souls* [or *selves*].* *Mt 11:29*

Rest of soul and pure prayer are in truth established by these two virtues, according to our Lord's word. When the two other virtues of the body, fasting and keeping vigil, are joined with them, according to

Mt 17:21

the sure verdict of our Lord, '*The species of passions and demons does not depart except by means of fasting and prayer*'* — the power and beauty of which are constituted particularly in vigils.

As for the fourth virtue, which Abba Mark calls perseverance of asceticism, he is accustomed to name it 'fasting'. In other words, when someone fasts, he will need to put up with less. This sense can be found in other Kephalaia, as when he says that 'the ascetic who perseveres is far removed from gluttony'.[7] From all this it is apparent that Abba Mark is everywhere calling the virtue of fasting and small amounts of food 'perseverance' and 'asceticism'.

These are the four virtues, two of the soul and two of the body, by which pure prayer is perfected into the first haven of peace. The solitary should meditate on these every day and take care to pray that he may acquire them, until he actually finds them.

This too one should realize: that the entire way of life of stillness is interwoven with the following three virtues: with faith that comes from listening, and with hope and with love, out of which real faith is made known. Once someone enters his cell and commences on the way of life of faith, that is to say, employing bodily labours, until he reaches the way of life of hope, which is the way of life of the mind, consisting in meditation on God, he labours and struggles by means of these four virtues indicated above against the four passions which sully pure prayer, hindering and preventing

him from arriving at meditation on God—
which is the way of life of hope. The
virtues, as I have said, correspond to the
'comprehensive commandments'[8] of every
commandment, out of which spiritual
prayer is constituted and established: fasting, vigil, humility, peaceableness. The opposite passions are love of the belly, sleep,
anger, vain glory.

When someone commences on the way
of life of hope, which consists of meditation on God, and until he reaches the way
of life of love which is the way of life of the
Spirit, in which is revealed real faith, which
is the vision of our Lord in the Spirit, this
person labours and conducts himself with
three great commandments, the most comprehensive of all commandments: they are
these—prayer without ceasing and without
distraction; instantaneous destruction of
evil thoughts the moment they begin to stir
in the heart; endurance of all afflictions and
every temptation that comes upon one in
stillness, originating from the passions or
from demons or from men.

When the solitary is fully perfected in
this way of life of hope, which is the way of
life of the mind, namely meditation on our
Lord, he is raised up and enters upon the
way of life of the Spirit, which is the spiritual way of life, in which all the fruits of
the Spirit are manifested and produced, the
ones which the Apostle laid out,* those   *cf Gal 5:22*
firstfruits, among which are these three: the
delight in the pledge of the love of our Lord
Jesus Christ and of the love of His Father;
complete humility; real faith, which is the

spiritual vision of our Lord and of the heavenly good things through the revelation of the Holy Spirit.

Eph 3:14
*I bend my knees** and I pray for you, says the apostle Paul, that you may be empowered with the Holy Spirit, so that Christ may dwell in your inner person in faith and in your hearts in love, in all humility of mind. These are the four virtues out of which the prayer of the mind is constituted, and these are the three great and binding commandments, by which spiritual prayer is constituted.

BIBLIOGRAPHY AND NOTES

A. The extract is translated from the edition by A. Mingana, *Early Christian Mystics*, Woodbrooke Studies 7 (1934) 232–4 (Mingana's own translation is on pp. 120–22).

B. A short introduction is given by A. Guillaumont in *DSpir* 2 (1957) cols. 2–3. Mingana gave a complete English translation of the *Discourse on Solitude* in *Early Christian Mystics*, pp. 76–143. There is a French translation, by R. Draguet, of Dadisho's *Commentary* on Abba Isaiah's *Asceticon* in CSCO 327 (1972), and of his *Letter to Abkosh*, by A. Guillaumont and M. Albert, 'Lettre de Dadisho Qatraya à Abkosh, sur l'Hesychia', in E. Lucchesi and H.D. Saffrey, edd., *Mémorial A–J. Festugière* (Geneva, 1984) 235–45.

1. Mark the Hermit, *On those who think that they are made righteous by works*, PG 65; 936A (no. 27) = *Philokalia*, p. 128 (no. 29). Dadisho has expanded the quotation.

2 Mingana in his translation understands the passage rather differently.

3. Mark the Hermit, *On those. . .*, PG 65: 936A (no 28) = *Philokalia*, p. 128 (no 30).

4. Mark the Hermit, *On those. . .*, PG 65: 936A (no 29) = *Philokalia*, p. 128 (no 31).

5. Mark the Hermit, *On the spiritual law*, PG 65: 924B (no 147) = *Philokalia* p. 120 (no 146); cf. Prov 14:29.

6. Mark the Hermit, *On those. . .*, PG 65: 944D (no 99)

= *Philokalia*, p. 134 (no 107). The word translated 'gentle' could also be rendered 'peaceable'.

7. Compare Mark the Hermit, *On those. . .* , PG 65: 933C (no 24) = *Philokalia*, p. 127 (no 25).

8. The term could also be translated 'binding commandments'; cf. Mark the Hermit, *On those. . .* , PG 65: 933D (no 25) = *Philokalia* p. 127 (no 27).

Chapter XIV

Joseph the Visionary
Abdisho

8th Century

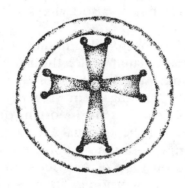

INTRODUCTION

J OSEPH HAZZAYA, or the Visionary, was born into a Zoroastrian family some time around 710. As a child of
seven he was taken captive during a raid, to be sold
first to an Arab, and then to a Christian in the region of
mount Qardu (north Iraq). Impressed by the example of
some local monks, he sought baptism, and when his
owner subsequently liberated him, Joseph became a monk
himself. For two separate periods in his monastic life he
lived as a solitary, but he also twice served as abbot of a
community.

Joseph has left a considerable number of writings, some
of which were circulated under the name of his brother
and fellow monk, Abdisho. A number of these writings
were included by A. Mingana in his *Early Christian Mystics.* Among his *Letters* is an important one on the three
stages or degrees of the spiritual life, wrongly attributed
in the manuscript tradition to Philoxenus. Although the
pattern is based on John of Apamea's threefold division,
Joseph adapts it to incorporate features from other writers, including Evagrius; we thus have the following main
correspondences:

(1) The first stage is that of the body *(pagrānūtā)*; this
is concerned with external practices, fastings, vigils, and
prayer centred on psalmody and readings. This corresponds to the cenobitic life and is symbolized by the Exo-
dus of the Israelites from Egypt (i.e. the world) and their
passage through the wilderness; it also represents the state

of a servant who is subject to commandments. The aim is purity, and the stage corresponds to the Evagrian *praktikē* and the Dionysian 'purification'.

(2) The stage of the soul *(nafshānūtā)* belongs especially to the solitary life, and is concerned above all with the practice of the interior virtues, in particular humility. The transition from the stage of the body to that of the soul corresponds to the crossing by the Israelites of the river Jordan, and the ensuing fight with evil demons reflects the Israelites' fight with the inhabitants of the Land of Promise. This is the state of a worker who awaits his daily pay. The aim is 'limpidity' or 'transparency' *(shafyūtā)*, and this stage corresponds to the Evagrian 'natural contemplation' and the Dionysian 'illumination'.

(3) The third stage, that of the spirit *(ruḥānūtā)*, is concerned primarily with the activities of the mind; it constitutes the entry into 'perfection' (or 'full maturity'), and represents 'the glorious Sion'. This is the state of a son (and no longer that of a servant or worker), and the most characteristic feature of it is the vision of the formless light of the Trinity and of the risen Christ. This stage corresponds to the Evagrian *theologia* and the Dionysian 'unification'.

Two excerpts from Joseph's works are translated here. The first is a short unpublished text on 'spiritual prayer'. Joseph's description of this exalted form of prayer indicates that he has in mind something rather different from Isaac's 'spiritual prayer'. The second excerpt (transmitted under the name of Abdisho) is taken from a longer work of advanced teaching on prayer entitled 'On the stirrings, or impulses, of the mind during prayer'. Here Joseph compares the soul to a ship at sea with the mind as the helmsman, trying to cope with the various winds, which are the impulses which arise in the mind during prayer. A detailed analysis of the different kinds of impulses is given, and the extract ends with a description of the vision of the light of the Holy Trinity.

1. JOSEPH THE VISIONARY,
On spiritual prayer

H E SAYS[1] 'What is the sphere where
spiritual prayer is prayed?' The
sphere where spiritual prayer is
prayed by the mind is the mind's natural
sphere: once the mind has reached that
pure sphere which belongs to its true nature, once its vision has been clarified of all
the imaginings and images of thoughts
which do not belong to its true nature, and
once the mind has been held worthy of an
illuminated vision of its own self, and there
has arisen within it the visionary spirit that
gives insight into spiritual understanding of
both corporeal and incorporeal beings, and
at the same time, of judgement and providence—it is at that point that the mind
prays with spiritual prayer, a kind of prayer
that is not prayed with the body's senses,
but with the inner impulses of the soul
which are entirely filled with illumination.
Then the mind can see the birth of things

past, present, and future, as well as the varied ordering of the worlds.

All these things are revealed to the mind in that sphere that belongs to the soul where spiritual prayer is prayed. For the mysteries of this stage are far exalted above the corporeal world, being made known in the world of spiritual beings. This is the sphere where spiritual prayer is prayed, and where sacrificial offerings are made to Christ our Lord. In the case of every prayer that is prayed outside this place, and likewise with every sacrificial offering that is made outside this sphere, and of every sacrificial offering that is made, from which no sweet savour pleasing to the Lord's* will *cf Gen 8:21* ascends, such a prayer is rejected, and it is an offering that contains a blemish.

At this staging point the fatigue resulting from the vehemence of ascetic labours is altered and finds an end: insights arise, and the mind's vision is extended with every kind of spiritual power from which the mind receives spiritual sustenance—and often enough the body too is sustained by it. In this place the body and the soul together receive knowledge, whether it be of the right or of the left. There are not two wills, one striving against its companion; rather body and soul cooperate with a single will of mutual consent. There is no image of the *old person* who was corrupted by lusts that lead to error; but rather, body and soul exist in unity with each other as the single *new person** who has been cre- *Eph 4:22–4* ated in holiness by Christ our Lord, just as the Apostle said.

lit. the right   All the changes for good* which I mentioned above take place for the mind in that
place. This is the place where the judges of
the worlds that have existed and will exist
are revealed to the mind; here all observance of the commandments and laws is
fulfilled. Beyond this place there is no
longer any law-giving or fear of trans-
gressing a commandment, since this place
constitutes the boundary between fear and
non-fear. It is not for everyone to be raised
beyond and above it, but many may reach
it. Below it there are many, but only a few
attain to it, while one in a thousand proceed beyond it: this is the person who takes
cf Mt 16:24   up his cross* on his shoulder and travels in
the steps of our Lord. A person does not
reach this stage through a partial keeping of
the commandments: no, it is only the person who obeys and fulfils in himself 'the
comprensive commandments' of which the
blessed Mark the Hermit spoke[2].

The powers that properly belong to the
soul are continually put into motion in this
place. Just as the air never ceases to provide
everything that lives and moves with breath
to inhale, so too when the Holy Spirit is
operating in the mind's movements, these
never cease from prayer, just as the Apostle
said: *He who feels out hearts knows what
the mind of the Spirit is, for he prays on
behalf of the saints in accordance with*
Rom 8:27   *God's will.* *

2. JOSEPH THE VISIONARY,
On the stirrings of the mind during prayer

BY THE SAME, concerning the operation of the impulses which arise in the mind during the time of prayer: which are material,* and which are immaterial† and which are uncircumscribed and without form.

*(*lit.* composite)
†(*lit* simple)

During the time of prayer the soul resembles a ship positioned in the middle of the sea. The mind is like the steersman in charge of the boat. The impulses convey the boat like the winds.

Just as it is the case that not all the winds that blow are suitable for the course of the ship, similarly, with the impulses that are aroused in the soul during the time of prayer, not all are suitable for the ship's course, enabling it without any cause for fear to reach harbour, safe from the waves. Rather, some of them are suitable, whereas others are not. The latter imprint in the soul some material form, and these hinder the course of the boat of the mind, the steersman preventing it reaching the harbour he is aiming for. The former impulses stirred up in the soul during prayer are immaterial: these are the gentle breezes which convey the ship of the soul over the waves to a harbour that is totally restful.

There are yet other impulses that arise during prayer, accompanied by light: these are called 'uncircumscribed'; they are

neither material nor immaterial, but uncircumscribed, as I have just said; for not all
immaterial impulses are also uncircumscribed. For the holy angels and the nature
of our souls are immaterial, but they are by
no means also uncircumscribed; for they
are immaterial things subject to circum-
scription, whereas out of all things there is
[only] one who is uncircumscribed. Now
the impulses which concern that Being are
uncircumscribed—just as the prophet said:

Ps 147:5

*there is no limit to his understanding.**

Material impulses consist in all the under-
standings that are stirred up in the soul
through the medium of the body's senses.
These are material, and they are harmful to
the soul's course during the time of prayer.
Even though at other times they may be
advantageous, nevertheless during the time
of prayer they cause the soul harm. This is
because during the time of prayer only the
immaterial impulses direct the soul towards
those that are without limit.

The immaterial impulses consist in the
hidden spiritual knowledge concealed in
the natural created world, wonderful insights concerning incorporeal contemplation, and insights arising from the
contemplation of Providence's judgment.
All these impulses may occur during the
time of prayer, and these are immaterial.
Therefore every time they are revealed to
the mind during prayer, they give a sweet
taste to the mind's palate, like a honeycomb, and they kindle all the faculties of
both soul and body with their warmth, so
that tears without measure pour down

from a person's eyes whenever these impulses are set in motion in his mind. These are not tears stemming from the passions or from sorrow because of wrongdoings, but rather they arise from joy and delight, and from a sense of wonder at God's creation, compassion, and care for everything—at how his compassion is poured out abundantly over us human beings, at the extent of our ingratitude towards him; at how, whereas we did not exist before, nor are we able to come into being of our own volition, yet in his compassion he brought us into existence and well-being, even though he was aware of our future ingratitude and wickedness even before he created us; at how, once we had sinned and incited his anger through our choice of evil deeds, out of his fatherly love he still does not hold back from us the gifts of his divine care for us and his providence; at how, when our nature had reached despair, he sent his beloved Son, our Lord Jesus, and handed him over to suffering and death on our behalf in order to save us who are befouled by sin; at how he tasted vinegar and bitter herbs for us, in order to render harmless the bitter venom of the serpent which slew us in Eden; and at how, after all the wickedness and blasphemies which we perpetrated against him, in his ineffable grace he prepared for us another world full of every imaginable good thing, decreeing for us the gift of resurrection by means of which we shall be raised up from the passions of mortality, and will become incorruptible, immortal, unchangeable, impassible, and

without needs, being continuously raised
up with him in an understanding of his
mysteries and in the glorious vision of him.

Thus as a result of recollecting all these
things the impulses of the mind are extended from the sphere of material things
towards those impulses which are without
limit, that is to say, wonder at the New
World, and the faculty of vision which belongs to contemplation of the Holy Trinity.
For when the vision of the mind is mingled
with the light of the glorious Trinity, all its
impulses become infinite. For none of the
visionaries or 'gnostics' is able to distinguish the identity of the mind as a result of
the vision of that glorious light that is seen
of the Holy Trinity, for all the innermost
chambers of the heart are filled by that
blessed light, and there are no shapes or
forms or anything material, or number or
colour; rather that Light who cannot be
separated out into shapes and forms is single owing to the simpleness of the faculty
of sight.

This too I have to tell you: at such a time
there is no longer any kind of movement
there, or any kind of thought, or any kind
of mental process, only a state of wonder
that is beyond all mental processes, impulses, or thoughts. This is the pledge of
the good things that are to come, which
have been prepared through the mediation
of our Lord Jesus Christ for the human
race; that is to say, for all rational beings, as
a result of the abundance of the compassion of the revered Father, who created us
when we did not exist, and allowed us to

share in a knowledge of his glory, so that we might become like him, having no end for ever, and that we might enjoy his glory. May he in his mercy make us all worthy of his glorious vision—here in pledge, but there in reality. Amen.

BIBLIOGRAPHY AND NOTES

A. The first text is translated from Mingana syr. 601, fol. 248b–249a, and the second from Mingana's edition in his *Early Christian Mystics*, pp. 272–4 (Mingana's own translation is on pp. 163–4). The second text is transmitted under the name of Joseph's brother Abdisho.

B. A good orientation is provided by R. Beulay in *DSpir* 8 (1974) cols. 1341–9. Other general studies include A. Scher, 'Joseph Hazzaya, écrivain syriaque du VIIIe siècle', *Rivista degli Studi Orientali* 3 (1910) 45–63; A. Guillaumont, 'Sources de la doctrine de Joseph Hazzaya', *L'Orient Syrien 3* (1958) 5–24; E. J. Sherry, 'The life and works of Joseph Hazzaya', in *The Seed of Wisdom. Essays in Honour of T. J. Meek* (London, 1964) 78–91. An English translation of some other works by Joseph (under the name of Abdisho) will be found in Mingana, *Early Christian Mystics*, pp. 145–84. The fullest collection of translations is into German, by G. Bunge, *Rabban Jausep Hazzaya. Briefe über das geistliche Leben und verwandte Schriften* (Trier, 1982), with introduction. A French translation of the Letter on the three stages, or degrees, of the spiritual life (wrongly attributed to Philoxenus) is given by F. Graffin in *L'Orient Syrien* 6–7 (1961–2); an English translation of the short version of this text will be found in G. Olinder, *A Letter of Philoxenus of Mabbug sent to a Friend*, Göteborgs Högskolas Årsskrift 56; (1950).

1. Who 'he' is is unclear.
2. For reference, see note 8 to Chapter XIII.

Chapter XV

John the Elder
John of Dalyatha
8th Century

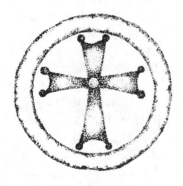

INTRODUCTION

A GOOD DEAL of confusion surrounds the name and writings of this John. It now seems likely that John the Elder (Saba) and John of Dalyatha ('the vine branches') are one and the same person. John evidently belonged to monastic circles of the Church of the East, living somewhere in the region of mount Qardu (north Iraq) in the early part of the eighth century. His most important writings consist of twenty–two homilies or discourses and a collection of fifty–one short letters; these show him to be an intuitive writer of great warmth and fervour, with a predilection for the imagery of the spiritual senses. For John the Elder, as for John of Apamea before him, the mystical life was essentially the anticipated experience of the resurrection life; as such, it is the true fruit of the Sacraments or, to use the Syriac term, Mysteries, of Baptism and the Eucharist.

Two of John's recently published *Letters* are translated here. The short *Letter 5* is an ardent invitation to the love of God; characteristically it breaks out into prayer at the end. *Letter 12*, specifically on prayer, describes the transition from active prayer to the receptive state of wonder which lies beyond prayer. Prayer is simply the 'knocking at the door', and it becomes redundant once entry has actually been made into 'the place of Mysteries'. There are many basic similarities here with Isaac's description in *Discourse* XXII (chapter XII.3, above); in particular it will be noticed that John follows Isaac in referring to the Syriac text of Evagrius which speaks of prayer as being 'cut off' by wonder.

John the Elder's writings, along with Joseph the Visionary's, were condemned by the authorities of the Church of the East at a synod in 786/7 on the grounds that they showed Messalian tendencies (a totally misguided accusation). John's works, however, continued to be appreciated in monastic circles and not just within his own Church of the East, for his writings are transmitted in a considerable number of Syrian Orthodox manuscripts as well, and they were translated both into Arabic (where he is known as 'the Spiritual Sheikh') and, in part, into Greek. In Greek four of John's homilies[1] have found their way into the edition, by St Nikephoros of the Holy Mountain, of the Greek translation of the First Part of the works of St Isaac of Nineveh.[2] John the Elder's *Letter 18*, containing rules for novices, also found its way into Greek, where it features under the names both of St Isaac (*Patrologia Graeca* 86: cols 883B–886A) and of St Dorotheus of Gaza (*Patrologia Graeca* 88: cols 1841D–1844B).

1. JOHN THE ELDER,
Letter 5

T O HIM WHO HEARS and obeys be the peace
of him who sanctifies.

1. O man of God, listen to the words of
your friend. No, my dear brother, let us not
impose our will upon Christ; rather, let us
submit ourselves to his will. Do you want
Christ to appear to you in prayer as he
would to his friend? Let love for him be
within you without a moment's break. Do
you want this love to be continually inflamed in your soul? Then remove from
your soul love for the world. Are you desirous that your abode would be in that place
which is without place, being in God?
Leave the world, as a baby leaves the
womb; then you will have seen reality. For
Christ cannot live with the world. I beg
you, listen to him as he demonstrates to
you with his own words, *'I am not of the*
world;* for this reason it chases me away
from where I would live, and I cannot live
with it, *because it hates me'.* But he is

Jn 14:23

Jn 7:7, 15:18

330

continuously overshadowing³ the soul and visiting it, so that if it become empty of the things of the world he can dwell in it.

2. Are you desirous of seeing the radiant beams of the beauty of the Holy Trinity in your soul? Keep the commandments of Christ, for he said, 'When *you keep my commandments,** it is then that my love shall be found with you' And with the fulfilment of these in the soul, he said that he and his Father and his Spirit *will come and make a habitation*;* and there he will dwell and be seen. He also said that his friends were *not of the world*, and that *the world has hated them.**   *Jn 14:15*

Jn 14:23

Jn 17:14

The fulfilment of his commandments is the cross, that is to say, the forgetting and obliteration of all desire for the world, and a yearning desire to depart from it in the flame of love, as was the case with Saint Paul. In openness of speech towards my God and in confidence I truly say that the moment the mind strips off the world it puts on Christ; the moment it departs from thinking about the affairs of the world it encounters God; the moment the soul cuts off from itself associating with the world, the Spirit starts singing within it of its ineffable mysteries. It is a *mystery for me** here, and a cause for fear; but to the true, truth is revealed. If only the pupils of the eyes could stir up tears sufficient to irrigate the land, the canals would be abundantly full! What is it we have exchanged this for? Alas, alas for me!   *Is 24:16 (Syriac)*

3. O Christ, who repaid with his own innocent blood the debt which our foolish

will incurred, open up our mind's eyes that
we may realize whither we are travelling.
May your light, which illumines the choirs
of your Sanctuary like the sun, lead me towards you; may your Spirit, Lord, place me
amidst them, both here and in the world of
light; may he instruct me how to recite,
with them, from their Book the praise to
you which cannot be heard. Create me,
Lord, a new creature that resembles your
beauty, so that we may forget and wipe out
the memory of our former nature.

4. Glory to the abundance of your ineffable love! Your door is open, Lord, and no
one is entering. Your glory is revealed, but
no one pays attention. Your light shines out
in the pupils of our eyes, but we are not
willing to see. Your right hand is extended,
ready to give, but there is no one who takes
from it! You entice us with all sorts of at-
tractions, but we ignore them. You instill
fear with terrors which are nevertheless intermingled with mercy, but we do not flee
to you. O our God who is good, have pity
on our miserable state. O our Father full of
mercy, urge yourself to force us to draw
near to you, seeing that we ourselves are
unwilling to urge you. Remove our soul
cf Ps 142:7   from prison,* for we have imprisoned ourselves, and bring us to the true light, even
though we are unwilling. May your might
put us in safe keeping, drawing us up out of
the submerged state towards which we are
heading. Remove, Lord, from before our
sight all the veils by which our soul's vision
is encumbered, preventing it from seeing
your true light. May we stand naked, with

open face, in that light continually and without interruption; may we continue in desire for, and delight in, its beauty, unto eternal ages, amen.

2. JOHN THE ELDER,
Letter 12. On Prayer.

THE MONK WHO continually prays to God accompanied by stirrings of one sort or another still stands below the consummate grade. You will object, saying, 'Do not blaspheme, brother; our Fathers exalt this form of prayer more than all other labours'. Indeed, I too am one of those who extol it, and I ask of my God that I may complete the rest of my life in such prayer; I acknowledge that it is something magnificent and much more exalted than all other labours. Though it is fatiguing, yet it gives rest to the weary, ensuring that, once they are rested, they never weary again.

2. Understand this well, my brother: Christ said to Simon, the head of the Apostles, 'To you do I give the keys of the kingdom of heaven,* so that you may close and open to whomever you wish.' It is not to him alone that he gave this authority, but to

Mt 16:19

all lovers of Truth. Now prayer is just the knocker on the door of him who gives. So how can the person who has entered the kingdom and received authority over its treasuries knock at the door? He enjoys the blessings within and is utterly astounded at the beauty of the Good One. It is ridiculous to say that such a person is actually praying: rather, he is completely intoxicated with the beauty of the most wondrous Bridegroom.

3. Evagrius says,[4] 'Prayer is purity of the mind, the movements of whose prayer are not interrupted except once the holy light of the Trinity has shone out in the mind.' For he says, 'Prayer is cut off by means of wonder at the light.' Thus the consummation consists in wonder at God, as we have said, and not in the continual stirrings of prayer. The person who has entered the place of the Mysteries remains in wonder at them, and this is the true prayer which opens the door to the treasures of God, allowing those who seek to have their fill of all they need. *Freely have you received, do yourselves give freely** too to everyone you wish. How could anyone dare to say of those who have been given authority over wealth, to give it as if it were their own to everyone they wished, that they are knocking at the door like beggars asking for alms to meet their needs? No; rather, they distribute life, raise the dead, convey hope, give light to the blind; *you are the light of the world*, he said: *I will give you the keys.** You are no longer someone who asks, for you have acquired authority—as

Mt 10:8

Mt 5:14, 16:19

though over what belonged to yourself—to bind and to loose, in this world and in the age of ages. How can such a person prostrate himself at the door and beg like a vagabond, seeing that the keys to the treasury are already placed in his hands, enabling him to take and give, have life and provide life?

4. But you will say, 'Why did *Simon go up to the roof to pray*,* and the great Paul say that he prays *continuously'*?* These apostles, brethren, employ words that are appropriate to us, in as much as they will be recognizable by us; by means of them they provide us with a type of things transcendent. These words are for us, and not at all for themselves. Did you not hear how, when Simon went up to the roof, wonder fell upon him?* And how does someone in a state of wonder and amazement actually pray? *It is the Spirit who prays on our behalf*,* says the holy Paul. Thus it is a question of the operation of the Spirit, and not of the movements of prayer, just as he said: '*God has shone out in our hearts*,* and *His Spirit probes his depths and reveals to us his mysteries'*.* We wanted to do this ourselves, but the Spirit of Jesus did not let us, for *we have the mind of Christ** in order to see the mysteries of the Father's house.

5. At that stage they have entered the place of wonderment, they have acquired authority in the world of visions; the Spirit has united them to the wondrous beauty. No more will they get weary in prayer, no more will they weep at the door, no more

Act 10:9

1 Th 5:17

Ac 10:10

Rom 8:26

2 Cor 4:6

1 Cor 2:10–12

1 Cor 2:16

will they cry out from afar, 'Show us your
beauty'; no more will they ask like beggars,
'Distribute some of your wealth to us'.
They give, because they have received; they
distribute, because they have grown rich;
they provide rest, because they have found
rest in the haven of Life. They rejoice, and
they give joy, for they are intoxicated with
love of him who is beautiful. *Rivers of living water flow from the belly of him who*
Jn 7:38   *believes in me.** Why do they flow, Lord?
Teach me. They give life to others and they
give the thirsty to drink.

6. And how can the person who has become one with Christ actually pray—as if
he was someone not acquainted with the
Master of the house? And to whom does he
pray, seeing that he is God's son? *Your Father who is in heaven knows what you re-*
Mt 6:8   *quire even before you ask Him.**

And why did Paul say '*Pray, and do not*
1 Th 5:17   *grow weary*'?* As long as he is a servant, he
indeed prays; but once born of the Spirit in
the world of prayer, he is a son of God, and
he has authority over the riches, being an
heir; thus he does not merely ask.

7. This prayer is the greatest of all
labours: it opens the door to the place of
wonderment, it gives rest to weariness, it
stills all movements. Maybe you will say,
'You are speaking about wonderment, and I
do not know the meaning of wonderment'.
let me adduce as testimony the words of a
certain brother, who is worthy to be believed; he used to say, 'When the grace of
my God so wills it within me, it draws my
intellect to wonder at the sight of him, so

that it remains the entire day motionless, in the place of wonderment. Then, once it has left there, it again prays and supplicates that the light of hidden Being that is hidden within him may shine forth in the world full of wonder.' From that point onwards there is no place for words, no place where the pen's torrent could travel along the paths of ink. Here the boundary is set, namely, silence. Only the mind is permitted to cross over and have a sight of that place where all symbols find their rest. For the mind is authorized to enter and wonder at the wondrous beauty which is beyond all, yet hidden within all.

8. Thus any prayer that is not from time to time transformed in wonder at the mysteries has not yet reached consummation, as we explained above. Nor can prayer consisting of stirrings last continuously if it has not tasted at all of the wonder which comes with the joy of God. Continuous prayer is wonder at God: that is the sum of our message. You may go on to say, 'Do not speak about things with which you are not acquainted; do not talk about matters which you have not explained.' I too hang my head in shame, and will keep silent, taking refuge in divine mercy. Assist me in prayer.

BIBLIOGRAPHY AND NOTES

A. Letters 5 and 12 are translated from R. Beulay, *La collection des lettres de Jean de Dalyatha*, PO 39, fasc. 3 1978.

B. A general introduction is provided by R. Beulay in *DSpir* 8 (1974). cols. 449–52, and by B. Colless, 'The mysticism of John Saba', *OCP* 39 (1973) 83–102. Beulay provides a complete French translation of the Letters; an edition, with English translation, of the Homilies is being prepared by B. Colless. There is a French translation of Homily 20 by P. Sherwood, 'Jean de Dalyata: sur la fuite du monde', *L'Orient Syrien* 1 (1956) 305–13.

1. Nos 1, 8, 20 and 22 in the numbering of Vatican Syriac ms. 124.

2. N. Theotokis, *Tou hosiou patros hēmōn Isaac episkopou Nineui tou Syrou ta heurēthenta askētika* (Leipzig, 1770); these are homilies 43, 7, 2 and 80, respectively, in the re-edition of Isaac's works in Greek by I. Spetsieris under the same title (Athens, 1895; 3rd edn. 1976).

3. See General Introduction, p. xxviii, with note 30.

4. See note 12 to Chapter XII.

Prayers
of the
Mystics

INTRODUCTION

A T THE END of his fifth Letter John the Elder burst out into direct prayer[1]. It is not uncommon for these writers to break into prayer in the middle of some disquisition and we have encountered several examples of this in the course of the selections in this book. Many of these prayers were later excerpted and collected together; indeed several are still in regular use since they feature in a selection of such prayers known as the *Shebīthō*, arranged for private use according to the pattern of the daily Office throughout the week.

To serve as examples of such prayers (which are often meditative in character) I have selected some prayers from four of the writers represented in the present book, John of Apamea, Isaac of Nineveh, Joseph the Visionary, and John the Elder. The long prayer by Joseph is specifically for use before Communion.

PRAYERS OF JOHN OF APAMEA

1. Praised are you
O Christ our Teacher,
for you enrich
with absolutely everything
those who cleave to you.
Lord, if someone gives his possessions to the state,
then he receives in return great honour;
how much more will you, Lord,
magnify and praise
that person who offers his whole self to you,
possessing nothing besides you!

Make our souls grow by your grace, Lord,
so that we may grow in you
and give praise to you,
for no one can grow
except in you,
and no one can excel
except in you.

Praise to you,
without whom everything is empty;
praise to you,
for apart from the praise of you,
all praise is but idle.
Praise to you,
the One who magnifies,
but it is you who are thereby praised,
for you are the object of praise
of everything.
Praise to you,
Perfecter of everything, O Christ.
By your divine teaching you gave wisdom

to all who are instructed by you
to deprive themselves of everything
that belongs to this world
—then they shall be attached to you.
Otherwise, as they travelled after you
while still cleaving to the world,
they might be drawn back by the world into it.
Praise to you who bade us release ourselves
and then cleave to you,
seeing that, when we are not bound up with anything,
nothing will separate us from you.

2. Direct the course of our lives, Lord,
straight towards you,
so that in you we may reach you,
and so that in you we may find you.
Make us worthy to attain to you,
in you;
and let us behold nothing beside you.
Hide everything from our mind's vision
by means of the manifestation of your glorious light.
For whoever gazes upon you
does not need to look upon anything else;
but whoever does not gaze upon you
is in need of all kinds of other sources of illumination
in order to be able to see.

Praise to you,
for you are the Light,
and in you our souls have illumination.
You illumine all
with knowledge of yourself.
Draw back the veil of falsehood from our souls
so that we can see your light clearly,
for our minds are not totally dark
owing to love of you,
for whoever desires the sight of you

does not see himself alongside you,
being deprived not only of his possessions,
but also of his very limbs
as he longs to take up more
than his human nature is capable of doing.
For whoever has really loved you
yearns not only after your poverty,
but also after death for your name's sake,
so that with his death
he may lose himself in order to find you.
He loses himself
and all that belongs to the world
in order to find you who have found him.
All the time he is eager
to take up your love for him
into himself,
so that with your help
he may love you.

Praise to you who have allowed us to love you.
Everything we have belongs to you;
we possess nothing of our own,
for everything has been given us by you.

If we reject the body's ease,
then life belongs to you;
it is you who have made us worthy to reject this.
For who can love his life more than you,
seeing that you loved his life more than your own?
Just as you gave your life for the sake of his,
in order that the mortal condition of his life
might experience resurrection
after the likeness of your life,
so by the shame of your cross
he should abound in the praise of the glory
which belongs to it.

How wonderful and great is your love towards us,
how abundant is your love for our human race.
You did not give something that belonged to you
for our sakes,
it was your very self
that you delivered up for our salvation.
You did not buy us for the price of something
you had created,
but with your very own blood that brings forgiveness
you have brought us freedom.

It is an amazing thing, Lord,
that you should be spoken of in our language,
when everything belongs to you.
You did not want to make use of your authority,
but instead you carried out everything
in gentleness and kindness,
declaring that you were giving
so that you might receive,
and handing over yourself
for our salvation.
With your very own priceless blood you bought us,
not wanting to make use of the great might
of your authority;
rather, although you have dominion over all
as God and Lord of all,
you made yourself lower than all,
in order to raise all up.

3. Praise to you,
O Christ the true Light,
for in you have our souls been illumined
so that we have gained perception
in our minds.
In you we have been made worthy of you,
in you we have found our lives,
and in you we have been acquired by you.

Praise to you,
for in you we have been conjoined to you,
and in you
your glorious Father has taken pleasure in us;
in you we have peace with him.
You nullified the fierce anger
that Justice had decreed against us,
annulling with your own handwriting
the document which Justice had threateningly inscribed
concerning us.

Praises be to you
who gave us life in everything.
Thanks be to you, O Lord of all,
for you are true and immutable life,
in whom our treasure will be preserved
and not snatched away:
our wealth will no longer be seized.
Our life is provided for by your care,
and all kinds of wonderful assistance from you
is proffered to us.
It is by these means
that you captivate humanity
to the love of you,
so that all may acquire you
and you may acquire everyone.
Praise to you who proclaimed and taught
that we were to be acquired by you in love.

4. All praise to you, O God,
who are hidden from all worlds;
all praise to your love,
for no one is able to recount its abundance.
For your greatness bends down
so that it may be seen by those who love you,
so that human beings may behold the sight of you:
this is the exalted position

to which you have brought them,
actually manifesting yourself to them.
How ardent and fervent is your love
for the soul which has become aware of you,
for the soul which is truly purified and cleansed
during her lifetime.
That person whom you have held full worthy
to look upon you
is raised up towards you in his lifetime:
but for his body, he would no longer be in the world!

What wonders has your love effected!
When someone is still alive
he has left this world:
though his bodily condition remains
with the world's bodily condition,
yet his spirit has been raised up towards you,
so that for a period of time
he is where he knows not,
being totally raptured and drawn towards you.

All praise to your knowledge,
all praise to your greatness;
thanksgiving be to you, O Lord of all,
who established your wisdom for us in wonder.
All this does your love bring about,
transporting us from this world to another world
in order to perfect us fully there,
allowing us to grasp there
things of which we are unaware here;
for many are the things which you have in store for us,
Lord,
things of which we do not yet even know
so as to ask for them.
Just as there are many things
of which a child is unaware in this world
and so does not know to seek for them,

similarly your grace
has prepared for us in the New World
things for which our minds have not yet conceived
of seeking from you or asking,
but which are hidden away in readiness
for that day when they shall be revealed
to everyone according to his capability:
the more a person has loved you,
the more you will manifest the wondrous sight of you.
Not that you refuse to manifest yourself here,
only that here this takes place
by means of the revelation of mysteries,
whereas at the end of time
it will be by means of the glorious vision of you.
Not everyone will behold you there equally,
but each in accordance with his capability.
For not even the ranks of angels
all have the same vision of you
in that world there,
but the degree of their vision
depends on the greatness of their rank.

All praise to you,
who bend down
in all sorts of different manners,
while remaining exactly as you are.
You are seen by everyone
in so far as they are able to see you.

I beseech you,
O God, Father of all,
cause our minds to approach this glory,
so that we may perceive in our understanding
and become aware of the greatness
to which you have called us,
and of how insignificant we are.

Grant us, Lord, to cling to you,
not in our outward beings
but in our hidden selves,
and may we follow you
until we behold your face.
For in this world, Lord,
a person continues to follow after you
as he becomes perfected,
but in the New World
you will manifest your very face to him:
then he will no longer be travelling after you,
but will be with you
in the Kingdom.

PRAYER OF ISAAC OF NINEVEH
(from a collection of thirty prayers)

1. As my soul bows to the ground
I offer to you with all my bones
and with all my heart
the worship that befits you,
O glorious God who dwells in ineffable silence.
You have built for my renewal
a tabernacle of love on earth
where it is your good pleasure to rest,
a temple made of flesh
and fashioned with the most holy sanctuary oil.
Then you filled it with your holy presence
so that worship might be fulfilled in it,
indicating the worship
of the eternal persons of your Trinity
and revealing to the worlds which you had created in
your grace
an ineffable mystery,
a power which cannot be felt or grasped
by any part of your creation that has come into being.
In wonder at it
angelic beings are submerged in silence,
awed at the dark cloud of this eternal mystery
and at the flood of glory
which issues from within this source of wonder,
for it receives worship
in the sphere of silence
from every intelligence that has been sanctified
and made worthy of you.

3. I beseech You, O God,
send me help from your highest heavens
so that I may keep afar from my heart
every evil intention and every carnal wish.

Do not cast me, Lord, from your protection
lest my adversary find me
and trample upon me just as he desires,
destroying me utterly.
It is you who grants repentance and a sorrowing heart
to the sinner who repents;
in this way
you ease his heart of the weight of sin
that is laid upon it,
thanks to the comfort which comes from sorrowing
and from the gift of tears.

5. O name of Jesus,
key to all gifts,
open up for me the great door to your treasurehouse
so that I may enter and praise you
with the praise that comes from the heart
in return for your mercies
which I have experienced in latter days;
for you came and renewed me
with an awareness of the New World.

6. I give praise to your holy nature, Lord,
for you have made my nature
a sanctuary for your hiddenness
and a tabernacle for your Mysteries,
a place where you can dwell,
and a holy temple for your divinity.

7. O Mystery exalted beyond every word
and beyond silence,
who became human in order to renew us
by means of voluntary union with the flesh,
reveal to me the path
by which I may be raised up to your mysteries,
travelling along a course
that is clear and tranquil,

free from the concerns of this world.
Gather my mind into the silence of prayer,
so that all my wandering thoughts
may be silenced within me
during that luminous converse
of supplication and mystery-filled wonder.

13. O Sun of righteousness
by which the righteous beheld their own selves
and became a mirror for their generations,
open up within me
the gate to awareness of you;
grant me a joyful mind,
one which sails above the rocks of error,
so that I may reach that serene haven,
as did our fathers of old who pleased you
with their discerning lives.

14. Sanctify me by your Mysteries,
illumine my mind with knowledge of you,
make your hope to shine out in my heart,
hold me worthy to supplicate for it,
O God my Father and Lord of my life;
illumine your lamp within me,
place in me what belongs to you
so that I may forget what belongs to myself.
Cast upon me the constraint
of wonder of you,
so that the constraint of nature
may be overpowered by it.
Stir up within me
the vision of your Mysteries
so that I may become aware of what was placed in me
at holy baptism.
You placed within me a Guide:
may he show me your glory
at all times.

You made me to be light and salt for the world:
may I not prove a stumbling block for my companions.
Seeing that I have left the world,
may I never again look back to it
and the things which I renounced
when I made my promise to you.
Cast reins of delight upon my heart,
so that my senses may not gaze
beyond the paths of your law.
Rig together my impulses
for the ship of repentance,
so that in it I may exult
as I travel over the world's sea
until I reach the haven of your hope.
When I am tempted, may my mind take strength
from the recollection of you.
Illumine before me
the path of darkness by means of the brilliance
of awareness of you.

19. The flood of Christ's mysteries
presses upon my mind
like the waves of the sea.
I wanted to be silent before them, and not speak,
but they proved to be like burning fire
that was kindled in my bones.
My mind rebukes me revealing to me my sins.
Your mystery stupefies me,
but urges me on beyond it:
in silence it indicates to me,
'Do not be slow to approach because you are afraid of
your sins, O sinner,
for it is by meditating upon this
that the dust of sin
will be shaken off your mind'.

22. O Christ who are covered with light

as though with a garment,
who for my sake stood naked in front of Pilate,
clothe me with that might
which you caused to overshadow the saints,
whereby they conquered this world of struggle.
May your divinity, Lord,
take pleasure in me,
and lead me above the world
to be with you.

23. O Christ, upon whom the many–eyed cherubim
are unable to look
because of the glory of your face
yet out of your love
you received spit upon your face:
remove the shame from my face,
and grant me an open face before you
at the time of prayer.

24. O Christ, because of our nature's sin
you went out to the wilderness
and vanquished the ruler of darkness,
taking from him the victory
after five thousand years;
force to flee from me him who at all times
forces the human race to sin.

27. May those who suffer from dire sicknesses
and grievous illnesses of the body
be remembered before you;
send to them an angel of compassion
and assuage their souls
which are so tormented by their bodies' terrible
afflictions.

Have pity, too, Lord,
on those who are subjected

to the hands of wicked and godless men;
send to them speedily an angel of compassion,
and deliver them from their plight.
O my Lord and my God,
send comfort to all those who are constrained
by whatever kind of hardship.

29. I beg and beseech You, Lord,
grant to all who have gone astray
a true knowledge of you,
so that each and every one
may come to know your glory.

30. In the case of all who have passed from this world
lacking a virtuous life and having had no faith,
be an advocate for them, Lord,
for the sake of the body which you took from them,
so that from the single united body of the world
we may offer up praise
to Father, Son, and Holy Spirit
in the kingdom of heaven,
an unending source of eternal delight.

PRAYER OF JOSEPH THE VISIONARY

To You be praise
First–born of Being,
exalted and full of awe,
for, by the sacrifice of your body,
you have effected salvation for the world.

O Christ, Son from the Holy Father,
to you do I pray in awe at this time;
of you, Lord, do I ask your will
and beseech your compassion,
that my whole person may be made holy
through your grace,
and that the enemy's constraint upon me
may be rendered ineffective.

Purify my understanding
in your compassion,
so that my hands may stretch out in purity
to receive your holy and fearful Body and Blood.

Cleanse my hidden mind
with the hyssop of your grace,
for I draw near
to the Holy of Holies of your Mysteries.

Wash from me all understanding
that belongs to the flesh,
and may an understanding which belongs to your Spirit
be mingled within my soul.

Cause to reside in me
a faith that beholds your Mysteries,
so that I may behold your sacrifice as you are,

and not as I am.

Create eyes in me, and so may I see with your eyes,
for I cannot see with my own eyes.

May my mind travel inwards
towards the hiddenness of your sacrifice,
just as you have travelled out into the open
and been conjoined to your Mysteries.

At this moment
may I be totally forgetful of myself,
and remain utterly unmindful
of my own person.

May every bodily image
be wiped away from my mind's eye,
and may you alone
be depicted before the eye of my mind.

And now, when your Spirit descends from heaven
upon your Mysteries,
may I ascend in spirit from earth to heaven.

At this time
when your power is mingled in with the bread,
may my life be commingled
with your spiritual life.

At this moment
when the wine is changed and becomes your blood,
may my thoughts be inebriated
with the commixture of your love.

At this time
when your Lamb is lying slain upon the altar,
may sin cease

and be utterly removed from all my limbs.

At this moment
when your Body is being offered
as a sacrifice to your Father,
may I too be a holy sacrifice
to you and to him who sent you,
and may my prayer ascend before you
together with the prayer of your priest.

Provide me with hidden hands
so that with them I may carry the fiery Coal.

Create in me a pure heart
so that your holy power may reside within me,
so that, through the power of your Spirit
I may in a spiritual fashion
inhale your salvation.

Fashion in me, Lord,
eyes within my eyes,
so that with new eyes
I may contemplate your divine sacrifice.

Lord, may I not see
the outward aspect of what I am now to receive,
but hold me worthy to see and recognize,
as did Simon the fisherman
who was called blessed for his faith.

Lord, may I taste not just the bread in your Body,
or just the cup in your Blood:
give me faith so that I may see your Body
and not the bread,
and drink your living Blood from the cup.

Grant me that spiritual palate

which is able to taste your Blood
and not the wine.

Wipe out from me
all the signs of my bodily nature,
and mark in me
the signs of your spiritual nature.

May I draw near to you,
and you alone be seen by me:
may I not perceive anything else that is next to me,
but may I walk in the house of prayer
as though in heaven,
and may I receive you
who live in the highest heaven.

You made me into a spiritual being
when you gave me rebirth from the baptismal water;
make me a spiritual being now too,
as I draw near to receive you.

It is a matter of great awe, Lord,
that your Body and your Blood,
O Christ our Saviour,
should be consumed and drunk
with that same mouth which receives
ordinary natural food and drink.

Lord, you did not give to the spiritual beings
what I am receiving now:
stir up within me at this time, Lord,
the sense of wonder at your Cross;
fill me with a fervour of faith at this moment,
so that my thoughts may be inflamed
with the fire of your love;
and may my eyes become for you
rivulets of water

to wash all my limbs;
may your hidden love
be infused into my thoughts,
so that my hidden thoughts
may flow for you
with tears and groans.

May my body be sanctified by you,
may my soul shine out for you.

May my body be purified by you
of every image and form here on earth,
and may my thoughts be cleansed by you,
and my limbs be sanctified by you;
may my understanding shine out,
and may my mind be illumined by you.
May my person become a holy temple for you;
may I be aware in my whole being of your majesty.
May I become a womb for you in secret:
then do you come and dwell in me by night
and I will receive you openly,
taking delight spiritually
in the Holy of Holies of my thoughts.
Then shall I take delight in your Body and your Blood
in my limbs.

You have revealed to me your hiddenness
in the Bread and in the Wine,
reveal in me your love,
cause a desire for you to shine out in me,
so that I may receive your Body in love for you
and in desire for you I may drink your Blood.

With the fulfilment of the sacrifice of yourself,
fulfill my request and accept my prayer;
harken to my words and sign all my limbs,
hidden and revealed.

Lord, I shall openly sign all my limbs
with the sign of your Cross,
as you have said, do you, Lord,
mark me in a hidden way
with the truth of your Cross.

May I receive you,
not into the stomach which belongs to the body's limbs,
but into the womb of my mind,
so that you may be conceived there,
as in the womb of the virgin.

And may you be revealed in me
through spiritual works
and good deeds that are pleasing to your will.

Through consuming you,
may all my lusts be brought to an end;
through drinking your cup
may all my passions be quenched.
May my thoughts take strength
from your sustenance,
and through the living Blood of your revered passion
may I receive strength for the course
of the service of righteousness.
May I grow in a hidden way
and openly prevail.
May I run eagerly
and attain the measure of the Hidden Person,
may I become someone perfected,
made complete in all my spiritual limbs,
my head crowned with the crown of the perfection
of all the spiritual limbs.
May I become a royal diadem in your hands,
as you promised, O true Lord,
Sovereign of all stirrings, Lord of all powers,
God almighty.

May I be intermingled with you
and with your love and your longing
on that day when your majesty will shine out,
and when the words find fulfilment that say
'To you *shall every knee bow,*
and it is you that *every tongue*
in heaven and on earth and beneath the earth shall
confess'.

And along with the spiritual beings
and all who have loved your revelation in spirit,
may I confess you,
praise you,
exalt you
in that kingdom which does not ever dissolve
or pass away.
Now and always.

Prayers of John the Elder

1. YOU WHO ARE HIDDEN and concealed within me,
reveal within me
your hidden mystery;
manifest to me
your beauty that is within me,
O you who have built me
as a temple for you to dwell in,
cause the cloud of your glory
to overshadow inside your temple,
so that the ministers of your sanctuary
may cry out, in love for you,
'holy'
as an utterance which burns in fire and spirit,
in a sharp stirring which is commingled with wonder
and astonishment,
activated as a living movement
by the power of your being.

2. O Christ, the ocean of our forgiveness,
allow me to wash off
in you
the dirt I am clothed in,
so that I may become resplendent
in the raiment of your holy light.
May I be covered with the cloud of your hidden glory,
full of secret mysteries.
May the things which divert me
from gazing upon your beauty
not be visible to me.
May wonder at your glory
captivate me continually,
may my mind become unable to set in motion
wordly impulses.

May nothing ever separate me from your love,
but rather may that desire,
which is in you,
to behold your countenance
harrow me continually.

BIBLIOGRAPHY AND NOTES

A. The prayers by John of Apamea are excerpted from his *Treatise on the Beatitudes* (as yet unpublished) in British Library, Add. 17170, fol. 16a, 17a–18a, 32b–33a and 42b–43a (the manuscript is dated AD 774/5).

The prayers from the collection of thirty prayers by Isaac of Niniveh, incorporated into Part II of his works, are translated from Oxford, Bodleian syr. e.7, fol. 112a–118b; the numbers are those given in the manuscript. Nos. 5, 22–26, 29–30 were printed (from another manuscript) by P. Bedjan in an appendix to his edition of Part I of Isaac's works (pp. 587–9).

The prayer by Joseph the Visionary is translated from Mingana syr. 564, fol. 178b–181b, of AD 1931. G. Bunge gives a German translation of this and two further prayers in his *Rabban Jausep Ḥazzaya*, pp. 357–66.

The two prayers by John the Elder are from his Letters 15 and 42, published by R. Beulay in PO 39, fasc 3 (1978) pp. 98, 182.

B. A description of some manuscripts of the *Shebīthō* is given by J. Sanders, 'Un manuel de prières populaire de l'église syrienne', *Le Muséon* 90 (1977) 81–102.

CHRONOLOGICAL TABLE

(Roman numbers after a writer refer to Chapters in this book)

	Greek writers	*Syriac writers*
Fourth century	Basil Athanasius, *Life of Antony*	Aphrahat (I) Ephrem (II) *Book of Steps* (III)
	Apophthegmata Gregory of Nyssa *Macarian Homilies* Evagrius (IV)	
Fifth century	Palladius, *Lausiac History* Theodoret, *Historia Religiosa*	John of Apamea (V)
	Abba Isaiah Mark the Monk Diadochus of Photike	Narsai
c. 500	'Dionysius the Areopagite'	Jacob of Serugh Philoxenus (VI)
Sixth century	Romanos Dorotheus	Babai (VII) Anonymous I–II (VIII–IX)
	John Moschus, *Pratum Spirituale*	John of Ephesus, *Lives of Eastern Saints* Abraham of Nathpar (X)
Seventh century	John Climacus Maximus the Confessor	Martyrius (XI) Isaac of Nineveh (XII) Dadisho (XIII)
Eighth	Andrew of Crete John of Damascus	Joseph the Visionary (XIV) John the Elder (XV)

INDEX OF BIBLICAL
REFERENCES

(Page numbers in italics denote direct quotations)

SUBJECT INDEX

Syriac terms

CISTERCIAN PUBLICATIONS INC.

Kalamazoo, Michigan

TITLES LISTING
THE CISTERCIAN FATHERS SERIES

Texts and Studies
in the
Monastic Tradition

* Temporarily out of print   †*Forthcoming*

THE CISTERCIAN STUDIES SERIES

MONASTIC TEXTS

CHRISTIAN SPIRITUALITY

MONASTIC STUDIES

CISTERCIAN STUDIES

Temporarily out of print

†Forthcoming

STUDIA PATRISTICA

FAIRACRES PRESS, OXFORD

---

* *Temporarily out of print*   † *Forthcoming*

Eight Chapters on Perfection and Angel's Song
(Walter Hilton)

Creative Suffering (Iulia de Beausobre)

Bringing Forth Christ. Five Feasts of the Child
Jesus (St Bonaventure)

Gentleness in St John of the Cross

Distributed in North America only for Fairacres Press.

DISTRIBUTED BOOKS

St Benedict: Man with An Idea (Melbourne Studies)

The Spirit of Simplicity

Benedict's Disciples (David Hugh Farmer)

The Emperor's Monk: A Contemporary Life of
Benedict of Aniane

A Guide to Cistercian Scholarship (2nd ed.)

*North American customers may order
through booksellers or directly
from the publisher:*

Cistercian Publications
WMU Station
Kalamazoo, Michigan 49008
(616) 383-4985

*Cistercian Publications are available in
Britain, Europe and the Common-
wealth through A. R. Mowbray &
Co Ltd   St Thomas House   Oxford
OX1 1SJ.
For a sterling price list, please consult
Mowbray's General Catalogue.*

*Cistercian monks and nuns have been
living lives of prayer & praise, meditation &
manual labor since the twelfth century.
They are part of an unbroken tradition
which extends back to the fourth century
and which continues today in the Catholic
church, the Orthodox churches, the
Anglican communion, and, most recently,
in the Protestant churches.*

*Share their way of life and their search for
God by reading Cistercian Publications.*

*A complete catalogue of texts-in-
translation and studies on early,
medieval, and modern Christian
monasticism is available at no cost
from Cistercian Publications.*

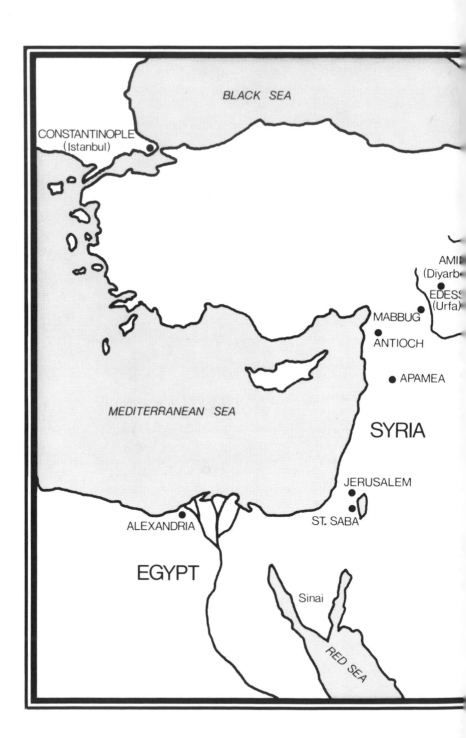

CASPIAN SEA

● BETH ABE

SIBIS
● NINEVEH
MOSUL ●

RIVER TIGRIS

RIVER EUPHRATES

● BAGHDAD
● SELEUCIA–CTESIPHON

BETH HUZAYE
(Khuzistan)

PERSIAN GULF

● QATAR